W. E. Caldwell: 1868.
From Mrs. L. S. Wood.
Lodi. Michigan.
January 1868.

*Geo. Shepard*

# SERMONS

BY THE LATE


REV. GEORGE SHEPARD,

PROFESSOR IN THEOLOGICAL SEMINARY, BANGOR, ME.


*With a Memorial*


BY PROF. D. S. TALCOTT.



BOSTON:
NICHOLS AND NOYES.
1868.

CAMBRIDGE:
PRESS OF JOHN WILSON AND SON.

# CONTENTS.

## IV.

### SALVATION IN NO OTHER.



## V.

### THE SHIPWRECK OF PAUL.



## VI.

### ELIJAH THE TISHBITE.



## VII.

### SAUL THE REGRESSIVE IN PIETY.



## VIII.

### CALEB; OR, FOLLOWING FULLY.

## IX.

### THOSE LOOKING BACK NOT FIT FOR THE KINGDOM.



## X.

### THE GIVER; OR, THE TWO MITES.



## XI.

### THE MORAL DISCIPLINE OF GIVING.



## XII.

### DOERS OF THE WORD, AND NOT HEARERS ONLY.

## XIII.

### JUSTIFICATION BY WORKS.



## XIV.

### CONFESSION OF SIN.



## XV.

### AND YE WILL NOT COME TO ME.



## XVI.

### ESCAPE FOR THY LIFE.

## XVII.

### THE METHODS OF THE ADVERSARY.



## XVIII.

### THE DEATH OF ELISHA.



## XIX.

### THE SON OF MAN IS COME TO SEEK AND TO SAVE.



## XX.

### THE GLORY OF CHRIST.

## XXI.

### SEEK FIRST THE KINGDOM OF GOD AND HIS RIGHTEOUSNESS.



## XXII.

### CHRIST'S BODILY AND SPIRITUAL HEALINGS.

*And again he entered into Capernaum after some days; and it was noised that he was in the house. And straightway many were gathered together, insomuch that there was no room to receive them, no, not so much as about the door: and he preached the word unto them. And they come unto him, bringing one sick of the palsy, which was borne of four. And when they could not come nigh unto him for the press, they uncovered the roof where he was: and when they had broken it up, they let down the bed wherein the sick of the palsy lay. When Jesus saw their faith, he said unto the sick of the palsy, Son, thy sins be forgiven thee. But there were certain of the scribes sitting there, and reasoning in their hearts, Why doth this man thus speak blasphemies? Who can forgive sins but God only? And immediately when Jesus perceived in his spirit that they so reasoned within themselves, he said unto them, Why reason ye these things in your hearts? Whether is it easier to say to the sick of the palsy, Thy sins be forgiven thee; or to say, Arise, and take up thy bed, and walk? But that ye may know that the Son of man hath power on*

XXVII.

DEATH ABOLISHED.



XXVIII.

SPIRITUAL BODY.



XXIX.

ETERNAL PUNISHMENT.



XXX.

HEAVEN.

# MEMORIAL DISCOURSE.

*We having the same spirit of faith, according as it is written, I believed, and therefore have I spoken; we also believe, and therefore speak.* — 2 Cor. iv. 13.

IT was the lamentation of one of old, and a lamentation strikingly indicative of having fallen upon evil times, "The righteous perisheth, and no man layeth it to heart." When a servant of God, who has been honored in being allowed to exert a mighty and conspicuous influence for good among the men of his generation, rests from his labors, it is a debt which survivors owe, not so much to his own memory as to the grace which made him what he was, to see to it, that, while those labors are not forgotten or passed lightly by, the qualities by which the great results have been achieved should be in some measure appreciated; so that not only may the desire be stimulated in others to pursue a course of like beneficence, but something be also done to show how the aspiration may be carried out to a practical and blessed end.

In attempting to trace the outlines of a character and a course of life thus calling for special commemoration, we naturally seek some point around which all that is most essential and distinctive may be grouped;

some principle which may serve as a key to explain the too rare phenomenon of a life greatly beneficent, and which, developed elsewhere, may afford a reasonable promise of the bright example being exhibited again.

The words of the text have been selected with no special reference to the direct application originally made of them by the apostle, but as conveying, when taken in their most general acceptation, a thought which was very signally realized in the life and labors of Professor Shepard, and the realization of which was emphatically central among all the elements which constituted his high pre-eminence as a preacher of righteousness.

George Shepard was born at Plainfield, Conn., Aug. 26, 1801. Of the earlier circumstances which contributed to the formation of his character, we have only a scanty record. One fact we are assured of, that is full of interest; that in his case, as in that of so many whose memory is fondly cherished in the Church, the foundations of usefulness were laid in the instructions and the prayers of a pious mother. His father owned a small farm, and the years of his minority were largely spent in farming operations. His aptitude and inclination for intellectual pursuits were developed at an early age. At the district school, as we are told, "he was a good scholar in all the branches; while in arithmetic he distanced all competitors, and yet was so unassuming and modest as to disarm envy and jealousy." We are further told "that it was the custom of the minister, Dr. Benedict, to visit the school on Saturday afternoons, and examine the pupils in the catechism; and this" it is added, "may be said to have been the commencement of his theological studies." With a view to qualify himself for a school-teacher, he entered the academy in his native place. His weekly compositions, prepared while connected with this institution, are characterized, by one who was a fellow-student with him there, as "containing more ideas than were commonly embraced in such efforts, expressed in a strong, vigorous, though somewhat sonorous style, *after the Johnsonian model.*" Meanwhile his leisure hours were assiduously employed in reading the old English authors, of whose works there was a considerable collection at his command. Up to the year 1819, there is no evidence of his having been the subject of any special religious impressions. His childhood and youth, however, had been singularly stainless. "He was always," as we learn from those qualified to testify upon this point, "a good boy. As a son, he was always dutiful; as a brother, affectionate; as a friend, warm-hearted and true." But during a revival of religion which was experienced in Plainfield in the year 1819, under the preaching of Rev. Orin Fowler, young Shepard was made, as he believed, a subject of renewing grace. There is no account in existence, so far as known, of the exercises of his mind at this period; but it is recollected that in the narrative, characteristically brief, which he gave of his experience, at the time he made a profession of religion, May 7, 1820, he expressed deep conviction of his own guilt as a sinner, and of the power and readiness of Christ to save, and a humble purpose to live devoted to his service. The young convert was soon subjected to a severe trial. He felt it to be his duty to give himself to the work of the gospel ministry.

But his father, who had no sympathy with his religious views, strenuously opposed the plan. He assured his father, however, that while he was willing to remain with him, as in duty bound, up to the age of twenty-one, it was his full determination to enter then upon a course of classical study. His mother, who was a woman of great gentleness of character, did all she could to promote his views; and as he entered Amherst College a year in advance, in the fall of 1821, his father's opposition must have been in some measure withdrawn. But his intellectual preparation for the ministry was gained by various and hard toil; and the recollection of his own experience in this regard, doubtless, bore an important part in making him, through life, the earnest and untiring advocate of the Education Society.

Soon after leaving college he became connected with the Theological Seminary at Andover, where he graduated in 1827. The intentness and success with which his studies here were prosecuted may be inferred from the circumstance, that he was urged by Professor Stuart to remain in the seminary as Assistant Instructor in Hebrew. This invitation he declined, and accepted a call from the First Congregational Church in Hallowell, Me., where he was ordained Feb. 5, 1828. Here was demand at once for the exercise of all his powers. Hallowell was at that time the centre of an extensive and flourishing business, and probably few places in the country of like size have ever contained so large an amount of intelligence and mental cultivation as were here concentrated. It was soon found, that, in the person of the young pastor, a power of no common magnitude was abroad in the community. His unaffected kindliness of spirit, his fervent, single-hearted piety, his untiring devotion to his work, combined with his commanding eloquence, gained for him an influence among men of all classes, more nearly resembling that possessed by some of the old Puritan pastors in colonial times than any thing that these modern days have often witnessed. In the few years of his pastorate, ties were formed which would have effectually prevented his listening to any ordinary solicitation to settle elsewhere. But when, in 1836, the trustees of the Theological Seminary at Bangor, then entering upon a new stage of its history, and one which opened a prospect of greatly extended influence and usefulness, fixed upon Mr. Shepard as the most eligible candidate for the professorship of Sacred Rhetoric, he felt at once that it was not a call to be lightly set aside; while the acknowledged importance of the work to which he was invited, and his own singular fitness for it, went far with a people that had been trained to take large views of things, towards subduing the repugnance naturally awakened in view of the proposed surrender of so highly prized a treasure. And the sacrifice demanded of them was rendered still less painful than it would otherwise have been, by the assurance which he gave, that it was his fixed intention never to leave the work upon which he was now entering, in order to become the pastor of another congregation, unless constrained by providential indications which could not be mistaken.

He came to Bangor. He gave to the seminary the labor of his life. In connection, indeed, with his duties in the seminary, he discharged, for a number of years, the duties of preacher and pastor to the Central

Church in this city, which came into existence mainly through his agency, and was built up into strength and efficiency by the blessing of God upon his labors. From time to time, also, he lectured, and performed other duties pertaining to the department of Sacred Rhetoric at various theological seminaries, where the stated provision for instruction in Homiletics had temporarily failed. But our own seminary continued to enjoy the benefit of his services to the last. The promise he gave his people upon leaving them was not an ill-considered promise, and it was faithfully redeemed. Nor was it at a trifling expense to himself that he redeemed it. Repeatedly was he solicited, by tempting offers from abroad, to leave his post. Theological professorships elsewhere were urged upon him. Overtures were made to him, on two different occasions, to accept the presidency of Amherst College. The Church of the Pilgrims in Brooklyn, N.Y., and the Mercer-street Church in New-York City, sought him for their pastor, and held out pecuniary inducements, which, especially at the time they were presented, it must have cost some effort to resist. All these invitations he declined, upon the ground, as he himself expressed it, that his work here was not done. That work he kept on doing for nearly thirty-two years. At length, on the morning of March 23, 1868, it was decided, by One from whose decision there was no appeal, that the work was done. Just how well it was done, the Great Taskmaster only is fully able to decide. But it involves no invasion of the divine prerogative of judgment, to imagine that we hear, as the toilworn laborer emerges into that dread yet loved and longed-for Presence, some faint echoes of the plaudit, itself an infinite reward, "Well done, good and faithful servant: enter thou into the joy of thy Lord."

It is a small thing, our brother would say, for me to be judged of man's judgment. Yet man *will judge.* In a sense, it is right, and it is necessary, that man *should judge.* In the case of Professor Shepard, man *has judged,* and therefore it is that we are here to-day.

Were it proposed, on this occasion, to institute a minute inquiry into all the elements of that power which Professor Shepard wielded in the pulpit, and which gave him for so many years in general estimation so high a place in the first class of living preachers, it would be necessary to attempt, at least, a perfect analysis of the man himself. In many cases, where great success has been achieved in any line of intellectual effort, the task of the critic is comparatively easy. The results accomplished are plainly seen to be attributable to one or two leading circumstances, a few at most; some one peculiarly felicitous endowment, physical, moral, or intellectual; some special course of training, some signal opportunity, some urgent motive accidentally brought to bear, some constraining necessity arising, of such a nature as almost to create the very power which it propelled and guided. There are often various drawbacks to be allowed for, arising from conflicting impulses, a divided style of effort, conspicuous deficiencies almost counterbalancing great endowments; and the inquiry is continually suggested, in view of what was actually done, How much more might have been accomplished, had there been a more harmonious combination of natural endowments, more of uniformity in their development, or of concentrated vigor in their application? But in the case of Professor Shepard, while there was a remarkable concurrence of certain of the most widely different elements of power, there were no signal deficiencies. What, indeed, in most men are elements of weakness, appeared sometimes, with him, to minister to strength. And it would be very difficult to suggest any material modification or re-arrangement of the elements of his character, that would have been likely to contribute essentially to his advancement in his own peculiar line of excellence. The chief spring, however, of the power so remarkably constituted and employed, lay, it may be affirmed with confidence, in the practical and all-pervading ascendency of *faith*. "I believed, therefore have I spoken," is the key which admits us to the interior of that life so distinguished by the beneficent influence which it exerted upon the characters and lives of others. Had Professor Shepard never come under the controlling influence of Christian faith, he would even then have been a man out of the common course. With a mind strongly disposed to thoughtfulness, and with natural sensibilities deep, warm, and comprehensive, to a degree not often met with, he would have been, under ordinary circumstances, distinguished as a kind neighbor, a good citizen, a wise and safe counsellor, a man of active and self-denying benevolence, the object of general confidence and love. With more of natural conscientiousness than most men, he would have found it hard to take any but the right side on any great moral question. It would always have been known where he stood. His reasons would have been known, and they would have had weight with others. His retiring disposition might have kept him in the shade; but, had any special emergency compelled him into public life, he would have stood forth a bold and strong defender of the weak and the oppressed. There was much in his natural constitution that fitted him to be a reformer. Perhaps not easily aroused, when once aroused it was to effective and persistent action. While he was not remarkable for rapidity in his intellectual operations, the truth once seen was seen clearly, and seen once for all, and became henceforth a part of himself. It was in his nature to be deliberate. Hence it was, that judgments once formed were not easily laid aside; and, so long as acknowledged in form, they were not likely to be overruled by momentary impulse. Such a nature furnished good material for divine truth to act upon. In the absence of all direct testimony upon the subject, the character of his own religious experience may be satisfactorily inferred from the whole character of his preaching. It must have been an experience which took firm hold upon all the leading truths of the Christian system, and reached to the very depths of his spiritual being. Every thing goes to show that there must have been the deepest conviction of the exceeding sinfulness of sin, of the greatness of the ruin which sin works, and of his own personal participation in that ruin. Thus was he prepared to receive, with the most implicit confidence, all that the Bible teaches of the glory of the Great Deliverer, and of the completeness of his salvation. These became to him realities, living, mighty, ever present. Not only was his own life habitually yielded to their power, but his convictions respecting them he must impart to others perishing for lack of knowledge. His whole manner of speaking betokened a man thoroughly in earnest. His words were plain, direct, graphic, strong. The things that he had to announce were things that he had seen. He had looked upon them as if no one had ever looked upon them before, and he told of them as if no one had ever told of them before. If he used the same words, in speaking of these things, that others had employed before him, it was not that he had taken the words from others, but just because they were the best words, the most expressive words, to set forth the things themselves. I need not say that his style of expression was peculiar to himself. He wrote an article for the press, occasionally, to be published without his name. But it was all the same as if his name had been attached. No one familiar with his manner, and possessing any power of discernment, could read a page of his writing and remain in doubt as to the author. Yet no man was ever more free from affectation of singularity. All that was peculiar in his style was simply the result of a strenuous and single purpose to make others see what he saw, and feel what he felt, combined as this purpose was with the speaker's mastery of language, and the common sense, the knowledge of mankind, which taught him to employ that mastery to the best advantage for the end he had in view. Professor Shepard's theory of the style appropriate to the pulpit was very clearly defined; and, in his own style, his theory was well illustrated. And yet it is felt by every reader, much more was it felt by every hearer, of his sermons, that he had but little, if any, conscious reference to theory in the composition of them. There is nothing in his style that has the look, at least to one acquainted with the man, of being artificial or made up. He attached great importance, in theory, to strength of expression; but he used strong language himself, because the strength of emotion which impelled him spontaneously suggested it. Commonplace was his aversion; but, in rejecting a commonplace expression, he was guided by the instinctive feeling that it was wholly inadequate to convey his meaning. The word that he rejected might be, as defined in dictionaries, the exact equivalent of that he chose: but the one carried its meaning as a dead burden; the other, winged, penetrating, pregnant with suggestion, was a living force, a servant that knew his master's will and did it. So, too, he condemned verbosity; but we feel that his own freedom from needless words is owing to the fact that, because they were needless, they did not occur to him. He remarked once in private, that, in the preparation of his sermons, he always had in imagination his hearers all before him. And we can readily believe it. His words and phrases, their combination and mutual adjustment, reveal the same thing. His sentences were written to be spoken; and they bear the marks of having been spoken, mentally at least, in the process of formation. Very often, on the other hand, more especially in those sermons which were not expressly prepared for the press, it is no less plain that the thought of how a sentence would read was something that the writer gave himself no concern about.

While in some respects Professor Shepard's style of writing is the very opposite of that of Paul, there is sometimes that in his sermons which very forcibly recalls to us the manner in which the impetuous earnestness of the apostle overrides all rules of speech. There is the like "disproportion between thought and language;" "the thought," in the words of another, "straining the language till it cracks in the process, a shipwreck of grammar and logic as the sentences are whirled through the author's mind." The one point is gained. The truth, as it presented itself to his own view, is made to stand out, in the view of the hearer, as clearly as language can make it; and all other considerations are given to the winds. This very disregard of logical and grammatical restraints heightens, if possible, the impression. It is as if the speaker could not stop to put into shape the thoughts which were struggling for utterance. It may almost be doubted whether the whole compass of literature furnishes any examples of a style more thoroughly expressive of the emotions of a full and burdened spirit than is found in some of these discourses. The very structure of the sentences suggests to the imagination — and the suggestion comes with tenfold vividness to those who remember the manner in which they were thrown out — the action of a massive engine driven by a gigantic force communicated from within by a succession of brief but constantly repeated impulses, any one of which, if protracted but a very little, would shatter and destroy the engine. At the same time, too, the measured regularity of the impulses gives us the impression of a constant and mighty self-control continually put forth to keep inside the limits of exertion within which alone it is possible to continue to exist and act.

Professor Shepard was in a peculiar manner fitted by natural advantages for the effective utterance of weighty truth. With a large and well-proportioned frame, and a countenance significant of a rare and attractive combination of seriousness, gentleness, simplicity, and strength, he possessed a voice which ranged, with perfect facility, from the most soothing tones of consolation to the thunders which are needed to arouse a slumbering world to the anticipation of judgment to come. And it is not too much to say, that, especially in his best efforts, he made the most of these advantages. It has often been noticed as a remarkable circumstance, that the same disciple who is habitually spoken of as the disciple whom Jesus loved, should have been one of the two surnamed "The Sons of Thunder." But a similar combination of qualities was exhibited in Professor Shepard. Where shall we look to find a man more nearly realizing than he did, in all beautiful and winning attributes of character, our ideal of the Apostle John? And yet what epithet could be more expressive of his power in the pulpit than "Boanerges"? Every utterance bespoke the resolute determination, *men shall be made to listen.* Preachers often seem to say to their hearers, I have that to communicate which you ought to listen to, which you ought to regard. If you do so, it will be your wisdom. If you do not, you will be the losers. But with yourselves alone is the responsibility. I have given you the opportunity to hear; and if you fail to hear, it will be no fault of mine. Professor Shepard was not satisfied with giving men the opportunity to hear. Hear they should. And not only so, but attend they should. Accordingly, attend they did. The habitual attitude of his hearers well illustrated what he himself says in his description of the Effective Preacher. "The hearers of such a one," he says, "will not be likely to settle down to their slumbers while he has them in hand. They will hardly dare to sleep; for they never will be able to conjecture what things may be exploded on their organs before they wake up."

One of the elements of Professor Shepard's power in the pulpit, and one not among the least of them, lay in a quality which under ordinary circumstances is apt to prove a fatal obstacle to all success. I refer to his constitutional timidity. He was naturally timid, self-distrustful, even to a degree that was almost morbid. In a letter to a friend who had expressed a similar feeling, he once remarked, "As to the shrinking and trembling and all that sort of thing, I seem to myself to have been doing nothing but just that very thing all my life. I have taken up no new duty except with dread and apprehension; but with God's grace I have worked my way through it so far." It was a very signal and triumphant manifestation of the power of faith, that, in surmounting this great obstacle, he was actually enabled to convert it into a direct source of augmented influence. Such a victory indeed brings always an accession of moral strength. It always implies a strenuous and invigorating exertion of the faculties, and the incorporation into the character of some lofty and ennobling end. When it comes, as it doubtless did to Professor Shepard, as the result of wrestling supplication, the strength by which it is accomplished is the strength of God, and is available wherever strength is needed. But it was not only through its general effect upon his character that this inward conflict, perpetually renewed, though always with the same result, contributed to his efficiency. It is no difficult matter to trace the very way in which this result was brought about. There was first the striking contrast between the preacher's manifest self-distrust, and the resources of power which he was found to possess. When he rose in the pulpit, especially to read a hymn, or to lead the devotions of the congregation, no words could have expressed more strongly than it was written on his countenance the feeling that he was nothing, and less than nothing. There was power enough there, obvious even to the most superficial observer; but it was power to all appearance quiet, undemonstrative, like the power which holds the planets in their orbits; a power which certainly gave no promise of any extraordinary appeal to the senses. And when such appeals began to be made, sometimes with a force almost sufficient to raise the hearers from their seats, they came with all the more effect for coming as they did, not only unheralded, but contrary to all the expectations that mere appearances had raised. Then, too, the mind of the hearer was very likely to revert, in part unconsciously, perhaps, yet with something of sympathetic interest, to the greatness of the apprehended motive, the strength of conviction and emotion, that must be working in such a nature, in order to impel it to such a demonstration.

But the great point to be considered here is, that the preacher's native timidity made it absolutely necessary for him to forget self. This was essential, not merely to his having any measure of comfort in his work, but to his doing it at all. If he thought of himself, it was not possible that his thought should ever take the form of self-complacency, or any other form than that of a painful, oppressive, almost paralyzing sense of his own insufficiency to do any thing like justice to the themes he was attempting to set forth. He must forget self, or sit down. And he did forget self. There was, as we have said, a degree of self-consciousness perceptible upon his first rising in the pulpit. But this lasted only for a moment. It was but the utterance of a few sentences, and the preacher was hidden in his subject, hidden from his hearers, hidden from himself; and, after that, all that had any tendency to bring him to the minds of others, or to intimate that his own mind had even for an instant turned inward upon itself, was that now and then in the midst of his most impressive passages there was seen a slight contraction of the eyelids, as if caused by the too near approach of some overwhelming vision of glory or of terror. I need not say how vast the advantage gained in respect to substantial power by this utter impersonality of the speaker. The absence of all self-assertion on his part made it impossible that any aversion the hearer might entertain towards the message should be re-inforced by the insinuations of wounded self-esteem, or of unwillingness to yield to the dictation of another. Men were made to feel that they were brought in contact with the truth itself, or at least with what purported to be truth. A large class of obstacles in the way of their reception of it were thus wholly put aside. They were placed in a position to judge it upon its own merits; and if it was ever to become a reality to them, it was likely to become so now.

Closely connected with the constitutional timidity of Professor Shepard, inseparable, indeed, from it as an element of power, and yet carefully to be distinguished from it in respect to nature and origin, was his profound Christian humility. The popular admiration of him as a preacher, and the respect entertained throughout the country for his character and talents, were manifested in too many ways to allow him to remain in ignorance of the fact that he possessed certain rare and high endowments. It is true the low estimate he habitually entertained, and which he was accustomed to express without reserve, of the grounds upon which pulpit popularity very often rests, would have effectually prevented him from drawing those inferences from the applause of the multitude which mere vanity would have been ready to accept. But while his own good sense in its deliberate exercise must have inevitably led him to something approaching to a just appreciation of his powers, the verdict of approval was too widely ratified, and had the sanction of too high authority, to be explained away even by himself as a tribute rendered to qualities that were merely superficial. Against any danger of self-exaltation, however, which might have arisen in this way, there was a powerful safeguard furnished by his faith in unseen realities. In the vastness of the themes with which he was habitually conversant, and contrasted with which all human faculties and achievements, considered in themselves, are nothingness, we may be sure he found the constant nutriment of that crowning grace by which his influence upon others was so greatly heightened.

It deserves to be particularly noticed here, that it was not only in the enforcement of generally admitted truths, and in the ordinary methods of their application, that the faith of Professor Shepard raised him above the fear of man and enabled him to speak the word with power. With all kindness and charity towards those who might differ from him he combined the utmost freedom in the formation of his opinions, the utmost confidence in them when once upon due deliberation formed, and the utmost firmness in expressing and maintaining them. He was an outspoken abolitionist when there was a stigma in the name. In an age of martyrdom, he would have been a martyr. Humble as he was, self-distrustful as he was, shrinking as he did instinctively from all the harsh contacts of outward life, and even from all needless conspicuity, it cannot be doubted that he would have been found equal to any of the great emergencies in which the might of spiritual truth has been most signally displayed. He would not have hesitated to confront an adulterous monarch with Nathan's or with John the Baptist's bold rebuke. With Athanasius, he would have stood against the world. Had he been in the place of Ambrose, like Ambrose he would have barred the approach of the imperial butcher to the sacred table, nor have abated one jot of the humiliation which must attest the depth of the repentance called for. It was, as we may well believe, in a spirit only such as his, and with like terrific energy of utterance, that Leo checked the progress of the "Scourge of God," and turned back the victorious Attila from the gates of Rome.

Among the elements of Professor Shepard's power as a preacher we cannot enumerate extraordinary skill in argument, splendor of imagery, a vast accumulation of recondite and curious lore, keenness of analytic power, or far-reaching grasp of thought. In any one of these respects, with his native strength of intellect, and his conscientious and indomitable force of will, he might probably have attained high eminence. He seemed, however, to have adopted a specialty, and, with characteristic good sense, to have selected that to which on the whole his powers were best adapted; the work, namely, of compelling men to see and feel how much of weighty motive was directly involved in the truths which they professed to receive. When he reasoned, he ordinarily reasoned well; but he had no special fondness for controversy, and rarely in his sermons pursued any lengthened course of argument. So far as illustration was needed to promote his main end, he employed illustration. He was not deficient in imagination. When he chose, he could draw a picture in a word. Yet there was no special cultivation of the imagination. On the other hand, there seemed often to be a studious repression of it, lest it should interfere with the purpose so sternly kept in view. As for nice distinctions in theology, they were not directly available toward the accomplishment of his one design; and therefore he ordinarily let them alone. He was fully able to appreciate them. He recognized their importance in their own place; but in his appeals to the consciences of men they would not have been in place.

We are apt to think, sometimes, that, without detriment to his practical efficiency, he might have taken a somewhat broader range of thought in dealing with the great themes of faith; but it may be readily believed that it was rather upon principle, than either from inability or disinclination, that he forbore habitually to venture into those regions of speculation which are so attractive to the thoughtful mind. He probably feared that his doing so might divert the attention of his hearers from what was most vital to their welfare, or at least impair that fixedness of view without which there can be no real depth of feeling. In revolving a subject to be presented from the pulpit, his mind seemed as if by instinct to fasten at once upon the essential, all-comprehending certainties connected with it; and all that could by any possibility interfere with the clearest, strongest, most effective presentation of those certainties must stand aside.

Professor Shepard was most emphatically a preacher of the cross. Whatever constitutes the glory of the Mediator, — his eternal power and Godhead; the divine purity of his life on earth; his humiliation unto death; the bitterness of the cup he drained for us; the exhaustless riches of his pardoning love; the reality and blessedness of his indwelling in every trusting soul; the fulness of joy that it will be to see him as he is, and to be like him, — these were topics that he was never weary of presenting, and by their connection with which the value of every thing else was estimated. Few men are better entitled than Professor Shepard, to that highest praise of a minister of the gospel, that he determined to know nothing but Jesus Christ, and him crucified. We are accustomed to look upon him as having been, more than most Christians, a self-denying man. It is not unlikely that in forming and adhering to Paul's sublime determination for the greater honor of his Master, and against all the solicitations presented by pride of intellect and the desire of human approbation, may have lain the chief self-denial of his life. And the promise was fulfilled in him, "Those that honor me I will honor."

In laying out so little of his strength comparatively in the line of argument, Professor Shepard reminds us still of the apostle to the Gentiles, who, with all his skill in dialectics as displayed in the trains of conclusive reasoning found here and there in his epistles and particularly in the Epistle to the Romans, yet dispenses with argument so much that he is even characterized by the great heathen critic of antiquity as "having first set the example of assertion unaccompanied by proof."

And might it not be an improvement in the prevailing style of preaching, were there within certain limits a more habitual and prominent assumption of the fact, that the natural man has ever in his own inmost spirit a witness to the truth? Does not this assumption often furnish the most effective answer to the objections of the sceptic, and prepare the way for what is at once the most intelligent and the most steadfast faith? "BELIEVE ME," was the demand of Christ, "BELIEVE ME that I am in the Father, and the Father in me, *or else* believe me *for the very works' sake.*"

Perhaps, however, it should here be said that Professor Shepard could, with more safety than many others, dispense somewhat with the forms of demonstration. As we have already seen, when he reasoned he generally reasoned with conclusiveness; and this of itself inspired confidence. Then, too, while the truthfulness depicted in every line of that open, guileless countenance made it impossible to doubt that the depth of feeling always indicated was the result of firm conviction, there was a manifest robustness in the whole mental structure of the man, giving strong assurance that whatever he was so firmly convinced of and felt so deeply, he must have had good reason for receiving.

And this leads me to say further, that, wherever

Professor Shepard was known, the profound confidence that was universally entertained in his unaffected goodness gave to his preaching a peculiar power that it is difficult to express in words. Men felt that, in speaking to them of Christian experience, he was only laying his own heart open. The tender, reverential, comprehensive pleadings with which he led the devotions of assembled worshippers could only have sprung from a heart in constant fellowship with the Father, and with his Son Jesus Christ. As he urged the necessity of a faith that works by love, his daily course of living at once illustrated and enforced his meaning. The burning words with which he denounced the insatiate grasping after wealth, the strong persuasions by which he sought to draw out the spirit of self-sacrifice, would have been comparatively ineffectual but for the re-inforcement afforded by his own example of an ever-active and self-forgetful beneficence. And it was a mighty vindication of the earnestness with which he ever insisted on the utter impossibility of justification on the ground of merit, that his own life presented to mere human view, in all its relations toward God and toward man, an aspect so unblemished.

Our attention has been thus far directed to the consideration of the elements of that power which Professor Shepard exerted in the pulpit. But as a professor he was no less eminent in his own department than he was as a preacher. And his success in both these lines of effort rested upon the same ultimate basis of a singularly vivid and unwavering faith. The clear views he had of the true objects of the preacher's work no one could more clearly or more forcibly set forth than he; while the directness with which, in his own practice, he ever kept those objects in view, made his preaching a model of such a kind as almost to constrain some measure of conformity on the part of those who were subjected to its influence, and yet at the same time forbid all servile attempts at imitation. In the great success which attended his ministrations, his pupils could not but discern conclusive evidence of the value of the instructions which he gave them. Nor was there any mystery in that success. The distinguishing excellences of the method he adopted for presenting truth were not far to seek. They lay upon the surface. To some extent they were capable of being imitated, and, as it were, invited imitation. And that unconscious kind of imitation, which is the only kind not wholly unworthy of a preacher of the gospel, was sure to result, with more or less of palpable distinctness, wherever a spirit, in any degree kindred with his own, existed. No one earnest to do good, whose mental conformation was not portentously unplastic, could listen day after day to his lectures on Homiletics, especially with the advantage of the commentary afforded by frequent opportunities to hear him preach, without acquiring something of that peculiar impress which always told the story of its origin.

In the review of Professor Shepard's life and character there is a lesson of great significance afforded by the very remarkable degree in which the eminence he attained, both as a preacher and as a professor, obviously rested upon moral grounds. Not only, as we have already seen, did his character give force to his preaching, but it preached continually, and with silent but mighty power, to those who rarely or never came within reach of his public ministrations. Those of his fellow-citizens who differed from him most widely in their religious views, rendered willing homage to the beauty of his life; and probably to no man among us would the hearts of the whole community have turned with more general accord, as to an example of what a Christian should be, than to him.

Let it not be understood that it is the design to represent him as a perfect character. Most indignantly would he have forbidden any thing like this. And, doubtless, if he could now speak to us from the heavenly glory, with a higher intensity of emphasis than ever would he assure us that the most humbling views he took of himself as a sinner, while on earth, are now seen, in the full blaze of the divine holiness, to have been far short of what the reality demanded. But whatever may have been his shortcomings, his infirmities, his sins, it would be very hard, even if it were desirable, to point them out. Not from any want of transparency in his character, but from the deficiency of our own discernment, they must pass untold. Twenty-nine years of intimate association have certainly left the speaker with as little ability as inclination to lift the veil.

Professor Shepard is gone. And what a void is left. What a void in that domestic circle, where, for the deep stillness of the outer world, the companion of his youth only hears with a yet quicker inward ear, the voices of memory and of Christian hope, and the accents of the Divine Comforter. What a void in that group of associated teachers, two of whom, for about the space of a generation, lived with him in a daily fellowship of interest and effort, unbroken by a word or thought of even momentary alienation. What a void in that sacred Institution, so tenderly cherished in his deepest heart, so faithfully and so variously served with his best strength, and for every member of which he always had the ready sympathy of a father. What a void in the church of which he was the founder, in connection with which so many souls have experienced the first pulsations of a new spiritual life, and so many others been animated and strengthened in the ways of God. What a void in this whole community in which his light has shone so long, in the churches of our State at large, and even among those of other States, that have been so often stirred by his eloquence, and guided by his counsels.

One void, however, we may conceive of, in this connection, which we may rejoice there is not and there cannot be. Suppose, for an instant, that he had never lived. Imagine all that sum of good to be annulled which, either directly or indirectly, he accomplished; all Christian life through him communicated, now extinct for ever; all stimulus by him imparted to the Church of Christ, withdrawn; all channels of benevolence closed up or narrowed back again, which have either been wholly opened by his influence, or along which, widened by his influence, there is poured a richer flow of blessing to the world,—imagine all this, and follow out the course of thought, as far as finite intellects can trace it, and then attempt to form some estimate of the nature and amount of loss to man, for time and for eternity, that such a supposition would involve, if realized.

Not only is the past secure. Not only did our brother do a blessed work in life, which can never be undone, but he is working still, working widely, working mightily, and will continue to work as long as the world shall stand. His was pre-eminently a moulding influence, and it was largely exerted upon those whose business it was to be to exert a moulding influence on others. To say nothing of the self-propagating impulses towards all good that may have been set in operation through the peculiar opportunities he had of preaching far and wide, when we consider in how many seminaries besides our own he labored, and at how many different times, and often in contact with large classes of young ministers, there is no extravagance in affirming that he is now giving character continually to the form in which the gospel is presented to thousands upon thousands in every region of the globe. Not only among English-speaking races, but to multitudes upon whom his own most impassioned exhortations would have been spent without effect, he speaks continually through those who have learned from him to speak with power. In Arabic, Turkish, and Armenian, in the tongues of Hindostan and China, and in savage dialects first reduced to writing by his pupils, words that to him would have been unmeaning are every Sabbath and every week day wrought into new and more expressive combinations, and convey the message of salvation with a more commanding energy, because he has lived and taught. The wisdom and the spirit with which he spoke will be transmitted. And it may well be that, long ages hence, the dwellers on the steppes of Asia, as they hear in their own tongues the wonderful works of God, and are moved to holy reverence and trust and love, while all unable to trace the origin of that inspiration which makes old familiar words to fall upon their ears with such strange power, will have reason, though they know it not, to be thankful for the grace that was poured into the lips of one that sleeps on the banks of the Penobscot.

# SERMONS.

---

## I.

### PREACHING TO THE MASSES.

*But we preach Christ crucified.* — 1 Cor. i. 23.

I PROPOSE, as the subject of this discourse, to speak of the gospel as having power on the masses: in other words, to set forth that type of preaching which is fitted to take effect on the less cultivated minds, — the more common minds of the world.

There is great complaint of failure on the part of preachers to reach the mind and heart of the people. There is alleged here a great defect in the result or fruit of their labors; and it is asked if there be not some serious defect in our theory and mode of preaching. Or must we take the ground that the gospel itself is incompetent, — is no longer the power it once was? It is alleged, from a highly authoritative source, that the preachers of this day are at fault in keeping to a refined and intellectual type of discourse, having too prominently in mind an *élite* and elect class of hearers. I do not undertake to pronounce on the justice of these statements or criticisms, but fall back on the theme already indicated; namely, that type of preaching which we find set forth in the first Christian labors, — prominently as exemplified in the apostle Paul, that most effective of all preachers.

We take for our text his own words, descriptive or suggestive of his own mode. His work was pre-eminently to preach the gospel; and he condenses the whole statement into three words: *We preach Christ crucified.* This mode, which was his power, is more expansively given in a statement which he makes in 1 Cor. ii. 2: "For I determined not to know any thing among you, save Jesus Christ, and him crucified. For I was with you in weakness, and in fear, and in much trembling. And my speech and my preaching was not with enticing words of man's wisdom, but in demonstration of the Spirit and of power." Again, he says, "I came not to you with excellency of speech or of wisdom, declaring unto you the testimony of God."

That the apostle's preaching was with great effect, there is abundant evidence. His work, in this regard, the results accomplished by it, — in its radical reforming efficacy; in the number of souls reached and saved; in its influence upon the condition of the age, and the history of the world; in its bearing upon the kingdom of Christ, and the repletion and the blessedness of heaven, — is without any parallel. And it was a work not only vast in compass, but also various and profound in detail. It was a work on the soul itself, changing the man at the very centre and spring of all his action, succeeding, as the apostle did, to make the gospel a power to do this wherever he touched, — showing it a power alike upon those almost at antipodes in locality, and quite so in character; upon the barbarian and the civilized equally;

upon the men of the Greek type and the Roman type; upon the men of any of the religions and of none of them; upon persons of all the philosophies, those of none: all these about equally felt the power of this man in the ministry of the word. If it is true, now, that the apostle was so signally effectual in his speech and preaching, then it may be well for us to sit at his feet, and subject ourselves to his influence, — at once receive some shaping at his hand, and catch some quickening from the impulsion of his enthusiasm.

This type of preaching, as set forth and illustrated in the mode of the apostle, we can speak of only in a few of the main features thereof. It is very evident, from the broken specimens we have, that preaching, in the hands of Paul and his co-laborers, was no set or formal affair, was held to none of the now recognized canons; but was rather in a somewhat loose, free discourse, drawn from the Scriptures, and aimed to establish in the minds before them certain facts, as being in the Scriptures, and also as being their doctrine and material of redemption.

1. I remark, then, in the first place, that we find preaching, in the hands of these early performers, to be very much announcement, the proclaiming, attesting, or declaring of a testimony, — a setting forth of knowledge and doctrine. It is a sort of heralding, a trumpet tone and service; a seizing and greatening of certain primary and essential facts, giving them an unqualified and unmistakable prominence, somehow making them obtrusive and adhesive to the men in hearing. Thus did this apostle preach. Nothing, perhaps, more surprises us than Paul's confined range, as he announces,

in one of the passages quoted, what seems an inevitable sameness of truth and topic. Evidently two master ideas successively had possession and ruled in him, — first, the old, fomenting, Jewish idea; then, this regenerated and baptized into the Christian idea, the seat ever after of infinitely purer and intenser ardors; — not now the bondage of law in the Pharisaic interpretation, but the largeness and freeness and opulence of faith as the justifying principle or condition. We are not to suppose or admit that this species of limitation, recognized by the apostle, operated to cramp or enfeeble his action; but the opposite. For we find, all down the past, that the great achievers, by speech and deed, have been more commonly of a like limitation, — a very few things, on their part, to say or do; but those few overwhelmingly put.

There is one quality which preaching, when it is thus announcing, promulging, witnessing, — one quality it secures; namely, that it is very clearly, strongly positive in its character. Of necessity, it must be strongly positive, — a very projecting forth of the great essentials in fact and doctrine. This must be done, in order that the minds which are to receive them may, in some tolerable proportion to the whole, succeed in receiving them; that is, really take them in, apprehend them, and not mistake concerning them. It is amazing how difficult it is to secure a clear lodgement, in the minds of people, of the most simple, rudimental truths, in morals, government, or religion. Take repentance, for instance. How many hear repentance preached through life, and at the end but imperfectly know what it is; so that, if their salvation turned upon their having the right intellectual idea or apprehension, they would not be saved. We bear in mind that it is the passions which cloud and hinder; and this holds everywhere, on all subjects, — especially religion. Hence the propriety, yea, the necessity, that the preaching deal in very clear statements, — not in thin or fine or equivocal, not the truth split into hairs, but endued with substance, and built into the concrete; and continue thus, and, if possible, succeed in getting a few leading, right ideas at once unmistakably in the head, and profoundly in the heart.

2. The next statement I offer almost follows from the preceding. It is, that the kind of preaching we are considering — preaching with the obtrusive and implanting intent — not only does not ask for the refinements of rhetoric, the mere æsthetics; but instinctively dismisses them. The very aim and tone of this kind necessitate plainness. And then the great precursor in this line has struck for us the key: he has given the pattern, who, in carrying through his resolve not to know any thing among the people, save *Jesus Christ and him crucified*, fell, as he tells us, upon the simplicities of language; abjured the high-wrought, the artistic, or what he calls, as given in our tongue, the excellencies of speech. He appears before us as one evidently burdened, and greatly hesitating on account of the disadvantageous, the homely, the enfeebling, lying in his case. And yet, when he came to the work, he did it manfully, and he did it mightily; because his preaching was not with the enticing words of man's wisdom, but with the opposite both in spirit and style, and therefore with demonstration and power.

It is remarkable how often the men with the defects have the most signally wrought, and swept on to the large results; as in the case of our apostle, whom we hear groaning, in his conscious meanness, at the same time the world and heaven were ringing with the fame of his deeds. While sinking himself out of sight, principalities and powers, the most hostile and audacious, were giving way before him. And it was done in his case *by the foolishness of preaching;* and also in the case of most who have come after him, in any like efficiency, it has been by the foolishness of preaching. And how have we all sprung to the rescue of this phrase of Paul's using, ready to show that it does not mean foolish preaching! Yet I confess, for one, that I have been somewhat shaken on this point, and, from later observations, am about ready to confess that it does sometimes, at least, mean foolish preaching. One thing is certain, — that to us of the rules and the forms it is foolish preaching. There is no linking of a process, or backing of an argument, or felicity of figure or phrase; only this: the great things of God are boldly given, done with a rough depicting, a vehement downrightness, a persistent affirming. The people are told, It is so, just as it is here written in the Book; and it is amazing. The eternal all with you is at stake. See the rage and swelter of the devouring fire! Behold the Lamb of God. Now is the time! Escape for your life. And the rugged and steaming words take hold; and men in crowds, that never heard before, hear now; and the weakness and the foolishness strangely become to them a power of redemption. This, when it is about certain that the far abler men, by the more authentic modes, and by a speech replete with all the selectest qualities, never would have reached them.

When we say that these inferior qualities prove, in the directions named, the most effectual, still we add, that we are to suppose or assume certain other qualities as also being there, which help minister to the strong effect. For this must be conceded,—that no man ever yet produced a great effect on the popular mind, without something marked and positive to do it with. We may not have the wit to find it: the people have the sense to feel it. Some of the most vital conditions of power are observed by him.

3. Another statement I now make is, that, while the order of preaching in hand almost of necessity takes to the coarser, ruder rhetoric, it also falls prominently into the briefer, because self-evidencing, mode of proof. Its third great feature, then, is, that it is self-evidencing. It is very obvious, that the result of argument is not always reached by the established paths of logic. Occasionally it is done almost wholly by another process. Very often is it so, in securing the admission of the primary, the cardinal ideas in morals and religion. What, for instance, did the most incontrovertible reasoning, pressed for a generation by some of our purest and ablest men, avail to convince this Christian nation, that a man is a man, and that the doctrine of right in enslaving him is of the Devil? Almost nothing,— except to bring contempt on the pestilent agitators. God at length changed the style of proceeding. He employed upon us the shorter and more palpable process; dealt in premises that were blows: and, in a single year, the extreme of the conservatives joined to intensify the conclusions

of the old fanatics; and our Wall Streets and State Streets rung out the cry, "Down with Slavery."

It seems to be a principle, that whatever partakes of the nature of message must have the conditions of its enforcement very much within itself. The word "fire" is uttered at early night in the streets of a peaceful village. No one cares. It is done in the sport of some boys. At another time, the word brings instantly every sleeper upon his feet and forth to the contest; because, from the very tones the man uses, from the very way of his speaking, all are sure he is proclaiming a terrible fact. The very announcement carries its proof. Longinus, the early Greek critic, sets down Paul as the first master of undemonstrated statements; utterances without the form of demonstration, and yet they go forth with the efficacy of demonstration. We have, in the main, the explanation of this fact or power in this apostle's history and experience; in the fact that he came to believe by literally seeing. He did not take the gospel, — receive it as truth from the teaching or testifying of Peter, and the other apostles who were before him. It was, I repeat, by beholding. It came upon him as a fresh and huge revelation, by no second hand. As a streaming and burning column from heaven it came, and entered him at once, in fulness as light and warmth. And, as he came to believe by seeing, he made others believe, because he ever spake as one who had seen. His very mode and temper of speech was his argument. His vast emotion before the revealings of truth was his argument. The scathing of his brow from the fiery revelation; the brand, or scar, it then took on; the blear and anguished eyes even,—were his argument. Words coming out of such conditions, without any other backing, fell with a convincing effect. It is true of no other eloquence, as it is of the preaching kind, that its seat is in the man. Christianity, in its great facts, is authenticated in the preacher's experience. It has become a concrete embodiment in his soul; and all objective truth becomes a visibility before him. The unseen and eternal he looks upon. It is superfluous to say how such a man, with the saving message within him and the massed auditors before him, will speak. It will be, very likely, with a process not hinted in the books; in the use of short links and abrupt connections,—the quick forging of his own heart; in the utterance of words and phrases, charged, as they go, with the very instincts of truth; and hence with authority they go; with strong impulsion he speaks; with bulks and points he speaks; at once heavy to strike, and keen to enter in.

Nearly all the singularly effective in speech have been memorable in the use of phrases; have wrought the contents of a volume into a sentence; have concentred the Divine gospel in a word, and let it forth. Paul shows himself one of the greatest of these masters of phrases. Two or three words,—and all the powers and mysteries of redemption are conveyed; and if you hear them once, they are ever within you. Where there is this short, cohesive putting, there is almost necessarily the central warmth and the experimental self-evidencing. It is something the heart knows assuredly, and feels profoundly, and then flings off. Then, also, it is something the hearts over against are eager to take in. This constitutes the true process, the electric line; this the expeditious preaching, and is likely to prove the potently missionary preaching.

4. We come now to a fourth step or statement. Preaching of the kind we are considering is, in the first place, promulging. Secondly, As being preaching with the obtrusive and implanting intent, it is with a brief and somewhat rude rhetoric. Thirdly, It is attesting and thus has the effect of proving. Fourthly, It is dispensing. The condition of effectiveness, in one particular, is the power of a bold, outstanding rhetoric; in another, it is the indwelling of a profound, experimental assurance; in a third particular, it is the actual and large possession of the gospel. In other words, the effectual preaching is the generously dispensing. Paul, as he was at Ephesus, may illustrate. He was, when there, so surcharged with the miraculous potency, that from his body were brought unto the sick handkerchiefs and aprons; and health and life were diffused. The same thing, I love to think, held spiritually; and it was the gospel in Paul, so opulently and massively in him, that constituted largely, in his case, the wonderfully productive preaching force; not in him merely as assured truth, and to go from him in some form of resistless demonstration; in him rather as a resource and wealth of blessing, as a divine treasury of good, as a fountain of saving efficacy. I do not give to the servant the prerogative of the Master. But I do conceive of the servant, under the flowing of the Master, as taking in quantity, as largely possessing gospel; and then, in the uttering, pouring it out as a power of salvation. It goes from him, because it is so richly within him. As Peter said, *What I have, give I*

*thee;* and it was a more enduring substance than silver and gold.

There is a mystery in these transmissions from mind to mind, from preacher to his hearers. It is not thought, opinion, argument, merely, he conveys. In all instances of commanding effect, it is of the nature of substance, and seems to act almost as a physical property, and yet finely ethereal. It wells up, and pours abroad, crowding, as it goes, every avenue and every possible egress, — limbs, eyes, mouth, every feature; letting forth, as it were, a diffused substance of eloquence. It is by volume and quantity the man thus rules over us. Dr. Chalmers was a marked instance of this. A friend and countryman of his, in accounting for that almost unequalled sway he bore over other minds, refers to the activity and quantity of the affections, and all vital possessions. It was the massive earnestness of the man, which worked hugely within, and worked out in expression, through all the openings; and so he seized you, overbore you, held you at his will: and by some commonplace truth, made grand by his imagination and bathed in his passion; by an intrepid iteration and a cumulative insistance, — he wrought the saving decision and action in the souls of many. On other rostrums this may be a sort of magnetic quantity. In the preaching place, it should be, and sometimes has been, gospel quantity, gospel wrought within, by experience, by faith's appropriations, into large and benignant possession. This resource of efficacy we all may have. If we have it, we receive it from the fountain above. It is the gift of God; at once a palpable instrument, a very substance of power, — the means exhaustless of blessing and saving.

It comes very obvious to remark, — first, in the way of inference, that, in respect to high pulpit power, we see in what direction it lies; namely, in the inner spiritual enduing, not in the external adjustments and accomplishments. 2. We see, secondly, how great is our liability, how strong is our tendency in the wrong direction; namely, to the externals. We come to regard preaching as a profession. We cultivate the humanities. We get steeped in the literatures; are trained to the peculiarities and niceties of style, — grow partial to the novel modes, phrases, expressions, and use them. Thus we carry away the religious discourse from the unalterable conditions of a large effect. Preaching does not lie, it never can lie, in these æsthetic conditions. The entire history of the Church, the failures and the successes in preaching, alike show this. Go back to that passage of more than a century ago, when the Wesleys and their co-workers broke in upon the broad, stagnant calm, the all but universal sleep of death, in the English Church. They took one great truth, — *Ye must be born again*, — took it as life and reality into their own souls; and with a few coarse words they spoke it, and it shook like the trump of resurrection. And, as they went abroad, hurling this one truth, *Ye must be born again*, — hurling it, in ungainly phrase, against the roughest and stoutest souls, souls turned by myriads, demonstrating by their turning the might of the truth and the mode. We have something of the like in our day, both in our own country and in England, — a style and spirit unusual, a palpable handling of truth, and a veritable pulling at souls, as though these persons believed them literally dropping into hell. The preaching and the modes both put us in doubt, and cause us to stand aloof; and yet we have to confess that there is something there we have not, elements of power there worthy our considering. And I cannot doubt that we ourselves should advance in power, by an infusion from these unauthentic quarters, if we would consent to modify our stately proprieties with some of those pungent extravagances; and if, in consequence, the damaging charge is cast upon us, as it was upon Paul, that we are mad, we can take refuge, with him, in his own summary vindication: *The love of Christ constraineth us.* Better, we may say, one surging sea of fire, than these vast arctic floats of ice amid which we now seem wedged and stuck.

I remark again, we have a great deal to teach and set us in the direction where the power lies. God has been putting us to school, and in this school giving us lessons on the genuine earnestness, such as Paul showed when he said: *One thing I do,* — an earnestness which is a totality; the whole executive mass gathered up and consolidatedly given to one thing. It is sad that there is so much more of this in the dominion of sin and of evil than of good. In rebellion and sin we have seen it in its intensest and firmest type. Every thing there concurs, and bends to the one issue, and what won't is made to. Well would it be if we would take this lesson, and do similarly for God and his redemption.

In the same school are furnished some lessons on giving. In the past, some two millions at the most, this great nation, in all its Christian denominations, has attained to give, in order to extend the kingdom of Jesus; and we quite complacently felt that we did what we could. But God proceeded to exact, for a single year at least, one thousand millions; and we had to confess to it, that we could. Then another thousand millions was added on, and again we had to confess to it that we could; and this, like the smaller sums that went before, to put down a rebellion. God certainly has been disciplining us to higher ideas both of doing and giving.

And let me add also to a more effective speech and preaching. Our ministers, who have gone out in the conflict, all testify that they have gained new lessons in working for souls; have come at once summarily to preach at men, in all brevity and directness. The result, all through the ministry, we expect will be, a decided advantage in strength and terseness of doctrine, giving, in bolder proclamation, the great verities of sin and retribution.

## II.

### THE DIVERSIONS FROM PREACHING.

*For I am not ashamed of the gospel of Christ: for it is the power of God unto salvation to every one that believeth; to the Jew first, and also to the Greek.* — ROM. i. 16.

IT is very certain that we live in a world where a power is wanted to put things right; and here we have a power presented which professes to be competent to meet the world's sad exigency. It claims to be a moral power, adapted to remove moral evils. It is a power as truth, having this prerogative, — to carry with itself the convictions of truth, and implant where it strikes the evidence of its own intrinsic verity. It is a power as a provision, a repository, exhaustless of resources for the poor and needy. It is a power as a remedy, a specific Divine, which meets the case of the sin-sick soul, which, wherever applied, — in due form applied, — is found to be always adequate to remove the disease. We consummate our description by saying it is the power of God, — a system of truth, a scheme and fountain of grace, proceeding from God. And when it goes forth thus attended, there is revealed on earth no greater power, — the power of God.

The gospel is a power as being promulged; specifically, as being preached. By being preached has it won thus far nearly all its signal triumphs; and it has won some great triumphs. It is very obvious, that the gospel, as preached, proves a much greater power at one time, in one set of circumstances, than it does in some other. And the reason of this lies mainly in the fact of the Spirit's presence and working where the power is witnessed. While this is the great and main truth, it is also true that there are circumstances which favor or hinder the appropriate results of the gospel. So that a greater moral force, or measure of the divine influence, is required to bring to pass the same results,—greater at one time than at another. The remark is often made, that there are, at the present, obstructions, peculiar and greater than formerly, in the way of preaching,—matters which operate to hinder the legitimate effect of the gospel preached. As it is well that these be taken into the account in the minister's preaching, it may be in place to state some of those things, circumstances, causes, which are operating to cut down the effects of our preaching. I waive entirely the great, the supreme consideration, embraced in the presence or absence of the Holy Spirit; and keep to those subordinate matters which have their influence, and which pertain to ourselves and society.

And one thing which here strikes the mind, and this of a generic character, is the increase of simply diverting forces.

1. It was said, a great while ago, that God hath made man upright; but they have sought out many inventions. The latter clause in this declaration certainly holds its way and its truth through all succeeding ages; and never did it stand forth in so unquestioned

and prolific verity as now. The things invented to attract, to amuse, to excite, to occupy time and the thoughts, come along in one compact and crowded succession. And when are we without the presence of something of the sort? These are mostly new things. The gospel is an old thing, — a periodic thing; revolves like the sun. We had it last year; we have it this. Be patient, and it will come around the next. Time enough to consider the gospel when there is nothing else to be considered. How natural that this last will commonly get the go-by! How plain that the great theme and interest, for which the Maker of the world upholds the world, really has a compressed and narrow chance!

There are also the diversions of business, and these have acquired new force by the new facilities created. Business has quickened its movements — it being done by steam, by lightning — by instant and large strokes; therefore the more eager and exciting. The strife of business absorbs the man, — sinew and soul. The zeal of business eats him all up. We might reason otherwise, *a priori*, and suppose a different process and result, — that, as men can go so far and do so much in a little time, they can afford to lay over, and they will lay over, some of the shreds and odd ends of their time to the service of God and the care of their souls. Such might seem a good argument; but the fact is just the other way. Men were never so voracious of time; never so impatient of the least delay or intrusion upon their progress, as they are since they can travel so far and do so much in a little time. All this hurry and stir, and eager achievement, and gainful reaching far forth of heart and hand for the world, are diverting and absorbing forces. All go to take the mind, the thought, from God's claim; from the gospel, that meets and would save him. And just so far as these diverting forces successfully exert themselves, just so far they operate to cut down the power, diminish the due effect, of the gospel.

2. I remark again, that, in connection with this growth of diverting forces, there exists in the ministry a diminished power or ability to get attention to the gospel. I refer here to no fault in the ministry. There may be a fault, — a falling-off in the essential and effective qualities of character and office. The case may, in part, be here, — that the gospel preached has not the power it once had, because preachers now are not, in intellect and heart, what preachers have been at some previous time. But this is not the point I am concerned now to present. Admit that the ministry, as a whole, is all it ever was: it is true there goes not from it the power of some former days to arrest and influence the people. And one reason is, the people have changed in their estimate, their views, feelings, bearing, toward ministers. They have not, as a whole, that respect which was once visible. I speak not now of the awful distance and the wide chasm which yawned between ministers and people. This was an evil and a hinderance, and we are glad it is gone. But something valuable may have gone with it. There was a reverence for the office, a certain wholesome authority conceded to the teachings of him who worthily filled the office, a disposition to hear, with something of the implicit frame and faith, — hear, because it issued from the oracle and the minister of God, —

very manifestly a position favorable to being reached and benefited.

Formerly, the advocate, the promulger of this gospel stood almost alone as the instructor of the people, the weekly orator, the public speaker. Now who is not a speaker? The sort of competition into which the pulpit is brought accounts, in part, for the relative depression of the occupants of the pulpit. They speak to those to whom everybody is speaking, on every sort of subject, and in all popular and captivating modes. How plain to see, that the preacher and his theme get on a level with all the rest that is going, — commonly below the level. Instead of having the field to himself, he shares it with a multitude of busy workers. Now, let him lag behind or fall off in the spirit of his endeavors, how plain they will go by him and over him; and the people will suffer them, and let him lie there in his sluggishness and ignominy! Let there be marked defects in his teaching, — subjects dropped from his ministrations which are vital to human welfare and to the scheme of redemption, so that others are heard where he is reverently silent; heard as supplying his lack of service; heard the more eagerly because he will not speak, — how inevitable that he lose still more in influence from the strenuous and fervid doings of others. This state of things will go on and increase; this competition will grow warmer and sharper; and the pulpit, and the gospel preached therefrom, will unquestionably be put by it at a disadvantage as compared with other days, — far more difficult to get a hearing and make an impression upon the souls of men; yea, more difficult for the great God himself to get a hearing, on account of the numberless creature tongues that are set a-going, not a few of which, in their own opinion, are able to talk more wisely even than He that made them.

3. But there is not only the competition of tongues: there is also the conflict of religions, — of the various schemes, theories, remedies which are brought forward, claiming the popular credence. This I adduce as another cause of diversion, or obstruction standing in the way of the gospel's just effect, — the many and various styles of religion. And I include here every thing which is brought forward as the soul's refuge or reliance, — whatever comes in the shape of a remedy or a revelation substituted for God's scheme, which is one for all the world and all the ages. The name of these is legion. They are very taking, many of them; very plausible in some of their aspects; supported by some remarkable reasonings, and still more remarkable doings. What, now, is the effect of these manifold schemes, these remedies and pretended revelations, brought forward, advocated, and sustained as they are? Manifestly, it is to distract and unsettle the minds of the people; to breed dissatisfaction with that scheme which is so unbending, which claims to be the only one, which repels and rejects all the rest, which shuts all souls up to this, — to be saved by this, or saved by nothing. In this day of multiplied devices to reform and to save, there are many whose quarrel and breaking off from God's plan is at this very point. They will not bear the restriction. Then this feeling naturally rises and spreads. Indeed, it comes to be said, They are all about alike. According as a man thinketh, so is he. If I only receive some one, my believing and receiving that will make it the right one

for me; and all will be well, no matter which I take. Is not this the precise state of the case very extensively in the community? And such an attitude of the popular mind who does not see to be powerfully adverse to the reception of God's gospel? The essential mischief and the virulent efficacy of this position, and inclining of the mind of the people, lies here, — in the fact, that it is a sceptical state of mind. And, Oh, what influences are at work still more to unsettle, to throw every thing, if possible, into question and doubt, — leading to the rejection of principles which have been established almost from the foundation of the world, — principles and verities upon which all the virtue and order and happiness of the world hitherto have been built, — principles and verities upheld by columns of evidence, based on earth and crowned with the light of heaven, — columns the ages could not crumble, which, after the wear of the ages, are fresh and bright still, all covered with God's inscriptions — reject all this, and then turn and believe what? Believe any thing. Believe and take down just what any arrogant and noisy pretender chooses to put down them. This I name as a disease of the times, — the rejecting of matters which stand on solid evidence, and the receiving of matters which have the merest sham of evidence. Matters not relished, because they cross the depravity, though they come with demonstration, many say, "We won't have them." Matters which come with a novelty, and deal gently with the depravity, and open another gate than God's contracted one to go out from our troubles, are received, all evidence wanting. This consideration is enough. They are somewhat new and various, and in some of their aspects or appliances quite likely to suit. Now bring along by the side of these that one ancient and immutable thing, — the glorious gospel of the blessed God, which utters no flatteries, and makes no compromises; which goes against all sin, which brings no other than a salvation from all sin; and which brings every receiver of it into a conflict and exterminating warfare with his own bosom sins, — bring this before those who have been fascinated and bewitched with these other kinds and the accompanying pretensions — how tame and stale, crabbed, antiquated, ungenial, uncourteous, because unaccommodating. And how strong the chance, in such conditions, that God's plan — salvation by the cross — encounter instant if not indignant repulsion.

4. There is another matter which may go into our detail of obstructive causes. It is found in the mental conditions increasingly prevalent, the growing want of good mental habits. These may be characterized as getting light, superficial, in distinction from the patient and solid; and are brought about, in part, by the causes already enumerated, by the multitude of things ever revolving. These call the mind outward, away from its own appropriate place and work, — earnest thought and reflection. The reading also contributes to the same unmanly state. As a general thing, it is light, — not invigorating and nutritious. There is brought along, first, an indiscriminating state of mind, — a blurred vision, — intellectual eyes which see every thing in a sort of confused and muddy conglomeration. Another thing is a state which shrinks from close thought and veritable argument; consequently shows but little patience before the discourse

which asks for continued thought in the hearer. This is a state which does not relish substantial preaching, — intellect, discussion, matter in preaching, — because grown incompetent to cope with such things. No mind is wanted in sermons, because no mind in themselves; both indisposed and incapacitated; indisposed, because incapacitated. A long reach of massive matter threatens to break them down. A chain of compact reasoning, forged out, linked together, and directed toward them is about as formidable to them as so much chain-shot. How much there is of this mental superficialness and imbecility, one almost fears to know. Very certain it has been advancing upon us. Hence the call in many quarters for smooth and easy preaching, — the fine and popular discourse, made pretty and shining by a liberal lay of varnish on the outside, and all the better for not having much of any thing inside. In carrying out this plan for a superficial and easy religion, it comes very natural to substitute the form for the power; a routine of form and ceremony is pretty much the whole of it. Bodily exercise, crosses, genuflexions, and manifold mummeries, — these the religion, what has efficacy, what saves. Salvation, then, is mechanical, — no heart nor intellect in it; no heart nor intellect required to produce it. Of course here is no place for preaching that is such. It is not wanted; gradually dies out. Here, let me say, we have a potent influence, working, in our time, against God's chief means of reform and redemption, and working, I am sorry to say, even amongst the descendants of the Puritans. I thought God made them men and women, not supple tools; endowed them with minds, souls, not mere knee-hinges. This altar tendency, in its extreme lurch, goes, if not to extinguish preaching, utterly to cripple the power of it. There are minds, souls, of the Puritan make, who will say to this puerile wave, "Hitherto, and no further."

Such are some of the obstructions to the gospel's due power existing in our time, as it seems to me, and tending to diminish the just measure of its efficacy. What is to be done? Let our confidence in the gospel, as the remedy for the world's ills, diminish correspondingly? No. God has his plan, his design; and will have his time. Though it may look dark now and then for his cause, and other schemes and doctrines stand forward in the popular lead; though it begins to look almost as though the gospel had had its day, done well in its time, indeed, but now has grown decrepit, and is left limpingly and far in the rear of the floating and vaunting banners of progress, — it is not so. No: it is God's; and God's time will come, and he will make his demonstration; and it will appear that what the gospel once did, it can do again, and on a wider scale than ever before, — working on a world-wide scale its wonderful and redeeming results. This, then, is to be done. Whatever the obstructions, whatever the delays, we are to be hopeful; having full confidence in the gospel, its vitality and conquering efficacy, wherever in faith and hope employed.

I can only indicate two or three particulars it will be well for the preacher to regard in his use of the gospel, if he would make it, in the circumstances, the power of God unto salvation. 1. One point is, that he preach this gospel in its immutable, unimprovable substance; preach God's scheme just as God has given it, in all its principles and applications, never adventuring to modify or diminish aught; never in any way to adjust the message to the clamors of any popular demand, or to soften and smooth it to please the more fastidious tastes. This we may settle in our mind,—that it must be God's gospel if it is to go with his power.

2. Another condition is, that the gospel be preached in its greatness, its mystery, its infinite resource of saving; that it be preached in that one ascendant feature of it which alone is the gospel,—which denied or reduced there is no gospel,—salvation by the Crucified. Greatness is here: the eternal Son given for the life of the world. Mystery is here: God the Son appearing in human flesh. Sacrificing love is here: the God-man, in the sinner's place, enduring an immeasurable woe. Here is that which stands out separate from all else; transcends, overtops, overmasters, in strangeness, in soul-grappling interest, all other works or exhibitions in the evolving drama of God's affairs. This doctrine of the cross the preacher is to greaten, and set commandingly forth; tax all the powers of his heart and mind, that he may approximate to do it. And when he does, it stands before every man in supremacy and as a finality. If we succeed in bringing out the glory and power of the cross, it will be a power unto salvation. This, if any thing, will make men pause and consider, will make them feel, will encourage faith and the soul's commitment to this foundation. They will trust their souls' vast interests to it as they see the fountains and oceans of mercy opened here; and they will not dare to resist and put finally from them the crucified Son of God.

3. In order to present such a truth as this, and those connected with it, there must be prayer, study, the mind's utmost tasking. If effectively done, it must be so done; all the better that it be vigorously intellectual, because of this lighter, popular tendency. Let there be at least this counteraction, — that the sermons are able, that they go to the foundations, that they show the basis and the reason of things, be inwrought with thought, fact, substance; and, in connection with this solid character, that they be fresh, and in sympathy with what is going on, dealing with the actualities of business and of life; bearing upon the very men now on the stage, taking them in their present modes of thought and principles of action. In times so flagrant, and so crowded with resisting and diverting forces, it is indispensable that the preacher become a master of that searching, palpable, business-like style of address which lays its significant hand upon the living and throbbing conscience, making, if possible, every conscience such that chances to be in attendance.

4. And, in order to the largest and best results, we say further, that the preaching must be with authority: it must come to the souls of the people with the infinite sanctions of Almighty God, — life if you obey, death if you refuse. He that believeth shall be saved; he that believeth not shall be damned. There is power in such words as these. True, many are coming not to like them, some not to endure them, but are bold to order away from their ears the disturbing sounds; and not a few so-called good people would have the preacher of this gospel, considering the prejudices so rife, very sparing in these ultimate and appalling utter-

ances. But no, thou man of God: yield to no such miserable squeamishness. Give no place to the sickly and puling philanthropy abroad. Go forth with a sound and an honest heart, — a heart tender in its spirit, but oaken in its fidelity, not keeping back where God has put forward, knowing well that your power is not in your own discretion, but in the word, the arm, the Spirit of Him who sends you.

This pulpit* has a most favorable record, in the past, of loyalty to the divine and also of fidelity to the human. Men strong and true have ever stood in it. May our brother who is to succeed in this ministry carry forward the work so auspiciously begun! We ask for him that he may have a growing experience of the gospel, and from the fountain within be prepared to preach it with all confidence as the power of God, — ever loving to set forth in their simple majesty those truths which are vitally and essentially the gospel, which have been so regarded through the ages, and that have wrought so signally, and accumulated all along down, uncounted trophies; and built these into columns and pyramids of demonstration, showing them to be of God. This is not the gospel to be ashamed of, nor this the time. Be it our trust, our joy, our instrument still of conquest and achievement; and may this particular field into which our brother now enters give perpetually fresh proofs of its transforming efficacy!

---

* That of the Third Church, Portland, Maine.

## III.

### THE ECLIPSED LUMINARY.

*If, therefore, the light that is in thee be darkness, how great is that darkness.* — MATT. vi. 23.

OUR Saviour, in this connection, brings an illustration from the eye. *If thine eye be single,* — that is, if it be sound, healthy, — *thy whole body will be full of light.* The individual will perceive clearly, and walk correctly; he will be not only a light to himself, but a safe guide to others.

But if the eye is diseased, double, wavering, then the whole body is full of darkness. Every thing is confused; and the individual not only stumbles himself, but all who depend upon him, or follow him, stumble likewise.

The light in a person, strictly speaking, is reason and conscience, — his intellectual and moral nature.

The conscience corrected, and the heart purified by truth, enable him both to see and to shine. The light of truth, of conscience, and a holy character extinguished, the darkness, — put where there was, and where from the very nature of the case there should be, light, put instead of light, — becomes truly very great darkness. The principle, then, is simply this: If where light was and light should be, there is put darkness, *the darkness is very great.* To one who has always been blessed with vision, who has looked freely forth upon all the beauties and wonders of nature and art, and who has always directed at will his own steps, but whose sight should be suddenly destroyed, and darkness at once fill and surround him, — to him who is the subject of the calamity, and remembers the contrast, how great the darkness. Or, take the case of one who has been spiritually enlightened, — enlightened from above, — who was filled with light, and became a body of light to others, — let all that light be put out, and darkness take its place, how great is that darkness.

This is the sentiment I propose to illustrate at the present time: *That when the Christian ceases to shine, and darkness comes in the place of his light, it is very great darkness.* This is a case which not unfrequently occurs. It is often an actual condition of things. But, if a true Christian, the dimness, the darkness, are but temporary; the foulness will be purged out, the cloud will pass away, and he will yet shine on earth, and shine yet brighter in heaven.

It is a sad truth, implied in our text and stated in our proposition, that the Christian does become darkness in the world sometimes; and the process is an easy one, and easily explained. If his faith is not corrupted, the great objects of his faith pass from his view; rather, he turns away from them; they are lost sight of for a season. Then his conscience falls into slumber, the heart grows callous and is soon defiled. Thus, becoming corrupt and worldly within, he is irregular and disobedient without; his conduct is a departure from the spirit and the precepts of the gospel; his life is wanting in all the clear manifestations of godliness. While the fact of the change is thus sad, the effects of it are far more so.

The Christian changed from light to darkness, — *how great is that darkness*. This appears, if we consider, —

I. In the first place, *the mere negative loss* in his forbearing to let his light shine. He has been made a luminous body, but he has ceased to shine. How much need of his light in the scene in which he moves. How much darkness to be removed; how little moral light shed for its removal; how much good he would do by steadily shining; how much did he do in the days of his soundness and integrity. The world are reminded of truth and duty, and the way to gain God's favor and final acceptance. They are made to see that there is a difference between him that serveth God, and him that serveth him not. They see the power of the religious principle, — the excellence and the loveliness of true piety. Impressions are made that are abiding. Some are convinced and won to the way of life; the clear and beautiful shining of that disciple at once draws them, and illumines the way of their return to God. Many may be — yea, often are —drawn to the path of peace by the attractive radiance of the pure, faithful disciple.

Another consideration is the great expense at *which he was prepared to shine.* He who was the brightness of the Father's glory, and who is now the light of the world, came down to the earth, and died upon the cross, that the sins of that disciple might be blotted out, that the Spirit might be sent to renew his nature, and so fit him to reflect the beams of the Sun of Righteousness, and be a living light in his sphere.

But when he ceases to shine, all that expense is so far lost. Christ's object in dying for him, and changing him by his Spirit, was not to save his single, solitary soul, but that he should be an agent in saving others. But when he ceases to shine, he ceases to do any good in the world. All the blessed effects we have considered, cease. There is a great and sad loss, — a loss in part of the Saviour's death for him, and the Saviour's work of renovation upon his heart; a loss, utterly, of all the good impressions and saving reformations which might and ought to have been produced by the power of his shining, the light of his example. In view, then, of the negative consideration, the mere loss experienced, we may begin to exclaim, how great the darkness. But the exclamation becomes more emphatic when we consider, —

II. In the next place, *some of the positive evils in the case.* It is not a simple subtraction of so much good which might have been done, — because there is no neutrality in influence. He that is not for Christ is against him. If we gather not with him, we scatter abroad. If we shed not light, we shed darkness; and how great must be that darkness.

Because it is a very conspicuous darkness, a darkness peculiarly visible. It is so on account of the change which has occurred. Yesterday, it is remembered, he was a shining body; to-day, it is seen, he is obscured, and sheds no ray. A change so great as from light to darkness is a very notable change. Multitudes who gave little heed to the shining of that Christian are all eagerness and wonder the moment he ceases to shine. Thus it becomes a peculiarly visible darkness.

It is an incongruous, unnatural darkness, inasmuch as it is a body of light, so to speak, radiating darkness, How strange! what has happened? Who can account for so monstrous a phenomenon? Were it the darkness of night, it would not be thought of; it would be congenial, and all would go to their repose. But it is the darkness of an eclipse,—how much greater in its effects than the darkness of the thickest night. To have the sun pass out of sight in the order of nature, is a trifle. But to have him turned into blackness in his meridian position; to have night, as it were, issuing from the face of the king of day,—fills all minds with amazement.

When the Christian becomes darkness, it is the darkness of *an eclipsed luminary;* and we know that men will gaze at such a sight, all eyes will centre there. How wonderful was the scene of the sun's momentary utter extinction which occurred early in the present century. All eyes, at that instant, were directed upward; the interest growing more and more intense as the darkness spread over the disc of the great luminary, until the last ray went out, when an involuntary shuddering seized every heart. The light that was in the sun then became darkness; and who that saw it has forgotten, and yet who can describe how great was that darkness?

The vividness of the impression which this sort of darkness makes is another consideration to be put into the estimate. It so infixes itself in the memory, the world gaze and never forget; they carry, it may be, the recollection to hell with them, and there curse for ever the memory of these eclipsed luminaries.

It is a darkness the wicked love to look at and feed

upon; they seem to have an intense relish for it. Like the owl at heavy midnight, they strain and distend their utmost capacity of vision, that they may drink in the congenial gloom. Not only do they love an interpretation of the Bible which blots out all the distinctive glory and searching meaning of this book,—they love, much more, a comment in the life of the disciple which contradicts the voice, or mitigates the light, issuing from these holy pages.

But I have not said the whole about this darkness. Not only is it a conspicuous darkness, an incongruous, unnatural darkness, an impressive darkness, an attractive darkness,—it is injurious upon the course of the world, fatal to the souls of men. We have seen, first, that it is a sight which brings all eyes to behold it; then it brings destruction upon multitudes who do behold it.

The influence of the lapsed, obscured Christian goes to accomplish all this mischief, because it tends to unsettle the minds of men as to the truth of religion, and of all the great doctrines of religion. His own principles become unsound, and this is the darkening of his own mind; then he diffuses these unsound principles, and so darkens others. His standing, as a disciple of Christ, enables him to do it. He gives currency to error, to false doctrine, as he could not do in other circumstances; for he is clothed with a species of authority for his work of corruption and ruin. He strikes a heavy blow, and it falls upon the very foundations. The sentiment is deposited in the breasts of many, to work there silent and deadly, that there is no reality in religion; it is an empty cheat; this great spiritual change so much talked about is nought but delusion; it has no power upon the character, nothing permanent in the results.

But his influence goes not only to corrupt the principles of men; it corrupts also the practice. Such an one leads the way in bad practice. He authenticates and gives currency to disobedience, the breaking down of God's laws. If he is a Sabbath-breaker, he brings, so far as he can, the authority of Christ and his religion to sanction Sabbath-breaking; if fraudulent, to sanction fraud; if impure, to sanction impurity. So he propagates his misdeeds; he rears up and draws after him a train to do as he does; and then to shelter themselves from rebukes without, and goadings within, under the wing of his religious profession, under the authority of his Christian life.

It is true, the Bible speaks differently, yea, oppositely: if these followers of the blind guides would go there, they would be instructed and corrected. But the Christian's life — the spirit, the conduct of the professor of godliness — is all the bible multitudes ever read. Here the page they gaze upon; here the text they quote; here the authority they bow to. They get their impressions and notions here, and so walk according to this rule. Some are made sceptics; the lapsed Christian's life, the argument, the dark demonstration which has turned them into infidels, and profane and bitter revilers. Others say, "If that be religion, we wish to have nothing to do with it; if that be a state of grace, the Lord grant that we may live and die in a state of nature." Others are put perfectly at rest on the great question of salvation. They think they see so little difference between men of the Church and men of the world, there is very little ground for alarm. If the former are safe, the latter cannot be in any great danger. God certainly will not predicate opposite destinies upon distinctions of character too small and too faint to be seen. Others, who feel some solicitude about their souls, and try somewhat for a better state, know not whither to go, nor what they must become. The way is all dark to them. They wander wearily about, and find no Saviour, no hope. They fix their eye, it may be, upon some dim, doubtful disciple, in order that their case may be an easy one; and then settle down upon something short of Christ. There can be no question but one false hope begets another. A low, uncertain character for godliness propagates its kind. The consequence is, that many who seem to set out for heaven lose their way, and lose their souls. How sad that the person who should have illumined his path, and led him onward and upward, was the dark impediment over which he stumbled and perished. Had that Christian been a light in his sphere, that friend, that neighbor, would have gone to heaven: his light being darkness, that friend, that neighbor, went to hell. How great was that darkness.

Suppose, now, that all the Christians in a given place were like him, — the entire Church in that place obscured, all her light put out, all distinctive truth blotted from her creed, and silenced in her pulpit, and wiped from the life of her members; and error and dishonesty, and all forms of ungodliness, put instead, and going forth, as it were, under heaven's great seal, — who can estimate the condition, or paint the blackness, of that darkness? We call it a sad condition in a community, if there is nothing in favor of religion, — no lights alluring to heaven, no lives speaking for God and the soul, no characters that are living arguments for his truth and cause. But infinitely more sad, if every thing in the name and form and profession of religion goes directly to discredit religion; the lives which should be arguments in favor of God's truth and cause are all arguments against it; the influences which should press toward heaven become not merely negative, but push positively and mightily toward hell. Native, full-grown, unregenerated sinners are comparatively harmless, let them constitute the great mass of a population: but this regeneration backward; this falsifying the true and the holy; this putting out light and putting on darkness instead, making men doubt, making them disbelieve, making them stumble, solemnly authenticating the way to hell,— giving a sort of sacredness to the broad road, and giving to multitudes, not the baptism of fire, but a baptism, a sealing, for the fire which shall never be quenched,— what mind other than the Infinite Mind can take in the whole extent of the evil?

I have made the supposition of a church all turned to darkness, and drawn the picture, and presented it to your imagination, that you may see and feel and exclaim, How great the darkness. In making some remarks upon this sentiment and discussion, it comes very obviously to speak,—

1. In the first place, *of the responsibility of the Christian*,— his responsibility as one always in view, belonging to a city set on an hill, having no neutrality, always either for his Master or against him; always shedding either light or darkness; if darkness,— darkness of a strange and destructive sort;— his responsibility as one shut up to this necessity, and to

abide under it for ever. He may go back, but he never can get back to be a simple, original, impenitent sinner as he once was. That condition was comparatively a negative one. Now he is chained to the necessity of doing, in a pre-eminent sense, positive good or evil. He is professedly regenerated; and it will be in its fruits, in a pre-eminent degree, a regeneration for heaven or hell. There is a great responsibility in this sort of necessity abiding upon him, and holding him, as with links of adamant, to these immense consequences. If he is right in heart, right in life, — living devotedly to him who died to save, — every thing — time, talents, property — consecrated to the cause of redemption, there is no telling what his Lord may enable him to do. Some vast tract of desert may become, through him, a well-watered garden; some hundreds, perhaps thousands, of souls may stand up in heaven, and point to him as the author, under God, of their mighty joys. If he pursue the other course, the consequences will be equally vast and interminable, but directly the opposite. Darkness will take the place of the light, death eternal the place of the life eternal. Oh the guilt of the perversion, the responsibility of the substitution. He who substitutes a base coin for a pure one does a slight injury. He who puts a deadly potion in the place of a healthful beverage does a great wrong, and incurs a heavy responsibility. He who extinguishes the beacon light on the rock-bound coast, amid the raging of the midnight storm, putting darkness before the mariner's eye and despair in the mariner's heart, brings upon himself greater guilt and a weightier doom. But he who puts out the light of truth and of a holy example, and puts instead the darkness of gospel error and Christian sinning, causing multitudes to make shipwreck of faith and of their souls too, — that person, with the vows of God upon him, goes up higher, far higher, in the scale of guilt, and will go, unless he repent, far lower in the gulf of fire beneath. How solemn, awful almost, the Christian's responsibility. Let me die and go alone to my place, rather than administer to any such results as these.

But there is no reason to shrink or be afraid. There is grace enough in Christ; strength enough there: you shall not ask for it in vain. There is light enough in that great Luminary of the world and the Universe. Go, live right under those beams, and you shall have light. We are only to go to the fountain there and take care of the fountain here, and we shall be full of light, and spread light, and do better for our Master than we sometimes have done.

2. I remark, secondly, we see how it comes to pass, that the faults, the sins, the derelictions of Christians and the Church, are so commonly exaggerated by men of the world. It seems, from what is said often in this quarter, that there is very little that is just or lovely or of good report in the Church, and every thing in it that is dishonest, contentious, and hateful; there is hypocrisy there, and every form and style of villany, — a very corrupt concern. Now this is gross and injurious falsehood, to be attributed, in part, to the world's hatred of godliness. They first wish to have it so, then they make it so. And they are helped to make it so by the operation of the principle in our text.

The sinning of Christ's subjects is very conspicuous

sinning: the sinning of the devil's subjects, very much more out of sight. In this latter case, it is a kingdom of darkness; they are deeds of darkness, done in an atmosphere of darkness. Who sees, or cares, or says any thing about it? But, in the latter case, it being darkness in a luminous body, as we have shown, it is clearly visible; and the strangeness and incongruity of the thing bring all men to stare at it. We know that a little spot in the sun gets more notice than all the sun's brightness; one single hour of eclipse induces more attention, more talk, than ten years of his glorious shining. Here, now, is the principle. Hence it comes, that the Church suffers so greatly from small departures, limited offences; hence, if one member suffers, all suffer with it; if one is charged with sin, all, in a sense, are charged with the same. The one sin becomes multiplied into a hundred sins. The little dim spot is spread and stretched, till it seems to cover the whole body with blackness.

It is admitted there is wrong in the Church; but I rejoice to know that the wrong, in most instances, is as nothing compared with what many in the world would make it. It is admitted there is not all the truth and righteousness in the Church that there should be, and will be; but I rejoice in the fact, that there is more there than in all other places beside. I do believe this is a fact: indeed, I believe that nearly all the heaven-accepted righteousness on the earth is in the Church; though there be some darkness in her, still nearly all the light is there. And yet it is true, that vast multitudes go down to destruction because Christians and the Church are not what they should be.

3. I wish to make a third remark on this fact; first, give the reason of it, and then, show that there is no reason in it. The reason of this fact, that so many perish on account of the inconsistencies of Christians, is found in the principle of our text, — *how great the darkness*. It may be in itself a little spot; yet it fills the whole of that perverse eye, so that it can see nought but darkness. The consequence is, religion is not recommended, but stands dishonored before him. He rejects it, perhaps he scorns it; he keeps his sin, he comforts himself in his rebellion; and in the end he is a ruined being. This is the reason of his course. But, as I said, there is no reason in it, because the Church is not the ultimate standard. Christians are not the Bible, after all, though they be the only bible multitudes read. God has another bible back of them, and that is the bible God will support, — that the standard he will bring and hold men to, and judge them by. His professed disciples may falsify every page, every doctrine, every precept; but that does not make it false. It abides notwithstanding, and will abide, as eternal truth; its promises, its threatenings, its uttered doom, will be accomplished. Now, cannot rational men see, have they not sense enough to see, that this is the standard they ought to come to? Though all the Church were unmitigated blackness, there is light here. Does not the caviller see it is not enough that he has reasoned down the Christian's life? There is no safety for him till he has gone beyond and reasoned down the Bible; not only blotted out the arguments arising from the Christian's practice, but blotted out the arguments, also, embodied in God's great and authoritative sayings. Even then, in this ex-

treme supposition that it is all darkness on our part, where is the reason of the caviller's course? There is none, — it is madness.

Take, now, the case as it is. Christians, as a body, do not falsify the Bible. Certainly there are those who illustrate all its spirit and teaching; there are many who do this. They are lights in the world; they perfect and point and clinch the Bible argument. They speak in their life, as God speaks in his Word. Is there any reason, I ask, in making all this nothing? — all this light nothing? — all the sun's shining nothing, his spots every thing? God calls attention to this light. Men choose the darkness; they might walk to heaven in this light; there is enough of it, and more than enough. They prefer to wrap themselves up in the darkness they find, and in that go down to death. They allow one professor's life that is wrong, to sway them more than ten or twenty Christian lives that are right. Is there any reason in this? Ye men of reason and understanding, is there any?

How this course must appear hereafter. I have thought, sometimes, how the lost must feel when they look back and consider on what foolish grounds they went to hell; with what contemptible sophistry they were led on; with what meagre, miserable bait they allowed the devil to take them.

O my friends, this is far-reaching business. You are fast moving to the eternal scene: there you will encounter a most searching light; there you will have to do, not with fables, but with the verities of God's unchanging word; there you will meet, not shadows, but solid and overwhelming realities. Look now to the right things. Yield to the dictates of reason, and to the urgencies of the gospel, and seek the things which are above, and perish not from that high position you occupy, of light and privilege and hallowed influence. If you do, yours will be a most fearful doom.

## IV.

### SALVATION IN NO OTHER.

*Neither is there salvation in any other: for there is none other name under heaven given among men, whereby we must be saved.* — ACTS iv. 12.

SALVATION, our deliverance from sin and death, the condition on which hangs the vast and hidden future, — on no subject, perhaps, are people more ready to listen to announcements than on this; and on this we might come forth to you with at once various and variant announcements.

I might come, gravely announcing to you, that this salvation is a matter in which you have no responsibility, and you are in no danger of missing it; for God who gave his Son will make it sure that every creature of his involved in sin, be a sharer in this salvation: God will bring you all to it. Thus to announce and say would bring the announcer and promulger into favor with a large class, and they would concede to him the quality of liberalness or generousness. But, really, does it not look as though he had very much overdone the thing, transcended the record, in making this absolutely unlimited announcement?

But suppose that he, or some one succeeding him,

puts in some sort of restriction, announcing that while you must have some Saviour, Patron, or Helper, must proceed on some mode of duty or service, still you may make your choice, — choose a divine or human Saviour, christian or pagan; or, discarding all systems and all helpers, do the whole within yourself, in your own way; do it by penance or by beneficence; only do something according to your own judgment and aptness.

It might be pleasant to approach you in this line of liberalness or proximate free-thinking, giving all this choice or scope to people, as to the grounds, conditions, modes of being saved. Certainly in many quarters it is even the demand of the people. But we have a higher allegiance. We have to deal with fact and truth as God has put it. We have to state salvation in the terms, the conditions, in which the Infinite Author of it presents it to the acceptance of the race. And according to this Authority it is by one name and way. The system or scheme is one of rigid limitation, made absolutely exclusive by the apostle through a most emphatic asseveration: *Neither is there salvation in any other: for there is none other name under heaven given among men, whereby we must be saved.* The meaning of this cannot be mistaken. It means that there is only one way by which it is possible for us to be saved, and that is by Christ.

This statement or sentiment so plainly laid down, is it to be proved by us? If that is asked, then we prove it.

1. We prove it by the words that declare it. Enough for the believer in God's Word, that his Word so teaches and affirms, that there is salvation in no other;

that there is no other foundation, *for other can no man lay than that is laid, which is Jesus Christ.*

2. The other proof is drawn from the salvation itself: that this *necessarily* is to the exclusion of all other schemes.

We first consider God's gift and sacrifice in the premises. He gave his Son, — gave him to humiliation and death. We next consider Christ's position before he came to our world, who and what he was; the greatness, the infiniteness, the supremacy pertaining to him. We consider what he parted with; what he endured; how he laid off the glory, took the infirmity, became a man of sorrows, and acquainted with grief. We read the description of him, as uniquely and sublimely constituted, — God in human flesh, — the God-man. We read the description of what came upon him, what was laid upon him, when he thus vicariously stood for a sinning race. He was stricken and smitten of God. For the transgression of God's people was he smitten. *It pleased the Lord to bruise him, and put him to grief. He was wounded for our transgressions; he was bruised for our iniquities; the chastisement of our peace was upon him, and with his stripes we are healed.* There is Deity; and, on the Divine part, the inconceivable of sacrifice and suffering submitted to, endured for the saving of men, that God might be just and holy, and yet save. So God declares, *just,* while he justifies the ungodly. All this was done by the divine wisdom and appointment; the amazing sacrifice, the boundless cost, was entered upon, was assumed, by his benevolent desire, that his creatures might be saved. We reason that it took all that, the illimitable of that, to save; and that nothing less was competent to save man. It cost suffering like that the Son of God bore in his own person to deliver or save the guilty from the suffering eternal of hell. If, now, God made such a provision of saving, it was because it was necessary, because no less one would answer.

We might put the argument on this ground, that, if God saw fit, it would be proper for him, as the great Ruler over all, to make his own condition, and hold men rigidly to it, and call them away from every notion or scheme of their own. But when we consider that his doing for our saving is not ARBITRARY, that we are to suppose and accept it all as strictly fitting, and as meeting the great difficulty in the way, and that God carried the infinite to its ultimatum, — that only divine qualities and powers could have sufficed in the exigency, — then how plain that no secondary can be admitted; no man may set aside the sacrifice of the Son of God, and place in its stead some work or contrivance of his own. But this is proving what is in itself plainer, more convincing, than any proof. God sent his Son to save the world. Christ, the Son of God, on the cross, met death to save the world from hell. This God declares to be THE WAY. Then, of course, the way was to the exclusion of all others. Then it becomes us to look to it, and see how we walk, what we trust to for the help of our souls.

There is one name; if we believe in it, we shall be saved: one way; if we take it, we shall be saved. There are many other ways, a portion of them seemingly right and fair. We may try any or all of them, and we shall not be saved, because it is written, *Neither is there salvation in any other: for there is none other name under heaven given among men, whereby we must be saved.* The Bible restriction is to one person, CHRIST; and to one mode of saving, THE CROSS. Christ and his cross, the grand theme and substance. Here the one grand centre and unity and power in God's scheme of redemption, specifically, essentially, and ONLY this. This exclusion of all else, this restriction to one person and act in order to be saved, is the doctrine of my text, — is the solemn affirmation of God.

Allow me, in what remains, to make a few practical remarks and applications of the subject.

1. And my first remark is, that there is wealth and largess in connection with this restriction. I say this because the opposite is often alleged. The limitarian scheme, as it is called, how many flings at it. We hear it denounced as partial, stinted in its promise, and still poorer in its performance. But mark the mistake: the restriction is the specific character and condition of the power. The power lies in the restriction, not in the compass or universality of saving. Here the opposer, the misrepresenter, puts it in the compass, the universality, of saving. Right wrong in so putting it; for while the thing is single, simple in principle, it is multiform in application; while the place is one, it is a broad place. Though it is one thing only, Christ's cross, that saves, it can reach all the cases, all the degrees. Any poverty it can supply; any soul-vacuum it can fill; any quantity and aggravation of guilt it can remove; any continuance of sin, even near to death's door, it can dispose of or surmount. It has to show a history of saving deeds, reaching along down the centuries, touching cases

like Saul of Tarsus, like John Bunyan, John Newton, Vanderkamp, Keopuolani, — of all countries, and all stages and measures of crime. All the differences are instantly answered to in the unity of the cross; all are harmonized in coming here, — coming to Jesus the Saviour. It is promise, history, experience, that in every case among men where the sinner has so felt his sin as to desire, and come to Christ humbly for salvation, to receive it as a gift, a thing of grace, that person finds salvation, not in the course of time, not by degrees, but instantly, perfectly, finds and possesses it. This one salvation that comes by Christ, this it is that comes to the souls of men in immediateness and fulness and completeness, to the amazement of the soul that receives it. And the same is accessible to all souls; is got here or is got nowhere. I ask, is it illiberal in God to treasure up in one spot infinite weal and good, then mark the spot, put his very hand on it, and say, Here, my creatures, it is, right here: come and take it freely; you all may have it and be my loving children? Is it not rather infinitely generous to make the provision, the deposit, and then designate the place, and open for all the path to reach it?

2. Another proof of generousness appearing in the restriction of the salvation is, that it abates all perplexing questions on our part; that we are not called upon to decide between competing remedies, or to fix what — this thing or that — we shall do, when do, how do, how much do. Were we left with the responsibility of an election on ourselves, when could we settle down in a solid peace? Never. We should go hesitating and trembling whether we had done the right thing, or done the right degree of the required thing. But now,

as God puts it, we know just whom and what we are to believe and do; then may calmly and immovably rest, and an opposing universe cannot shake us.

It also abates our labor of search. We are not to traverse all worlds, go up to the heights and go down into the depths, or go over the sea, and hunt through the snarl of multiplicities, to find that boon, — salvation, life. *It is nigh thee*, so God says; nigh thee, and clearly known by thee, if thou admit the Word of God. How kind in God, that he makes it thus feasible for us. We are simply to cast aside every thing else, and come, unwearied, direct to the only and the central place where the salvation exhaustlessly abides, and we shall have it.

3. This restriction, I remark again, this exclusion of every other, this limiting to one thing, while it makes the salvation so feasible, is attended with the greatest sureness in its operation.

It renders fatal mistakes gratuitous: they need not be. It furnishes a criterion, a touchstone, for every one looking for heaven on any basis called Christian; calls upon him to apply in his own case the test, and says, Is there revealed this in your case? — namely, a leaning of your soul implicitly on Christ for help; a resting of your soul sweetly on Christ for pardon; are you conscious that it is thus with you?

We are willing to grant that you may be in error on some points of doctrine, defective here, defective there; but if true at this pregnant spot, — Jesus the crucified your hope, — then all the rest will come right, or all else will be passed by. I come to you to-day with no captious argument, in no spirit of contention, nor to assail this dogma or that, this *ism* or that; I would waive all these to-day. I do not say but you may believe this theory, this scheme, this *ism*, and reach heaven. I do say, if you ever reach heaven, you must believe Christ; that his life, death, blood, righteousness, saves the soul, and this only saves. Receive this as your hope, and I know not what measure of heresy on other points it may not lift you out of, up to heaven. To this point I press you: I cannot stop to debate the other schemes. On this point I must insist; and you must let me insist on this. It is not dogmatism to say that there is salvation only in Him. It is God who says this, and puts it on every minister of his, evermore to say it, and never cease to say it, and puts the mortal curse upon him if he dares to say any thing different. My hearer, I dare not say any thing different: I have no desire to say any thing else. Oh, that I had the gift and the grace and the power worthily to set forth the infinite of gracious resource abiding and ever flowing here. How would I exult in setting forth to you the literally unbounded wealth of this message.

Let me in my concluding remark apprise you what, at the present time, is the great competing foundation as against Christ; what, ever and everywhere, is the grand decoy from Christ and his cross. It is a charitable life. How common the opinion, that it is well with those who do a great deal of good to the poor and the suffering. It is maintained to be well with them, on the ground that they have so abounded in good offices. If these flowed from love to Christ, *because ye did it unto the least of these my brethren*, then you will be saved; and not because of these kindly deeds, but because of your trust in, your love to, and your union with, Christ.

Mere charitable deeds, how did Christ put them as a merit of salvation, in that scene he drew of the two men who went up into the temple to pray? One could say, doubtless truly, *I give tithes of all that I possess.* The other could say nothing of this; could only say, *God be merciful to me a sinner.* And he was the accepted one; the other was the condemned one, because he had no faith, penitence, love. Paul settles this matter with a final and crowning authority when he says, *Though I bestow all my goods to feed the poor, and have not charity, it profiteth me nothing.* The apostle here settles it that one may give his whole time and his whole property in charity to the poor, and be found wanting; not having love to Christ, be a castaway. One may be a great lover of his species in this outward sense, and be a bitter hater of Christ. A person may go the whole round of commendable things, and knock and ask at the door of every one for salvation. At the door of strict religious observance, of prayers and sacraments and forms,—Is it with you? Answer—Not in me. At that of beneficence and all noble living: Not in me. Blameless morality, an uncorrupt honesty, just and faithful doing, answer, Not in me. Temperance, anti-slavery, heroic reform, Not in me, not in me.

Most presumptuous for the little creature of a day, a sinner at that, to go into a rivalry on this matter with the great God himself, and get together before him his little heap of questionable goodness or merit, and present it to take the place of what the Eternal Son has wrought out and amassed.

Behold him standing, at the last day, on his trial, a competer with the Judge who so wonderfully undertook our cause, and exhausted a divine capability to meet it, — this man, a worm, braving to outdo that Infinite One in the article of merit and saving power, saying to him, Thou couldst not save this soul of mine; and I have brought a wealth and an efficacy that will. And will it, when the echo of these words shall be filling the universe, *There is none other name under heaven given among men, whereby we must be saved?* It will not. Then let all other names and ways go, and come and be saved by this, an ample way, an open way, a blessed way; but, my friend, terrible if you don't.

## V.

### THE SHIPWRECK OF PAUL.

*And now I exhort you to be of good cheer: for there shall be no loss of any man's life among you, but of the ship.*
*Paul said to the centurion, and to the soldiers, Except these abide in the ship, ye cannot be saved.* — ACTS xxvii. 22, 31.

THE precise time in this memorable storm at which Paul uttered his assuring words cannot be definitely fixed; probably, near the middle of it. It is evident, that, throughout the days and nights that gloomily succeeded, the peril seemingly increased, till the end of the fourteen days during which they tossed up and down, drifting through the sea of Adria. The first indication of approach to land probably was the roar of breakers, so peculiar, and so readily detected by a practised ear. This it was which led to the precaution of sounding; which being done, they found the water twenty fathoms; a little farther, it was only fifteen; a fact which indicated a rapid approach to the shore. Now came the order to clear the anchors, which they did, letting go four by the stern; and in this position they waited anxiously for the day. At this juncture the sailors undertook to flee from the ship, and would have succeeded, probably, but for the interposition of the apostle, through the centurion.

The soldiers, however, at once cut the ropes of the boat they had let down, and it drifted away, leaving the company still more in peril through the loss of this their only boat. But, the seamen retained to work, and Paul there to encourage and to cheer, it was accomplished as the apostle said: they were all brought safe to land. The entire cargo went into the sea, and the ship went to pieces; but not a life was lost.

How admirable appears the character of Paul through all this terrible scene. A model of conduct in circumstances which develop, commonly, only fear and petulance. With him it was calmness, self-possession, patience, through those fourteen days and nights without sight of sun or stars. The benevolence of the apostle, also, perpetually shone. It was the benevolence his religion gave him. He was ready with his counsel, which they heeded not; and, when they were brought into trouble by this disregard of his words, ready still in their extremity to do what he could for their benefit and relief. As his words of counsel directed toward them failed, he directed words of prayer toward God. It was after a night of prayer, that Paul came out with those words assuring all of ultimate safety. It was the prayer of the apostle that saved these lives. Said the angel to him, *Lo, God has given thee all them that sail with thee.* We may safely paraphrase and add, For thy sake, in answer to thy prayer, they live; they are debtors to thee for life. And may we not suppose they were given to Paul, at least some of them, in a higher sense? On account of Paul's intercession, his fidelity in teaching, his example of calmness, his excellent and radiant life, we may suppose that some of their souls were saved. At such an hour, they must have felt the need of something to stand by them, sustain them; something they had not; something they saw the prisoner had. Softened now by that providence, impressed by that teaching, won by that life, how probable, even, that some who sailed with Paul also took passage with him in the saving ark.

In this history, then, we have illustrated before us, — 1. The efficacy of Prayer. Prayer reaches the ear, and brings forth the mighty working of God; brings his blessing down; saves the life, saves the soul. The promise is not only made: we behold the performance, God hearing, interposing, redeeming.

2. In this whole scene and transaction, we have an illustration of the benefit the bad derive from the presence of the good. Paul, we may suppose, was the object of sly, if not of open, ridicule. Very likely they despised and even hated his religion. But he loved them, and strove to do them good; and to him was it owing, we repeat, that they came alive out of their difficulties. And this, which was so palpably the fact on board that vessel, is the same the world over. From the time ten righteous would have saved Sodom, and three righteous actually saved this imperilled company, the bad owe it to the good, beyond what they think, that they live and are blest.

3. We also find in this account an example or illustration of the truth of the Christian records. We find that they are ever holding true under the severest examination. An English gentleman of the highest scholarly and nautical attainments has given years to the study of the two last chapters of the Acts of the

Apostles. He took up his residence in Malta and vicinity for some time; also visited and thoroughly examined all the libraries in Europe which could furnish any thing to illustrate the incidents of this memorable voyage; and, as the result, he brought forth a work so replete with new information, that it became necessary to reconstruct previously written commentaries. And one result of these investigations is, to confirm the exact truthfulness of Luke's history. In coming to this result, one point made certain is, that the ship was laid to. Another point is, that the storm beat upon her from the east and north-east. Another, made certain from ample *data*, is, that she was laid to with her right side to the wind. These three things being known, it is ascertainable upon established nautical principles in what direction she would drift. The line of her drift—in other words, the course on which she fell to the leeward—pointed west by north. This is determined by naval authorities from the precise *data* Luke furnishes. From the same authorities we have it, that, in a storm of this character and intensity, a ship would drift on an average a mile and a half in an hour, thirty-six miles in twenty-four hours. Then we have this conclusion,—the course of this drift, as scientifically ascertained, continued, would bring this ship out at Malta, where she did come out. And drifting at the rate of thirty-six miles a day for the space of thirteen days, the time she actually was drifting, would take her over a distance of four hundred and sixty-eight miles, which is very nearly the distance from Clauda to Melita. And have we not here refreshing confirmation of the truth of this Scripture? This species of proof comes palpably home to us; and the like keeps coming from various quarters with advancing science, making still bulkier and higher that huge column of demonstration which has been constructing through the ages. This is the book, this the mighty pillar of proof, which some people have presumptuously calculated, and others timidly feared, would ere long be overthrown by the knuckles of the spirits.

4. In this historic scene or transaction, we discover some light and relief falling upon a certain difficult point of doctrine, deemed the Gordian knot of theology. In touching on this point, I refer particularly to what is found in the two passages selected as my text. In the first of these we have the unqualified declaration that every life shall be saved. Paul received the assurance from heaven, and he uttered it for the relief of the distressed company, *There shall be no loss of any man's life among you.* In the second, Paul, seeing that the crew were making arrangements to leave the ship, says to the centurion, *Except these abide in the ship, ye cannot be saved.* We have here, first, the absolute declaration from above, that all on board should be saved; the unqualified declaration direct from God being, All who sail with you shall get safe to land. This, thus absolutely uttered, of course, was determined, fixed, by the Divine Being. If not, how could even the all-knowing One know it, or cause it to be uttered? Having resolved to bring it out so in the end, he could declare it through his servant, as he did. The declaration was based on his foreknowledge; and the foreknowledge was based on the determinate purpose. There is no other way to account for or present the matter, without encroaching upon some

Divine Perfection. It was the purpose of God that all on board should be saved; and that purpose he made known, in the height of the peril, for the relief of the company. Then, after, comes from the same Divine Source the discordant utterance, as many will deem it, *Except these abide in the ship, ye cannot be saved.* But what Paul said before was the prophetic fact; God will deliver the whole company. What is said in the second instance is the indicating of the means,— Except these abide. Abide in the ship, and ye shall be saved. God's high purpose on the one hand, man's instrumental agency on the other,—both have their relation to the saving to be effected. This, now, is one point we have illustrated by this inspired narrative; viz., that these two things are consistent,—God's purpose to bring to pass, and man's agency in bringing to pass. These two are consistent, because they are both co-existing facts.

But these two positions, stated in the abstract form, have made a great deal of trouble. It is said at once, If God ordains, it must come to pass, and will; the doings of the creature, whether brought to hinder or to help, are a grand impertinence. But if we look at the two, in a concrete form, in the actual occurrence, it appears differently. First, we have the absolute statement, they shall all be saved; then the qualifying condition,—Except so and so, ye cannot be saved. Any difficulty here? Practically, are they not, seem they not, consistent? Was the centurion, or were the others, probably staggered by any appearance of inconsistency? or did they raise any objection on the score of inconsistency? or was the purpose of God endangered by the enjoined condition,—the seamen not abiding in the ship, — consequently God's purpose frustrated? No: God, who fixed and uttered the purpose, could secure the condition as he did, and that by the free working of the minds of the company. As a fact prophetic, they were saved by an absolute decree; as a fact resulting, they were saved by a conditioned obedience, — both indubitable facts under God's administration; and, as facts, both dwelling in perfect harmony.

Another point or aspect of this matter, receiving illustration from this case, is, that these seemingly conflicting facts are not only really consistent, but the one is helpful, even necessary, to the accomplishment of the other. This, too, appears in the narrative before us. God's purpose was, to save this ship's company. God's plan was, to save the ship's company by the ship's crew, by their skill, their courage, their stalwart strength. Therefore it was that he moved his servant to say, Ye cannot be saved, except these abide, simply as the natural and provided means of saving the ship's company. They were to be saved, then, by the appointed means of deliverance in such a case; the means were necessary to their deliverance, unless they were to be delivered by means wholly supernatural.

It appears, then, further, in the unfolding of this case, that God's purpose to deliver, and his announcement of that purpose, went to encourage and sustain the efforts which were to work out the deliverance. They were told two things from heaven: first, that they would be saved; second, that they would be saved only through their own exertions. There, now, is the case, there, the facts. Let common sense interpret. Suppose the case your own, a case of imminent peril,— what will you do? Throw yourself supinely on the purpose of God, whatever that purpose may be? Not a man in his senses would do any such thing. Doing this would prove him to be out of his senses. In the case before us, the centurion based no plea of safety on the naked ground of God's declared purpose of deliverance, but minded Paul, retained the men, put them to their duty; and they could work, and did, with mighty vigor, sustained and nerved as they were by the encouragement of the announced decree of their salvation. Let any man know that his striving will avail to his rescue, he has, in that assurance, the strongest of all motives to strive.

It is very obvious how all this applies to the process and the interests of salvation in the higher sense,— the soul's salvation. Let us take these facts and principles and pass with them into this more spiritual region. And, first, we state the truth, that God has a purpose respecting the salvation of the souls of men. We should naturally infer this from the boundless perfection of his character, the infiniteness of his attributes. It certainly seems to be so from the teaching of his Word, in which the calling and salvation of Christians is said to be, not according to their works, but according to his own purpose and grace. God's purpose is not merely that he will save those that believe, but that, by his grace, he will bring some to believe and to be holy. The purpose is to make holy, to save,—a purpose eternal and irreversible; not extending to all, as in the ship's company, but to a definite and a vast number. God, we believe, could write out the names, complete the roll, and spread it before us, and say in our ears, Each of these shall be saved. The second fact or principle brought out in the historic case holds precisely the same in the process of the soul's rescue; namely, the condition, the human performance, as made indispensable. Except ye do it, ye cannot be saved. Except ye repent, ye shall all likewise perish. He that believeth shall be saved: he that believeth not, is condemned already. Strive to enter in. Work out your own salvation. The phrase is varied, indeed, but all goes to show us, that if any of us are saved, it will not be by relying on the secret purpose, but by obeying the open, palpable counsel and precept of God, repenting, believing, obeying.

Another point of the parallel is the consistency, between God's purposing and the necessity of our doing. Multitudes will have it, that, in such a case, there is no need of any endeavor on our part. We can only say to this, how like a fool a man reasons, when his soul, the interests of his immortality, are at stake; and persists still in reasoning, when all nature, all actual things, all veritable facts and events, lay bare his sophistry, and rebuke his folly. His crop of grain,—God's decree fixes it, God's blessing produces it. He admits it to be so; and yet he ploughs and plants and weeds, and fosters the growth; and, by so doing, he reaps the harvest promised. Was God's purpose here a hindrance? Did it bring a blight or a blessing on the seed sowed, and the toil put forth?

Another point in the parallel, and the efficacious and practical one, is, that God's purpose, his decree of election, stands in his administration as an encouraging consideration. And this simply because the gospel, in this doctrine, says to every man, You may be saved: not, you shall; but, you may be. So was it on board that ship. An assurance of deliverance, indeed, was given. But it was added, Consider the means: employ them, and you live. Perform the condition, and you are safe: disregard it, throw it overboard, and you go after it into a watery grave. How plain. There is something here to nerve to exertion. How much more in the other case, where the life of the soul is concerned; because it is not known, in this other case, who or how many God's saving purpose embraces. This is one of the secret things which belong to him. The thing revealed, that which belongs to us, is, Repent, and believe the gospel. Here, now, is our point of interest and of working, if we would come out right. Here, too, the place for us to make — in a sense to create — the evidence that God's saving purpose embraces us. The evidence is simply this, that we are about the work, are performing the condition. Thus, you see, the motive to put forth endeavor is about doubled. The business on my hands is to make out the case that I am one of the ship's company who is to get to the heavenly shore. We do not know beforehand precisely who will reach it; but we do know, that those who are serious, who make effort to be saved, are more likely to prove the ones whom God has purposed to save. We see this, then, that God's purpose of election does not take a man's salvation out of his own hands: it puts it into his hands, just as, after he announced the decree of deliverance to that whole ship's company, he put their salvation directly into their own hands: Except ye abide and work, ye cannot be saved. God makes the election. The creature is called upon to make the election sure, — to bring it to the test and proof. The mischief is, that multitudes begin at the wrong end, prying into the election. First, they try and satisfy themselves that they are elected: that made out, then they will do something. That cannot be made out in this way; indeed, we have none of us any thing to do with that matter. It is God's prerogative to elect, "having mercy on whom he will." It is your privilege to make out the evidence, each in his own case, to make your calling and election sure. The favoring evidence that you are one of the chosen of God, begins to form the moment your soul earnestly turns with filial listening to the heavenly Father's call and claim. The evidence brightens as you forsake all vain associates, all obstructing practices or employments, and come humbly to be taught from the Book of God, and, in the secret place of prayer, beg for light and for mercy. Still, all this may prove as the morning cloud and the early dew; all may come to nothing. The evidence rises to demonstration when you come and give your heart to Christ, and bind your all to him as his disciple. This you may do, are called upon to do. The way is all open to this. Out of yourself, not the least obstruction. On God's part, there is every thing to encourage and to aid, especially the blessed fact revealed of God's mind and purpose to save. An angel this, brighter than the one Paul saw. And he stands with smiles and beckonings by the side of every soul that has seriously meditated its own salvation; assures you salvation, if salvation such as God proffers, your soul truly desires. If, then, you have begun, we say, Go on, and make your case more hopeful by still more decided doings on the platform of God's gospel. And if the balking thought comes up, I fear I am not one of the elect, crush it out by proceedings still more profoundly resolved and earnest, that if there are to be but ten from this drifting Sodom to reach that heavenly shore, by God's grace and my own sinew, I will be one. In a certain lazy sense, there is an excess of reliance, an utterly false reliance, upon God's power or grace. A vast many go in for that grace, the goodness divine, that alone, to get them into heaven. They have yet to find it won't do it; have yet to learn, that it takes some human tug and stuff to get a soul there.

It is safe to say, Better to put trust in God than in bolts and planks. It is prudent to add, Notwithstanding your trust in God, look well to the soundness of your bolts and planks; and, if the bolts part and the planks rip off, then, in your desperate resolve for the shore, cast yourself upon the severed and floating timbers. So did that wrecked company. Notwithstanding the soothing word of Paul, that they should all be saved, it was by an awful struggle they did it; with frightful buffetings amid the foaming, curling breakers; some on boards, and some on broken pieces of the vessel. *And so it came to pass, that they escaped all safe to the land.*

## VI.

### ELIJAH THE TISHBITE.

*And Elijah the Tishbite, who was of the inhabitants of Gilead, said unto Ahab, As the Lord God of Israel liveth, before whom I stand, there shall not be dew nor rain these years, but according to my word.* — 1 KINGS xvii. 1.

IN giving a discourse upon this prophet, one might open with the statement that Elijah was a remarkable man; and the statement, as predicated of the subject, would be a very tame one. There are many remarkable men in the Bible; but Elijah seems to stand on a height far above most of them. His character has an element of the preternatural, and his history a pervading tinge of the romantic. Indeed, there is nothing more stirring and more captivating to the imagination in the world of fiction, than we find in the story of this man, all of which is sober historic truth.

His first deed was a wonder, and the narrative is a string of wonders — wonders sublimely wrought — all through his course; the finishing one the most sublime of any in the train.

He bursts suddenly upon our view. His origin, his education, his commission, all abide in darkness; this only we know, *Elijah the Tishbite.* He comes up with spectral grandeur; with the majesty and authority of a being of another world. His first standing forth is in the presence of a king, proclaiming in that presence a three-years' famine throughout the land. He then passes away, to be hidden for a season near a small brook. There the ravens fed him, till he became an inmate in the poor widow's home, where for two years he made the meal and oil increase as fast as they were consumed. And when death smote down the widow's son, — as she, probably, little thought with a prophet at her board, who could keep the famine at bay, — and her soul was filled with the bitterest sorrow, the man of God undid the destroyer's work, called back the departed spirit, and gave the mother her son alive. While the prophet abode in this place, the king was in earnest search for him; and soon we see him in the presence of the enraged monarch, retorting upon him the charge: *Thou art the troubler of Israel, thou and thy father's house, in that ye have forsaken the commandments of the Lord, and thou hast followed Baalim.* Next we see Elijah gathered with the prophets of Baal, — four hundred against this one man of God. And he there confounded them all, and brought down the fire to consume the sacrifice; an achievement which convinced the people, brought from them all the shout, *The Lord he is God*, and ended in the overthrow and destruction of the priests of Baal. Soon we see him again, — the man who had the power to shut, by the same power opening, heaven; and the rain fell freely, and the earth was clad in beauty. Next we see our hero fleeing before the infamous Jezebel, terrified by her threats, and hiding himself from her ire in an Arabian cave. In a little while we see him again, appointing and anointing kings and prophets; breaking, by the authority given him, two time-honored royal successions,— one in Syria, the other in Israel. This maker of kings, in a little while, comes before us again, as the reprover and denouncer of a king; and, soon after, an arrow, thrown at a venture, smote that king, and the dogs licked up his blood. Then his more infamous queen fell by a still more disgraceful death, and her carcass was more completely eaten by the same commissioned dogs,—all in fulfilment of the stern prophet's word. The holy man journeys on till fifty men, sent by another incensed sovereign to apprehend him, meet him; when the prophet speaks, and a shower of fire descends and consumes them all; another fifty, and another shower buries them also. The dread, mysterious personage passes on till the Jordan opposes. He smites the stream with his mantle, the waters divide, and he and his companions walk over on dry ground. We see them journeying on still, Elijah and his anointed successor; and, as they talked together, behold, there appeared a chariot of fire, and horses of fire, and parted them asunder; and Elijah went up by a whirlwind into heaven. His companion saw it, and cried, *My father, my father! the chariot of Israel, and the horsemen thereof.* A marvellous ending of a most singular and marvellous life.

In glancing over the field of the prophet's doings, the one thing which stands out, arrests and impresses us, is this, namely, Power,—the power of the man. So inspiration, with its customary absence of epithets, describes him,—using but two words,—*the spirit and the power of Elijah*, — power based upon, derived from, the spirit of the man. It may not be amiss to designate a few things in the spirit, the gifts, the endowments of this man.

Severity stands out as one trait in the spirit of Elijah. When he spake, very commonly was it to denounce, to doom, to destroy. Elijah, — we should not like to be judged by him. We should be almost afraid to go into his presence. We should all the while be thinking of the fire, lest it come down and consume us also. And yet I have no doubt there went alongside this severity a deep vein of Tenderness; that he felt deeply for the Sareptan woman in her bereavement; that he wept while he prayed the prayer which brought back the son's precious life. These contrasted qualities you will commonly find in the great, achieving characters; namely, severity and tenderness. Yea, the model is found in the Divine character, — these there lying together: *The goodness and the severity of God.*

Decision is another quality which went deeply into the spirit of Elijah. This everywhere, and in the very highest degree. We see it in his prompt utterance and action: the word he speaks is so unqualifiedly spoken. The work he performs, is done at once, — no wavering, but direct, strong, absolute, authoritative.

Another and kindred quality is Boldness, — boldness to meet his foe, though his foe be a king; boldness to utter the truth and hurl the dart, strike where it might. Israel's impious king had opportunity to learn the prophet's boldness in both these respects. There was also the boldness of adventure, daring to take risks, to assume any measure of responsibility. How does this appear in that first utterance: *No dew nor rain for these years, according to my word?* And again, most especially when all Israel was on Carmel, together with the prophets of Baal; when he staked every thing — his own life, the religion of his country, the reputed existence of God — upon that marvellous test, the answer by fire. What a spirit of adventure, — one against such a multitude, and all to turn on such a portent. It is the spirit of Elijah, without a single quavering fibre, ready to risk it.

Another thing, intimately related, most deeply inwrought, was Confidence in his position, therefore Strength of position. He stood firm, strong, because he knew where he stood. All these qualities were his, we say, because they were made with him, — were the native endowments of his soul. God laid in him, at the beginning, the foundation for such words and works. All these qualities were his, we say again, and especially, because he had faith, unshaken trust, in God. How strong and firm these were, with Him to sustain him in every emergency. He spake, he struck, he adventured, because he believed in God, — trusted that God would take care of his own cause; that the God who had commissioned him would carry him triumphantly through. Thus faith heightened and perfected all the commanding qualities of his spirit; did not alter them; carried them forward and higher; made them vastly greater, stronger.

1. And, first, it may be worth while to notice, for our encouragement, the nature and extent of God's resources in the matter of raising up men for his service. "Of these stones" he can make them; he can bring

them, full grown, from the womb of vacuity and oblivion, — men who shall rule kings and change the aspect of the world. They come suddenly on the stage, and utter a truth and do a deed which fills all attending minds with wonder. And when the question is started, Who are they, and whence? nobody can tell. *Elijah the Tishbite,* — that is all. Their whole previous history is put into a word, without father, without mother, without descent: — *Elijah the Tishbite.* There you have it; and so it has been from the beginning, and so it is now. The men who have had the qualities to impress and bless the world have commonly come up from obscurity. They have struggled with hardships, and have made themselves, — rather God has had the ordering, and has made them, and they show the marks of his workmanship. How obvious and common a truth do I now state, that the overwhelming mass of reliable and useful, influential and controlling men of the world have had this sort of origin. How rare that distinguished men have been followed by distinguished sons. How very rare that families, distinguished for their wealth, nurture those who are disciplined in spirit, who prove strong in manly service, and blessings to their friends and the race. The difficulty lies in the temptations and expectations of the too-favored lot. And it is strange that the world so abounds with those who, to the last, will strain every nerve, that they may bring about in their own family circle this luxurious and expectant condition, which, the world over, goes to feed indulgence and foster effeminacy.

2. I remark further, That, in the case before us, we have an instance of God's adaptation of men to the

times. It is as we expect, — that, when he undertakes to raise up men for a particular service, they are sure to be fitted, qualified, for that special service. We see also what is God's judgment in regard to a fitness. He furnishes men of stern and bold qualities for times of great corruption, — an Elijah for the time of an Ahab. It is true that such come with a jar and a dissonance, and for a season they make trouble and commotion; for there is no other way. It is the light meeting the darkness; the truth conflicting with the error; the piety reproving and denouncing the sin. Whatever may be true in medicine, God's system of moral cure is by contraries. He puts forth the truth to crowd out the error; and what if it does happen, in the fierce antagonism, that there are seasons of confusion and trouble? What though the tempest twirls every thing into disorder, if it only blows away the miasma? There are some people who are exceedingly alarmed at the presence or the prospect of agitation. But it is not well to be frightened or to be angry or to threaten to go out of the world, for this reason; because agitation is God's economy, and so long as sin, with its legion train, has its present hold and supremacy, and the men God makes and means for the world are in the world, agitation there will be. The great Ruler will overturn and overturn, until he whose right it is shall come and reign. Rarely has there been the time when some characters, some actors of the spirit and stamp of the old prophet, have not been needed and been useful. At all times there are persons who will carry an influence, wield a power, and command respect. They are often of a rough, hardy, almost a forbidding, character: they can live anywhere or anyhow, — in a cave or in a palace; can receive their food from a crow's beak or a silver fork. There is close, firm consistence of spirit, — strong, compact, because of their faith in God. They are men we are obliged to respect. When we come before them, we cannot help feeling their presence. The truth lies within them; often it is as fire shut up in their bones, and they can throw it forth in living sparks, to stir the consciences and warm the souls of others. How different from another sort the world breeds and brings before us, — delicate and self-indulgent, living to please themselves; your pliant, willow men, your silken men, prim-toilet men, who carry their fire and smoke between their teeth. What will such accomplish for God and humanity? Our expectations are very low in that direction, and we cannot help its being so.

3. I remark again, It is wonderful, in regard to the men God prepares and brings forward in his providence, to see how naturally and easily they accomplish the greatest things. They lay foundations for all coming time; they strike blows which are felt the world over; they shed an influence which will not expire till moral causes cease to act. But they seem to think nothing of it themselves; they think very little of themselves; they seem and act as though doing the most common, every-day things in the world. And why is it all so natural, so obvious and easy? Simply because they are in the current of God's providence. God goes before them, and works through them and with them.

Here, let me say, we find an important practical hint for the Christian, — for him who would use his abilities in a way to do something for the world. It is that he learn to discern the time; and to catch, as far as he can, the foreshadowing of the Divine plan and purposes, and learn what God probably means to have done,—what, for the glory of his name, and the cause of redemption, must be done; so study and move, that his power may come in concurrence with God's, that he shall be a co-worker with him: then, a little power, a little human capability, will bring to pass astonishing results. And here faith will help us wonderfully; for faith is a wonderful discoverer, especially where God's mind and movements are concerned. Faith can see them in the far distance, and in the shadowy dimness, just as the prophet saw the rain; almost before the cloud began to form, when it was the merest speck in the horizon, he admonished the king to seek shelter from the deluge that would soon be upon him. He foretold its coming, he saw it coming, and still he continued to pray for its coming,—prayed as earnestly as though there had been no promise, no prediction, no certainty in regard to its coming. Though predicted and so made certain by the unqualified Word of God, it was the prayers of the prophet that brought the rain. Predicted as it was, had not the prayer gone up, the rain would not have come down. And there is no mystery, no inconsistency here. Prayer is the appointed means. The blessing shall be, the world shall see and know it; but not unless my people pray. God says absolutely, I will do it. God says conditionally, I will be inquired of by the house of Israel, that I may do it for them. Thus we see what one of the Fathers says: "That the promises of the Almighty do not discharge our prayers, but suppose them. He will do what he undertakes; but we must sue for what we would have him do. Our petitions are included in the decrees, the promises, the engagements, of God."

4. We see the power of a man, as consisting in faith. Here lies his highest power of beneficence and achievement; because, as we have said, such an one is more likely to be timely in his endeavors; and especially because such an one has God with him, and works the work given him by the abiding power of God.

There is this that I wish to note in this connection; namely, the power, the moral efficacy, of the man of God, — as bringing to the minds of the people the thought of God, making them to realize the presence and authority of God. This, I doubt not, was the case pre-eminently with our prophet, that wherever he went there went with him, there was diffused about him, the reverent realization of the great God he served. He made the people feel that there was a God in the world, and a God nigh at hand. This same sort of impression, made deep and constant in the minds of the people, is wanted exceedingly at this time. How it would sober and regulate and elevate society; for our disorders, frivolities, and crimes grow largely out of our atheism, — not theoretic, but practical, atheism. God is not retained in the mind. No God, is the wish of the heart; the open, emblazoning label of the character reads: *Without God in the world.* Now the great and difficult work is, to have God restored to his place, — God abiding in the thoughts and affections of the moral beings he has made. There is but one thing we can hope to do instrumentally for this, — godly living; better far than any miracle or portent ever wrought or witnessed. This, everywhere that God's people are, the silent and strong influence of godly living, would do much to make God realized, thought of, and feared, if not served.

5. In my next remark, I wish to note the fact of the good man's death as being characteristic often, — as flowing legitimately and specifically from the tenor and temper of his life. But before speaking of this, there is another resemblance or congruity I will just refer to, — a resemblance between the traits of the natural and the renewed man: the fact that grace does not wholly blot out native traits; that it does not wholly overcome the constitutional temperament. There will always be passages in the renewed character in keeping with the former and the general character. Hence it was that even the faith of Elijah could not always hold him up, and keep him bright and cheerful. See him on one occasion. A woman threatens him; and this prodigy of valor, this pattern of faith, who had confronted opposing thousands and made kings tremble before him, frightened, flees for his life; and in his desert cave lies, all unstrung and dependent. Hear his answer to his Divine Lord and Master: *The people of Israel have forsaken thy covenant, thrown down thine altars, and I alone am left.* And what does this mean? It shows a man of variable moods, given now and then to fits of depression and melancholy; when every thing is going adversely, seems to be taking a very plunge into ruin. It is something in the physical character and constitution, which even the grace of God has no power fully to reach and remedy. We see the power of the malady, when it could bring down and unnerve such faith and strength as Elijah commonly showed. But we have only one record of this

sort. Prevailingly, with this man, it was doubtless "spirit and power," — an ardent, achieving spirit; a very soul of fire. He died. No; he did not die: he passed away characteristically, — a perfectly fitting translation. Enoch walked with God, — a very quiet, calm, silent sort of a man, probably; and his translation was as quiet as his walk. Only the fact is recorded in the shortest and simplest phrase, *God took him*. But this prophet of fire is caught and carried up visibly by the horses of fire and chariots of fire, — heaven's splendid equipage, let down for the purpose. This chapter I have opened, of characteristic dying, — the calm, even, quiet, dying quietly; and the reverse, too, appearing, — the ruling traits or passions symbolized in the death, — there is not time to pursue it.

But there is another sort of connection between the life and the death, far more pregnant and solemn than that just before indicated. The other is accidental and varying; sometimes it is not so: this always so, — a godly life, a safe death, God has joined them together. And God is present when his people die, — if not with his visible chariot, with what is far better, — with the Spirit of his grace, and an invisible retinue of convoying angels. We do not behold it, but it is real. The reward we do not perceive, but it is amazing.

How God does honor and reward his faithful servants, we see in the magnificent ascension of his prophet. It was not for his own sake alone, that the prophet went up in that manner. We can now look over the line, and see the agents and powers of that commonly hidden scene. We see the soul living right on, when passed over the dividing stream; and living, seemingly, a mightier and a vaster life. We see, too, a rising body. Tell me not there are no bodies like these in heaven. I see one, — our ancient and venerable brother, — as it tracks its wondrous way, and enters those sublime portals. I see the beginning of its glorified state. As the old mantle drops, I see, succeeding, the radiant vestments of its immortality. Brethren, followers of the Lamb, let me say here, that that favored man shall have no pre-eminence over you, if faithful, cleaving fast to Him who is the Resurrection and the Life. Wondrous morn, — and soon it will come, when all space shall be filled with still more gorgeous translations, when the elect of God, gathered from the four winds, from one end of the atmosphere to the other, shall be seen, passing together in triumphant procession, with their Glorious Leader, through the gates into the Eternal City.

O world, wealth, honor, pleasure, how despicable thou art, when our eyes rest upon such a sight as this. We shall see it. Shall we be it? Resolve that you will, with somewhat of the old prophet's decisive strength of purpose; and then hold on your way, look up in prayer, persisting still, and fail not to be one: and so help you God.

# VII.

## SAUL THE REGRESSIVE IN PIETY.

*Is Saul also among the prophets?* — 1 SAM. x. 11.

THIS, we are told, passed to be a proverb. It was originally uttered by the people, as an expression of their surprise at seeing Saul with a professed company, engaging in religious duties, in the utterances of devotion and praise. Afterward, when any one was seen suddenly, and contrary to the previous habit, in religious connections, and, with seeming heartiness, religiously employed, this proverb leaped forth, *Is Saul also among the prophets?*

We must admit these are touches of a divine pencil, this whole character a divinely drawn character. And let me say, in the use of the modern phrase, Saul, thus set before us, stands as a representative man.

The words of my text introduce us only to his religious character; and in this he represents a large class, found in every age, — perhaps never more plenty than now; a very large class, marked by a certain type of experience. For the better understanding of this subject, let us turn to the religious character of Saul, marking the occasions, the causes, the qualities of it.

The first developments of the character were bursts of devotion, the utterance of thankful praise.

And I observe here, —

1. That there was a providential reason for this. I mean, a course of providence toward Saul, adapted to awaken this order of development. It was a course of singular, separating, opulent distinction and benefaction. Owing to tribe, family, birth, it was altogether unexpected, an astounding surprise, that visit of the prophet to him, under a regal burden and gift. How poor was Saul on the occurrence of this interview. Fivepence was all he could raise to hand as a present to the prophet. But the prophet handed back to him a kingdom; giving him the signs which were to prove to Saul that the hand of God was in the gift, and the seal of God upon the transaction. And every prophetic sign turned out just as Samuel said. So that, when Saul came to the last of the signs, the pent fires of his soul broke forth. Such lavish generousness called out from his nature something like gratitude, worship; so like, that in that stage it would have been difficult to have judged them any thing short of the true.

We are to take into account, as in part the reason of this religious development in Saul, a peculiarly susceptible nature, — a nature that made short turns, quickly variant in its moods, relieving itself by starts and bursts. This appears in his conduct in the cave, in his savage hunt of David. At one moment there was the fury of murderous passion; then, under the sign of David's filial and forbearing love, a perfect tumult of tenderness: *Is this thy voice, my son David? And Saul lifted up his voice, and wept.* Then what words of conciliation and entreaty followed. Some have doubted as to the antiquity of nerves. I think it quite evident that they are as old, at least, as Saul.

This seems to have been his order of temperament. Hence his quick turns and susceptibilities, his ups and downs, his brief sunshines, his longer and deeper glooms.

2. I remark again, that there were, doubtless, reasons for these better moods, and these advanced stages of character, in a divinely imparted influence. What God did for Saul in his physical and mental structure and endowments, we know very well. What he did in the way of specialty to fit him for the high place, is not so clear. Still, it is evident that he did something; and this something suddenly and summarily. For the record says, *It was so that when Saul turned his back to go from Samuel, God gave him another heart.* Precisely what and how much is meant by this, does not so readily appear. It evidently did not mean, in the high, Bible sense, a new heart. For Saul never did any thing distinctively and exclusively appropriate to such a heart. The phrase, doubtless, included a certain measure and character of religious sentiment and action; for Saul evidently felt and acted religiously. And this experience and expression, so far as it went, was doubtless the result, the product in part, of spiritual influence divinely imparted to him. God certainly, in undertaking to endow a man with kingly qualities, that he may act in his stead, would not altogether withhold the religious. Then, doubtless, there were other endowments giving him that inspiration of character, that largeness and elevation, that tone and bearing of authority, divine impartations, embraced in the phrase, *God gave him another heart.* There were what we may call the semi-religious endowment and qualities. And what were these qualities?

In the beginning, there was an admirable self-distrust and humility, that greatness and dignity of soul which does not allow itself to be lifted up by sudden prosperity. Ordinarily, it would be enough to turn the head of a country youth to precipitate a kingdom upon him. But with what strange reserve and meekness did Saul bear this great honor. He shrunk from speaking of it even to his familiar friends. And when the hour for the inauguration came, and all were gathered to witness the pomp and the ceremony, the elect monarch, on whom all eyes were eager to feast, had, in his excess of modesty, hid himself among the stuff. And, after the recognition and the formal setting apart, he went back to his old home, to the care of his cattle; showing, in connection with this, not only his humility, but the noble quality of clemency; interposing, as he did, to spare certain ones guilty of insult to him, whom the people would have summarily despatched but for Saul's interceding grace. And not only humility and mercy, but worship, sacrifice; evidently a marked fervor in the utterances of devotion, and pretty certainly a uniformity, a steadfastness, in his devotions. The religious rite or service he seemed very unwilling to neglect or put by; on one occasion refusing the risks of battle till he had gathered around himself and his army the shield of the Divine favor, which comes of observing the prayer and the sacrifice.

But let me say here, that the material bearing on the favorable side of Saul's character is exceedingly scant. It all dwindles down pretty much to one item; namely, that he stood strictly for the observances of religion. So far as the kingdom of God was in form,

Saul went pertinaciously with it. After a little while we find that all his scrupulousness was for the form, the triviality. He ordained a fast when the salvation of the kingdom depended on the strength which comes of food. He was for putting his patriot son to death for a sin of ignorance, that was no sin at all, — only this, that a senseless vow had been infringed; and he spared the Amalekites, brought under sentence of death by God for their sins, and he himself commissioned and sent as their executioner, — in the face of the commission and the command he spared them. He could not forego, on one occasion, the offering of sacrifice, — so very religious was he; but he could trample down God's rule and authority, in arrogating to himself the priest's function, in order that he might do it. Again, he went directly contrary to God's specific and solemn word, — taking upon him to keep alive what God had commanded him to destroy: still, only in small part did he save what was thus doomed. Soon the prophet comes, and the king advances to meet him, saying, I have performed the commandment of the Lord, except that a few of the best cattle are reserved for sacrifice, — his damning formalism here obtruding again, to be rebuked on the spot with a scathing force of words, enough, we should think, to have wilted it down for the ages, never more to rise again: *Hath the Lord as great delight in burnt-offerings and sacrifices, as in obeying the voice of the Lord? Behold, to obey is better than sacrifice, and to hearken than the fat of rams.*

This religion of Saul, being very much in the expression and form, was a religion of appearance, — stood more for the appearance with man, than for the reality before God. Hence his impassioned cry to Samuel, when the old prophet was wrenching himself away: *I have sinned: yet honor me now, I pray thee, before the elders of my people, and before Israel; and turn again with me, that I may worship the Lord thy God.* His kingly standing, his reputation with the people, was first with him, — not God's judgment of him.

The defect of Saul's religion, we see, lay in the temper and habit of his heart, and in the spirit of his obedience: the heart not right, the obedience not thorough and entire.

Let me state here, in gathering up some of the practical instructions of this case, that there are two kinds of piety, which may be described as the Regressive and the Progressive. The first is not valid; its more common sign being from seeming good to bad, and from bad to worse, though not always, perhaps not commonly, running into downright immorality. The other is sound; and its sign is growth, advance from good to better, and on to the perfect. Passing the more genial and pleasant topic, I propose, at the present, to draw what light and quickening we may from the gloom and the deadliness gathered in the other.

The Regressive in piety, — there is such a character. Oh how frequently found. How many, who, for a time, were in the prophesying ranks, in the prayer-meeting, the assemblies of worship and praise, interested, and uttering that interest: but not now. Ye began and did run well seemingly; then came the reverse step. Are there not those here to-day before whose minds these remarks call up a vivid passage of their lives? And I venture to say you then pronounced it the best, the happiest passage. Oh how happy, if it only had held on. How sad, as it is now going with you. How sad, that so blessed a beginning should, almost at the threshold, have been swallowed up in abortion. How sad, I imagine, some of your thoughts, in the still, retrospective hour; and sadder yet, in the dread foreboding hour. How sad, when you come to the end and to your reckoning with God, to hear your doom from his lips.

Think of Saul's course, written out for your warning, — his early and blushing honors, and dawning hopes; then his faltering distrust, his politic disobedience; then his gloominess, his soul-laceration, his spasms of frantic agony, his enmity, his malignity, despair, — the God who once heard hearing him no more; then the crowning daring, of a resort to the spirit-world, and thence coming the mutter of his destiny; and in that, the finish and climax of his soul's horror, the symbol of what succeeded, the soul's self-destruction, consummate and eternal.

This character and end, I repeat, is written out for our warning. And for one I feel it to be salutary. And if it have its due effect upon us, what will the effect be? I answer, —

1. It will make us afraid of the beginning of sin, the first dropping from duty, the first symptom of departure from our profession and allegiance. And, back of this and as preventive of this, it will put us on the watch, and suggest to us the wisdom of great sharpness and severity of self-scrutiny. This being deceived about ourselves, taking ourselves for something when we are nothing, is most wretched business. And we cannot but fear that there is a great deal of

it. It is not falling from grace: it is being nothing in the start. Consider this as held forth in our teaching character to-day, — namely, the tenacity of this self-deceiving. How it held on in Saul through all his moods of rebellion and reeking murder, — ever and anon the interlude opening when he would whine the saint. This delusion of character and hope, it seems sometimes as though it would kennel in the soul with avarice and lust and treason, and with the father of all these, — the Arch-fiend himself.

This fact, while it admonishes us to enter on the work of self-scrutiny, admonishes also to a thoroughness in it. Better not to do it at all, than not do it profoundly and rightly, — avoiding what is so common with us, a resting in the superficial testimony and evidence. "Is Saul also among the prophets?" Yes. And himself prophesying? Yes. Then write him down a saint. Sometimes, I fear, our judging is about as shoal and summary as this.

2. I wish to say here, that the deceptive marks, those which more commonly do minister to the deception, are the obtrusive marks, — pertaining to the surface, and so ever protruding themselves; whilst the deep and vital and real are the hidden ones, down in the place that is out of sight. Let me repeat and be emphatic here, for here is the rock of uncounted wrecks. He appears well, he speaks well, prays well. Suppose I should now say to you, that this fact, taken apart, — I say, taken apart, — is among the most unreliable of the evidences that he is a Christian; nothing here necessarily conclusive that he is; nothing here that necessarily brings out the vital centre of the man. We do not see that, the vital centre, in his lip-service. God alone can see that pregnant inside.

A man in certain moods and with certain gifts can transfer that inside into any form and show of outside sentiment and testifying he pleases. "Some of you," said Dr. Chalmers, in one of his grand and dissecting strains, — "some of you have heard of the individual who, under the oppression of melancholy, seeking counsel of his physician, was advised by him to attend the performances of a comedian who had put all the world into ecstasies. But it turned out, that the patient was himself the comedian. And, whilst his smile was to all the signal of merriment, his heart stood uncheered and begrimmed before the gratulations of the applauding multitude, evening after evening, a poor, helpless, stricken mourner, amid the tumults of the high-sounding gayety himself had created." Whilst the kingdom of God is in power, there is a simulation of it in word only; and so well simulated, that, if you do not go below the words, you cannot tell the difference. But, if you go down to the silent and salient centre of the man, there is a difference world wide. It is where Saul did not go, and where none of his type at this day go. He consecrated himself to a certain extent, and so far became religious as to pray, praise, prophesy, go to meeting, observe the forms. And so far he stood to it. But the outer cuticle and the remotest fibre of his selfishness was not touched by all this; though he was sincere in it all, very likely, and thought quite well of himself, with his nice outside dress of religion, and his silken, ribbony words, venturing to say, *I have performed the commandment of the Lord.* And it came back from the old prophet like a shaft of granite whelming him, *What meaneth then this bleating of the sheep in mine ears, and the lowing of the oxen which I hear?* It means that the sheep and the oxen are left out of his bill of consecration. What his soul's selfishness craved he kept for himself, — all of that he kept for himself. And this is the core of the difficulty, the inmost centre of his rottenness. And right here, let me say, abides the vitiating defect now. The sheep, the oxen, the logs, the stocks, the moneys, — whatever will contribute to the gratification and the pride of life, — is left wholly out, I fear, of many and many a pretended Christian consecration.

My friends, there is a chapter here, in our professedly religious doings and not doings, which it frightens me to think of looking at the headings and titles of. The man comes well attired, grave, in good seeming to make the offer of himself to God in the house of God; when that same God sees and knows, that at least nine-tenths of all he solidly values and vigorously lives for is outside of the pale of his consecration. The safe iron box is at home, under his own key and keeping. He means it shall be, and probably it will be. I tremble on account of our superficialness. I include myself in this remark, and personally tremble; and pray God to probe down into us, and so fetch us nearer to his own standard, to the making our all over to him. We can have no assurance as Christians till we do this. The probability is against us that we are Christians, if we know this and do it not.

And let there be the repentings and humiliations for past shortcomings. Let us come before God for these things, and deal directly with God, as Saul did not do. He confessed to David and to Samuel, and begged forgiveness of the prophet, — none from God; showing by this that he had no thought or sense of the enormity of his guilt. May God help us to thoroughness. May his law come home to us, that we may know, in the phrase of President Edwards, "the infinite upon infinite of our sin;" and then let us not faint or despair, but, knowing the Saviour revealed, his boundless compassion, and his unlimited capacity and reach of forgiveness through his sacrifice and blood, let us go to him, and in faith cast all upon his mercy; and in truth devote all to his service in a spirit of wholeness and in a rigor of fidelity that will never retract and never falter.

# VIII.

## CALEB; OR, FOLLOWING FULLY.

*But my servant Caleb, because he had another spirit with him, and hath followed me fully, him will I bring into the land whereinto he went; and his seed shall possess it.* — NUM. xiv. 24.

IN the fourteenth chapter of Joshua, we find a record of the accomplishment of this declaration or promise, as follows: *Hebron therefore became the inheritance of Caleb the son of Jephunneh the Kenezite unto this day, because that he wholly followed the Lord God of Israel.*

We have here presented, briefly but clearly, the religious character of Caleb. The service by which his character was tested, and in the performance of which he won this marked distinction and approval, was his thorough search and true report of the condition and resources of the land of Canaan. The individuals sent on this search, twelve in number, all agreed in reporting that the land was a land of great beauty and fertility; but ten of them went on to discourage the Israelites from attempting to take possession of it as God had directed them to do, because the inhabitants were numerous and strong, and their cities impregnably fortified. Upon hearing this, the people murmured on account of the dangers that awaited them. Joshua and Caleb rent their clothes, protested against the pusillanimous report the craven ten had made, and contended that the country might be easily subdued in the name of Jehovah. God was displeased with the murmuring and rebellious multitude, and passed upon them, with the solemnity of an oath, the sentence of universal excision in the wilderness; then added, But as for my servant Caleb, who has faithfully followed me, him will I bring into the land, and he shall possess it, he and his children. We see that the description of this ancient disciple is slightly varied in the different places. In one, it reads, He hath followed me faithfully; in another, He hath followed me wholly; and again, He hath followed me fully: all the descriptions, however, bear the same meaning, and that meaning very obvious. The main idea is that of the wholeness, entireness, totality.

Following God wholly: it means with the whole heart. Great account is made of this in Scripture,—the heart-service, service with all the heart. This God everywhere insists on,—unvarying, unfaltering singleness of purpose and affection. Thou shalt have no other gods before me, is not only the first, the beginning, of the commandments; it lies at the foundation of every thing that comes after. Ye cannot serve God and Mammon, is not only a declaration of Scripture, but an axiom of our common sense.

Following him fully: it extends to all the faculties we possess, takes in all the talents, all the powers, God has given us. Inasmuch as they came from him, their strength and influence should revert back to him; all made to terminate on his kingdom and glory.

Following him fully: it extends to and embraces all

the requisitions of God's Word, the entire circle and detail of Christian duty. In the character described, there is no disposition to make exceptions; to pray to be excused in regard to certain matters; to think a great deal better of the Bible, if its strictness could only be abated, somehow explained away. The one following fully does, indeed, come short, — and none so keenly sensible of it as he; yet never is it matter of calculation with him; never the springing up of the desire to be relieved from a portion of that enjoined upon him. His aim is to be thorough, conscientious in little things, in all things, and to love duty in all the wholesome severities of it.

The following fully, extends to, takes in, all times and all circumstances. It is a following God when scorn points her finger, and obloquy hurls its reproaches, and persecution builds her dungeons and kindles her fires; professing him, adhering to him; come what may, neither fearing nor faltering. And what is more difficult, and more decisive of the following fully, is the adhering to God, faithful to the spirit and duties of religion in times of prevailing indifference, coldness. This, indeed, was the very test-point in the case of Caleb and Joshua. Ten of their companions broke away from their allegiance to the truth and to God; and the whole body of the people followed these recreant ten. But these two stood firm, stood alone; resisted the overwhelming torrent of iniquity; maintained their integrity, and persevered, and blenched not. Thus it was they won the encomium of following fully. This is very plain; namely, that it is one thing to follow the Lord at such a time, quite another thing to follow him when all things favor;

when the current sets that way, so that it is popular to put on the seeming of religion; religion being the talk in the house and the shop and in the very mart of business. Many will fall in at such a time, who have no good foundation, no abiding principle planted in the heart; and who will fall off in the time of spiritual drouth and dearth. When the popular interest is in another direction; when some gilded bauble, some scheme of gain, some flaunting amusement, is the grand attraction, — then where are the Christians? Then is the time to find them out, to count and set down the reliable ones.

Circumstances of a more limited character furnish the opportunity of reaching this rare distinction of following fully. The havoc of circumstances, how sad, how terrible, as witnessed on every hand. Some, in changing their business, will exchange away the spirit and hope of their religion. Some, in leaving their old place of abode, will put off, or wear very loosely, in their new residence, the garb of piety. Some, by entering into new domestic alliances, or connections more unfavorable to religion than surrounded them before, will compromise, and gradually give up, their Christian profession. There are others who will not, but will take their religion, a humble, faithful piety, wherever they go themselves; at least, silent reprovers in the presence of all wickedness, shedding some heavenly light, though dwelling in the thickest darkness of error; imparting some savor of Christ under the very seat and throne of Satan himself. Such come into the rank of followers fully, disciples, Christians altogether, at all times and in all circumstances. And the reason they are such is, that they have another spirit with them, as Caleb; another spirit, one altogether different from the spirit found in worldly men, in the great majority of men; a spirit, a principle, a consecration, which is the work and the fruit of the Spirit of God; not nature, but grace; a gracious renewal, the heart's deep change, the love of God implanted as supreme. Out of this springs true soul-courage. The soul, loving, fearing, the Infinite One, is thereby ready for any emergency. The scorn, the threats, of hostile millions are as nothing when against the will or the honor of God. This is what sustained that ancient disciple when he stood so sublimely alone; so firmly stood when all others quailed and fell. The people were ready to stone him, but the glory of the Lord flamed between to prevent them. This same spirit, the love of God made regent, the fear of God casting out all other fear, is indispensable as a prerequisite in carrying through our religion in a corrupt, time-serving age, when interest is stronger than conscience, and when the honor derived from one another is more highly prized than the honor which cometh from God only.

It is obvious to every one, that there are many things to be said in favor of setting up this standard of striving; many motives that persuade to this thorough-going style of discipleship.

1. And one consideration is, that any thing decidedly short of this will endanger our salvation; short of this, perhaps fatally, eternally short. Of those old disciples or professors, we read this fact, that the whole mass who fell below Caleb's standard were doomed to lay their bones in the wilderness; not one permitted to enter the earthly Canaan. How true is it, that most of us called Christians are living far below

the Lord's standard of privilege and duty; thus we are living in a condition of fearful uncertainty as to what is our character and destiny, because living to work out the problem how little piety will succeed in getting the soul into heaven. And who can solve this problem? Where the oracle that will give us a response? where the balance that will weigh out for us the smallest amount of questionable religion that will suffice to secure the soul's standing in its final exigency? This whole region is spread with gloom and doubt. What will come to those occupying it, none can tell till the Judge shall pronounce. Very likely some will be saved from this section, this dubious ground, but they will know very little about heaven till they get into it; and know there but little as compared with some others. Though this is a common way of getting along, we must all confess it is a very poor way. There is certainly a better one, and we know what it is,—to be Christians wholly. Then no question about the present or the future, on our own part or anybody's else. The promise is unqualified, Such shall possess the land. They shall possess it as an inheritance, and also as a conquest. This leads me to another consideration, in which I pass from the question of personal safety to that of influence, achievement.

II. The power of influence and achievement, on the part of the follower of God, lies in his character, then in his actions: 1. In what he is; 2. In what he puts forth. So far as it abides in the personal character, it essentially lies in the completeness of the character. Let it be otherwise,—a sort of half-and-half character; some good things in him, about as many questionable things; engaged in religion one day, buried in the world, furiously rapacious after its gains, the next; a saint in his closet, a villain at his counter, — what the influence? what the impression coming from his character? what the balance between the seeming good and the unquestioned evil? In such a case, we must say, the influence is all on the wrong side; all goes to swell the tide of sin, and help on the work of death.

But take a somewhat less objectionable case, one where there is but little that is wrong, still a little. What the beneficent force of the character in this instance? Need it be said, that it is exceedingly impaired, — on the principle inspiration recognizes, and all experience confirms, that *dead flies cause the ointment of the apothecary to send forth a stinking savor:* so *doth a little folly, him that is in reputation for wisdom and honor?* And so, we may add, does a little sin in him who is in reputation for piety. The principle lies in the incongruity, the deep offensiveness, of an ill odor coming out of a fountain of sweetness; of a foul blot upon a fair and beautiful surface. Hence it is in religion, that little things test the character. Thus, too, little things spoil the character, and nullify all power of good from it. On the other hand, the efficacy of the character, its emanating influence for good, depends upon the fulness and the rightness of it; always obeying, doing, giving, shining. Such characters carry conviction with them; such make it known and felt that there is a difference between him that serveth God and him that serveth him not; and make it felt, too, in the souls of ungodly men, that they must be radically changed, or they never can see life.

The man who thus accomplishes good by what he is,

will also accomplish it by what he does. The character that sends forth an influence to impress, will dictate the deeds that will achieve. There is a spirit there that will carry him forth in earnest endeavor; no matter how hard the field, ready and eager is he to enter upon it; and for that reason, because forbidding and resisting, — even as Caleb chose Hebron for his inheritance, because the Anakims were there, and there was contesting and heroic work to be done. Not only does the field that has work in it invite him, but, when in it, he is there to show the mind and the sinew to do the work. And the work, the action, the sacrifice, backed up by such a spirit and such a character, one of the whole-hearted stamp, one the whole world knows to be of God, and to stand in the right; the labor of such an one will never be in vain. Where the labor goes, the life will go with it, and give it authority and force. Where the tongue strikes a blow for the Master's cause, the example follows it with another; the weight and force of the example deepening and infixing the impression of the tongue. All pertaining to the man is concurrent and persistent, all compacted, and directed to the one end for which he lives, to serve God's kingdom and the world's welfare. That is following fully; and that is the way to bring something to pass; something the rust will not eat, nor the fires burn. The measure of good done, God will recognize at the last, and crown it with awards the Infinite alone can mete out, and the Eternal alone be the theatre of. It is obvious to remark, in view of this subject, —

1. That being a whole Christian is an exceedingly great advance upon being half a one. Indeed, the case

is such, that no addition or multiplication of the half will make the whole. One of the latter sort in moral prowess and strength, will chase a thousand of the former, and two put ten thousand to flight. By no rule of arithmetic or law of morals are the two sorts in any way comparable. The fragment of a Christian doomed to this diminutiveness, who is he? The Christian a little for God, and not a little for Mammon; a Christian only by church-enrolment, — only known to be such on communion days; a Christian, rarely, if ever, at the prayer-meeting; never in the field of self-denial, in the front of the conflict and the peril.

2. It is further obvious, that what is wanted in our time is not so much more Christians as more Christianity; not more in number, but more in quantity. I have thought, sometimes, that we might say of religion as is said of learning, — that a little religion is a dangerous thing; dangerous in its bearing upon others. I mean the half-and-half sort, the attempted mixture of the good and bad, the strong patch on the old and rending garment; a medley of inconsistencies, a bundle of contradictions, a problem dark with enigmas. The men who live thus are good men some of them, we fain would believe, back in the secret place of the soul, and will get to heaven, we earnestly hope; but there are so many foibles and detractions and downright failures to be and do, and so many harmful things emanating from them as they pass along toward their final rest, so little that is the Christian, so much not the Christian, that it seems a decided misfortune to the world that they are so long getting through and getting home. Oh for Christians of the other pattern. Oh that God would bring us all to be

such, by discipline, by suffering, by persecution, by any thing.

And if any are meditating a beginning in the Christian life, let it be a full-hearted beginning, on no plan of division or compromise, but laying your all at the Master's feet. Many there are who try long and try hard, and then wonder they are not accepted as Christians. Not accepted. Why they have brought nothing for God to accept. They keep back all that is vital and central. What wants he of the dead and flimsy shell? The moment you go with your all, your life and love and possession, make that over, how quick will come the response of reception, and how radiant on your soul shall fall the beams of his light and favor. And this, let me tell you, is the Christian beginning that will be succeeded by a happy and prosperous life in Christ. Every thing laid down at the outset, then every thing comes easily afterward. Self-denial, sacrifice, is easy, most cheerful and blessed, because such have one and the same interest in God. Try to be, and may God enable you to be, a follower of him, a disciple, a Christian, like that.

# IX.

## THOSE LOOKING BACK NOT FIT FOR THE KINGDOM.

*And Jesus said unto him, No man having put his hand to the plough, and looking back, is fit for the kingdom of God.* — LUKE ix. 62.

THIS is the reply of the Saviour to one who said unto him, *Lord, I will follow thee; but let me first go bid them farewell which are at home, at my house.* And Jesus said unto him, *No man having put his hand to the plough, and looking back, is fit for the kingdom of God.* The Saviour, by using this proverbial expression, evidently meant to say, that those who came and offered themselves to be his disciples, with minds divided, irresolute, were not fit for his kingdom; not fit to meet the duties of it; not fit for the employments and rewards of it. There is a similar passage in the Epistle to the Hebrews: *Now the just shall live by faith; but, if any man draw back, my soul shall have no pleasure in him.* Indeed, there is a great deal said in the Bible on this subject of faltering and falling back; looking back and drawing back; beginning to build, and not being able to finish: and the reason, doubtless, of there being so much said is, that there is so much of this in fact, in the actual world of religious experience and endeavor, and that it is so unsuitable, so unworthy. Hence it is, that the great admonitory mnemonic of antiquity lifts up and utters its short, sharp warning to all the successive generations, *Remember Lot's wife.*

And why is it, how to be accounted for, that there is so much of this beginning and not continuing, — so many who put their hand to the plough, and then let go their hold? Almost every one, indeed, brought up amid religious privileges and influences is at some time more or less earnestly induced to move in the direction of, to take some steps in the way of, religion. They more diligently and seriously read and study the Word of God; they kneel in the place of secret prayer; they give an unwonted attention to the means of grace; and they have feeling and interest in the great concern. The fact that there is very much of this sort of movement in the world, — a movement in the souls of men toward religion, — shows that the souls of men were made to be religious, and with capacities to be satisfied with nothing less. When startled by the action of conscience, or agitated by foreboding fears, or stirred by generous aspirations, they put their hand to the plough. This fact is so. Then the other statement finds, too, its verification: they look back, and by and by they give up and go back.

And there is a reason for this faltering and reversing the step, as well as for the hopeful setting out. And the reason is in part found in the conditions of discipleship. These conditions are not what was at first imagined: they are somewhat more uncompromising than was supposed, laying the unqualified requisition upon the whole man at the present moment. This was what made the difficulty, the faltering in those cases of proffered discipleship described in the context. One says, *Lord, I will follow thee, whithersoever thou goest.* Christ said in reply, *Foxes have holes, and birds of the air have nests; but the Son of Man hath not where to lay his head.* In this reply to the forward, eager man he said, My kingdom has nothing of this world to offer. If you enter, you share with the Master poverty, reproach, toil, and conflict. There is a good, but it is invisible; reached, possessed, by faith, remote and reversionary. When the seemingly earnest applicant saw this, very likely he hesitated and drew back.

When, to the request, filial affection and respect would dictate, *Let me first go and bury my father, then I will follow thee*, came the answer from Jesus, *Let the dead bury their dead;* cut clear of all else, and enter on your work now, — it was a vastly severe testing of the strength and the purpose within; too severe for multitudes to abide it, stand true to the Master, and follow the Master, bearing such a cross. It is this unaccommodating feature, as many will regard it, in the gospel, this almost uncivil, certainly not very gentle, proceeding, this squareness, this downrightness, this blunt rigor of claim and condition at the threshold, which is the reason many go no farther than the threshold. They look in, but enter not. They gayly make the beginning; they miserably balk in the progress and the finishing.

It is intimated in the Scripture account that these failing ones are wanting in certain qualities of character, — even of natural character. This, in part, the reason of the failing, — that they are thus wanting; have not the nerve, the soul, for the conflict and the work. Hence the judgment Jesus pronounced respecting them: They are *not fit for the kingdom of God.* The kingdom of God, it is here on the earth, it is also there in heaven. On earth it is a place of labor and conflict; the good, the pure, the right, contending with the evil, the base, the wrong. In heaven succeed the reward and the rest. Such the place and state, the kingdom of God. All those designated in the text, — the hesitating, the faltering, beginning and not going on, entering and not going through, — all alike, are pronounced not fit for the kingdom of God. And why are such not fit? They are not fit, because they are in heart, in spiritual character, unsound, not converted. Their entering on a religious life, and then quitting it, turning away from it, proves in their case superficialness, utter unsoundness. The apostasy is ever from the seeming, never from the reality, of principle and holiness. The faltering and falling off is never by feet truly planted on the rock. The falling savors of sand, not of rock. Then this vacillating quality of character stands in the way of one's getting inside,—into the fortress and the kingdom. In one sense, it is a reason why he is not converted. Not that it is of him that willeth, nor of him that runneth, but of God that showeth mercy. Still we must believe that the willing is something. Indeed, man's willing and God's purpose of mercy are evident counterparts, one over against and answering to the other. The resolved willing of the creature becomes a sign of the gracious purpose of the Creator. Whilst the resolved willing is thus effectual, and, through grace, brings the contesting soul onward in the path of salvation, it is also and equally evident that failure accrues from the want of this positive and decided attribute. So wanting are some in this regard, that it almost amounts to an incapacity to attain and maintain a Christian footing; hardly long enough of one mind for the grace of God to take possession. Here it is an unfitness to enter; not enough of manly strength to enter, making probable an unfitness for the work they will meet after they have entered. When the Saviour said to that man, in two words, *Follow me*, and the person with all his manly nature rose right up and followed Christ, he thereby showed himself to be the man for the service and kingdom of Jesus Christ. So was it with Andrew, Peter, Matthew, and all those drastic men who laid the foundation stones and timbers of this kingdom.

Again, we say of the cases and characters before us, Not fit, because there is betrayed in their action a want of enlarged comprehension, lack of the ability and disposition to take in the distant and the future, and make the broad and right estimate of, and to live and make sacrifices for them. It is an element of faith that does this; that which believes and feels beyond what it can see; a sort of natural quality with some; but, in its truest and most potent possession, religious, and the gift of God. Upon that is based all this strength, manliness, steadfastness, and persistence against perils and discouragements; a quality such as the world has sometimes seen, and admired wherever seen. This it was in the great Navigator which kept his soul and the prow of his boat pointed to the land he felt assured was ahead; more steadily pointed that way than the needle to the pole. Whatever the enterprise or the cause, no person has ever yet done worthily, who has not caught a truth and an energy from the unseen, from the far-away and the far-before. If the mind, the soul, the affections, are shut in and held right here, in this little locality, — its first and chief thought being of the treasures here, — the comforts of the present, the home, the burial, the farewell; there is necessarily a blighting or obliterating of the forward, the resolute, the accomplishing qualities. Every thing is contracted, withered, impoverished, by this lowness and limitation of view. Whereas the enlarging, the comprehension, help make the man fit — elevate and nerve him for the work he is called to. In this case, it is the faith and scope of his soul, the felt powers of the world to come, that bring him out; make willing, loving to devote strength, life, all, to the enterprise and the kingdom.

It comes to this, that there are certain causes, which, if men once put their hands to, they must go forward and go through. The principles, the interests, involved, are so immense, so illimitable in their reach, that it is worth all the cost and sacrifice; and craven are we, traitorous to God and his creation, if we do not go through. The fact of holding on is the soul's testimony and declared judgment of the untold greatness of the stake. Our fathers in the Revolution constituted such a case: they put their hands to that plough; thereafter there was to them as men but one possible course, — plough it through. They did; and the fact that they did, showed the style and the quality of the men.

A like case has come upon us at the present time, to finish the work not then wholly finished; though they went through with what they undertook. The Divine Providence has been calling for the doing of the rest; and was there ever such a work committed to the finite before, bearing such costs of treasure and of blood? It was laid upon the men of the present. They had no election other than to put their hand to the plough; and, having so put, but one thing remained, to press to the victorious end, no matter what is to be endured, before the great work is finally and unalterably done. Otherwise it will be pronounced not fit for the realm we are reaching toward. This lost through our recreancy, the doom of a witnessing universe is upon us as not fit. The failure comes in this case from a want of comprehensiveness, — not getting hold of the vastness, the immensity, of principles and interests at issue.

I will add, in this connection, that there is a significance in the primal meaning of the word, rendered in the text *not fit*. That word denotes *not well put*. Looking back is not well put for the kingdom: face forward, unblenchingly on, is well put. That means, beginning with a soul set to finish; a soul set, God helping, — and God will help such a soul, — and fixed to finish. That is what is meant by well put: all in the man put in the line and expectation of the conquest and the kingdom. Well put, — the phrase reminds us of that noble Christian hero in our late war, by dint of merit passing from a humble private to the rank of general, — one of our ablest and bravest, — who, when mortally smitten in his twentieth battle, and just ready to die, requested the attendant to turn him once more, that his might be the privilege to die with his face to the enemy. That was the heroic spirit, well put, fit for the conquest; and such can hardly fail to attain, though they die to attain. I use these facts to illustrate Christian truth and duty: how striking and inspiriting are the analogies.

We see in them that one of the conditions of getting honorably through, after undertaking, is, that we believe and understand, when we begin, that the work is great and most arduous, the warfare perilous, the enemy not to be despised.

Then, again, in connection with a clear comprehension of all that is formidable in our prospect, it is important that we be believers and enactors of the doctrine of perseverance. The importance of this lies here, that the doctrine, if believed and brought into the soul, is far more likely to secure the perseverance than the opposite doctrine. Entering on the work, understanding its vastness, resolved in God to do it, then, God helping, do it; that is the doctrine in God's Book; that the fact in man's experience which contributes and leads to the success. Once committed, hand on the plough, God calling to the service,—ever after no such thing as fail: no such word in our vocabulary. Such a thought we may not think, for our eternal all is at stake. That is the view which will help a man to the end, and fetch him a victor there; whereas, the opposite sentiment or doctrine—that of failure, or failing from grace—wakes the expectation of it, operates as a premium on feebleness and imbecility, and brings to pass the soul's greatest peril and shame.

It follows, from the preceding, that everybody is not fit for the kingdom of God, because every thing people imagine does not constitute a fitness. The profession, the form, the ceremony, does not, the giving heed to the pastimes of religion, the matutinal shows, or the twilight entertainments of song and prayer. Nor does the saying, "Lord, I will follow thee," or the hanging out some label or sign of being a Christian. Not these,—

none of these. It is only character that makes fit,—the work and state within, the faith and some fight in the soul, the decision that presses ahead against the rudest resistance of the enemy. Such things are the proof of being Christians; the things Christ acknowledged when on the earth.

We have, then, a test to apply to those who present themselves at the door of this kingdom, and ask to be admitted. It is simply the requisition put upon those three proposing disciples. The test then is the test now. It can be no less at any time.

Many before me have had some experience under this claim. How have you answered to it? We may all respond, How have we answered to it? Are we satisfied, steadfast, true, and without any regret that we have undertaken to follow such a Master, without any glance back to the pleasures that have been left? Or has there been some lurking wish that we might have more liberty with the world that is, and still keep hold, in faith and hope, of the better world to come? The evidence that we are Christians, under this practical test of Christ, is, that we are following, getting forward, against all decoys back, or threats to drive back. Nearer, my God, to thee, nearer to thee, even though it be a cross or flame that brings me on. That is the spirit that will make trials and adversities set the soul ahead, nearer to Jesus.

It is plainly suggested in our text, that radical defects in the character are first indicated by little things. An apostasy does not leap forth at once: no one, by an instant move, wheels round and goes back. He first thinks of the good that lies behind; then the heart lusts; then the eye looks; then the feet turn; then the man is an apostate. What we are concerned to know is, whether there be the slenderest inception of this in the case of any of us. If there is, deal with it so as effectually to arrest it, or those terrible letters begin to form, and ere long will blaze against you, — Not fit for the kingdom of God. There is an awful efficacy and doom of evil wherever those reprobating words do light. Such cast out as worthless, — mere refuse material, — not fit for the kingdom of God; not the stuff to make a Christian of, not he; therefore no likelihood that he will ever be made a Christian. He has been up to the place, has been put to the test; and he did not stand it, — not the stuff, not he.

The failure or unfitness may be, in part, as before intimated, in natural or material qualities. It is also, and more especially, in moral qualities; unsuitable in spirit, in temper, — impure, unholy. This quality we receive from Christ, ever and bountifully from him, whenever we ask it of him and open our souls to receive it. And now is the time, the gracious opportunity; a day of privilege, that will find its close; soon, suddenly, may it reach that close. Then those who have neglected it, and yet are flush with fancied hopes, will come, as this Book says they will come, to another door, the door opening into that realm above of life and joy; and then and there, as they cry, Lord, open unto us, those debarring words will meet them, *Depart: I never knew you.* Then and there shall they be pronounced not fit for the service or the place. Only the pure, the holy, are here. Not fit. Only the loving, the loyal, are here, — hearts all joined and knit as one. Not fit. It is a peculiar throng, entranced, exalted, crowned, all; and *unto him that hath loved us and washed us in his own blood*, they sing the song which none else can learn. Not fit. These brief and fearful words, shall they meet you there? Say, No: God helping, no. Rise up to-day, in the utmost power of your soul's resolve; or, what is far better, in the felt extremity of your own weakness, in the girding grace and strength of Christ, rise up and get ready. Understanding what you say, putting your mind into it, your heart into it, your compacted will into it, say with deepest humility, in faith and holy trust say, *Lord, I will follow thee whithersoever thou goest.* Follow him, and through all be his. Then shall that other word meet you at the gate, — Fit, — your blessed passport there. The King shall say it; and all that countless throng shall repeat it, — Fit for the kingdom. Victor, thy struggles are ended. Soul, heaven is before thee: enter thou into the joy of thy Lord.

## X.

### THE GIVER; OR, THE TWO MITES.

*And Jesus sat over against the treasury, and beheld how the people cast money into the treasury: and many that were rich cast in much. And there came a certain poor widow, and she threw in two mites, which make a farthing. And he called unto him his disciples, and saith unto them, Verily I say unto you, That this poor widow hath cast more in than all they which have cast into the treasury: for all they did cast in of their abundance; but she of her want did cast in all that she had, even all her living.* — MARK xii. 41–44.

"WHAT more tender," said Mr. Webster, in one of his most remarkable forensic efforts, "what more tender, more solemnly affecting, more profoundly pathetic, than this charity, — this offering to God, of a farthing? We know nothing of her name, her family, or her tribe; we only know that she was a poor woman and a widow, of whom there is nothing left upon record but this sublimely simple story, that when the rich came to cast their proud offerings into the treasury, this poor woman came also, and cast in her two mites, which make a farthing."

The scene of this was the temple. In certain departments, or courts, it appears, there were placed coffers, or receptacles, for the gifts of the people of moneys to be devoted to religious uses. Into these receptacles the gifts were continually thrown, as those came in who were prepared to make their offerings, and desirous of making them. With the others came this poor widow. Among the qualities of character, indicated in the account given of her, there very obviously and delightfully appears, —

1. Humility. It is said that many that were rich cast in much. It seems that the offerings of all were in full view; how much they gave, the munificent and the mean, alike in view. Now what a force was here, considering what human nature is, to deter, to keep back, the very poor and meagre offerings, so eclipsed would they be by those princely ones: how hard to confess in this comparison the deep poverty, perhaps incur the imputation of covetousness, bringing so contemptible a sum, — two mites, which make a farthing. But this poor widow, conscious of her integrity, not caring for the imputations or the shame of the comparisons, comes along, very likely in the track of some one or more who cast in their thousands, and heroically puts in her two mites. I think I see an admirable humility in this proceeding. We certainly see, —

2. An unquestioned benevolence in it; a height of benevolence not often attained in this world. The benevolence is not brought out in the statement that she gave two mites; but in this, that she of her want did cast in all that she had, even all her living. Observe here what significance there is in the circumstance that she gave two mites, two pieces. Suppose the fact had been, and the narrative had read, she gave a farthing. True, it was all she had, but there was no piece below this, and she felt that she must give something. And

so by a species of compulsion she gave her all, the farthing. But no, there were two pieces. She might have given, and gratified her benevolence by giving, one-half her living; and would not that have been noble? — certainly prudent to have kept half. But for prudence she had faith. She trusted God, and gave the whole. I wish you to note here this instructive circumstance in her case, — I might say, most reproving to many. I refer to this, that the possession of small change did not diminish this woman's contribution; that the fact of her having two bits presented no temptation to cut down her offering one-half. How shamefully different is it, not unfrequently. When the Lord's treasury-box is passed around, with what intensely elective affinity, sometimes, do the niggardly fingers, in their parsimonious fumbling, strike upon the very small bits, careful to take but one; often descending to the baser coin, and so lumbering the treasury with it that the Lord of the treasury might express his grief and chagrin in the phrase of one of his own servants, — Alexander the copper-smith did me much evil. And then, not unfrequently, the memory of this blessed woman is insulted by calling these stinted gifts, these infinitesimal atoms broken off from respectable estates, calling these the widow's mite. No, no: the widow's mite was a mountain of benevolence, a very Andes in the comparison, whose heart and ribs and head of gold reach to the heavens, so high that all the world has seen it, and will to the end of the world.

Let us now pass, a moment, from her and her offering, to another character in the scene, the Lord Jesus Christ. He was there an interested and discriminating spectator. He beheld how the people cast into the treasury. He separated the gifts, marked the amount in each case, and especially marked the spirit. And may we not suppose he does the same now, in his higher abode? How grateful the thought, that our Lord is mindful even of our labor and sacrifice for his cause. How stimulating the motive lying in the fact that he does see, and loves to see, every sincere heart-gift made to help on his kingdom. And how he prizes a little, into which enters a great amount of heart. If it is to the extent of the ability, and goes with true self-denial, yet most freely goes, no matter how small it is in comparison of others, his eye not only follows it with admiration, his lips lavish upon it words of strange commendation. *Verily I say unto you, that this poor widow hath cast more in, than all they which have cast into the treasury.* These words seem to be extravagant. Are they so? Or are they capable of an unquestioned justification? Are they not pregnantly true, and so come to our souls with the producing force of truth?

Let me say, first, they are obviously true in this sense; namely, that this poor widow gave more in proportion to what she had to give from, than any or all of them. For they did cast in of their abundance, she of her penury. They had left an abundance, probably no perceptible diminution made by what they gave. It was not diminution in her case. Her great and full heart swept her whole living into the treasury. On that footing the case is made out undeniably in her favor; she gave more than they all.

But, again, there is another light in which her offering may be put, and so the case made out in her favor. I mean in the light of the immortality of her offering, making up in reach and continuity what it lacked in magnitude at the time. And it was the embalming of the Lord's commendation which gave it this perpetual and ubiquitous living; living as long as the moon shall measure time; living and acting wherever gospel truth has traversed and Christian hearts are found to beat; living an example of power which can hardly be contemplated and not be felt,—an example which has unlocked coffers which otherwise would have remained locked, and made wider than otherwise would have been, the openings for the disbursements of charity, carrying deeper and farther the blessing streams. Could we write in our figures the amount of good, as God embraces it in the sweep of his knowledge, the sum total of generous giving and doing, produced by the poor widow's offering as the moving cause, this total sum would doubtless exceed, not only all that all they, who cast into the treasury with her, gave,—I know not but it would exceed all that any one generation of givers have as yet given into the treasury of benevolence. This is the view the great lawyer took in the celebrated argument against an infidel charity, to which I referred in the beginning. This example, so vital and eternal, read, told, gone forth everywhere, sinking deep into millions and millions of hearts, this has done more good than a thousand or a myriad marble palaces could do. We should not doubt this, if we could trace in their inception and history, side by side, the two mites of this Christian woman, and the paraded millions of the infidel Girard; the gift of the one drawing to itself the warm admiration, and the loving sympathies of Jesus: the stately charity of the other, saying to Him whose name is love and whose office it is to bind up and bless and save, virtually saying, Off, away from these premises; thy spirit nor teaching nor touch are wanted here. We do not know but millions such as these may be overruled for good; indeed, they have been in this very case, showing how wonderful in working is He on the throne: still who does not say, for greatness, and boundless beneficence of results, give me, rather, the poor widow's two mites?

But there is a presentness to these words somewhat remarkable. May we not suppose that the Saviour meant to affirm an equal, yea, a greater, present efficacy residing in the widow's offering, than in all the others? I conceive that it is so, and that the principle may be this, that just in proportion to the heart's vitality, which is the heart's sacrificing love, entering and pervading the gift, just in that proportion will the Divine efficiency and the majesty of the Divine working go forth with it. He who sat over against the treasury, and whose eye penetrated to the spirit, saw, doubtless, more of the heart's vitality, the heart's sacrificing love, gathering about and entering into the widow's farthing, than there was in connection with all the rest. On this ground may it not have been, that the Lord pronounced her gift to be greater than all the rest?—on this ground that there was more of this vital element, a greater depth and volume of charity, in the farthing than in the proud pile of thousands of pounds?

On the same ground or principle, it would accomplish more: having in it more of the heart's vitality, it would therefore carry with it more of God's power than their whole put together; for assuredly, it is

God's prerogative to work and to save by few or by many, by little or by much. And his eye follows that mite so charged, saturated with heart, wherever it may go; follows it and the page of gospel-truth purchased thereby; the Spirit and the Power divine join in with that page, and travel with it over the line into some realm of utter gloom and satanic oppression, — and the Spirit and the Power use that humble page of gospel, the purchase of that mite, as the rod of a great revolution, the spring of a glorious renovation, and the instrument of eternal redemption to hundreds and thousands of souls. I cannot deem it a mere fancy, that there is on the part of God this singling and honoring and empowering of specific gifts thrown into his treasury: and this is one way in which we make it out, that the farthing, as given, was more for all the purposes of charity than the pounds in uncounted thousands by its side.

This, then, my brethren, is the sort of distinguishing and labelling we would do well to get on the money we devote to the Lord. Of very little importance is it that we designate it and have it marked, — this parcel for India and that for Africa: but oh, how important that we so give our gifts that the blessed Master, who knows us altogether, himself shall distinguish and label this offering, as charged to the full with heart-vitality, and that, as saturated all through with the heart's sacrificing love.

I come now to indicate, in two or three particulars, the practical bearing which this case should have upon us; or wherein we may be instructed and incited by it in our privilege of giving to the Master's cause.

1. And, first, we are reminded of the great responsibility which this idea or doctrine of heart-vitality lays upon us; the fact being, that this — the heart-quality — possessed, no slenderness of gift shall fail of good; this wanting, no greatness of gift will suffice. If, now, it be so, then let us consider it, and see that the heart is alive, is interested, and train our hearts to the right affection, while we train our hands to the generous bestowment.

2. But, secondly, we are further instructed by the case, that quantity, the amount of the gift, taken in connection with the ability of the giver, is intimately associated with the heart-quality, is even indispensable to the producing of it; so that you cannot have this quality of power in the gift, unless you conform to certain conditions in respect to quantity, or to the amount given. This appears very readily. The vitalizing power of the gift is the love that prompted it; and so intense that love for the object, we will suppose, that it prompts to the giving of all that could be. But change the giver and keep the gift the same. The individual hands out two mites from his abundance. Did it cost him any thing? As it left him, did it go, as sometimes even the farthing does, with a wrench, and a pang of self-denial, while yet the feeling was, it must go, because such the love to the Master and his cause. How plain it is, that if you give a detached trifle from your profusion, your gift, so failing in quantity, fails also in quality, — misses the condition of power. It is nothing to you as it went: it is nothing to God as it comes; and nothing to the world as it goes forth. You make nothing of it, and God makes nothing of it. But come up in the quantity, to a gift of

such a size, that, as it goes from you, goes with a sensation, carries something with it, showing your heart to be in and to go with it, then that offering will be crowned by God's approval, and be pervaded by God's efficiency.

3. Again, we learn from this example, that with most of us, in this matter of charity, the danger probably does not lie in the direction of excess. We are very little exposed to the fault of giving too much to Christian objects. If there ever was an instance of overdoing in charity, it was this poor widow, who gave her whole living. But she was fortunate in the judge who pronounced upon her action. Had it been somebody else, almost anybody else, she, doubtless, would have gone away with the character of one beside herself, not competent to take care of her own affairs, a fit subject for an overseer. But He who gave himself for us thought differently of her, who gave her all to him. It was right, was noble, what she did. Shall we, then, be likely to err in that direction? Possibly it would be no error, should we, some of us, give our all. And if an error, this literal giving of all, the peril in our case, I take it, is not very imminent. It is altogether in the other direction: a selfish begging off from the standard and the measure to which duty, philanthropy, religion, are ever summoning us; and assigning reasons and pleas for a reduction of the claim. Suppose we could bring these reasons and pleas into the light of this woman's spirit and example, I have no doubt the greater part of them would be wholly incompetent and unworthy. For example, this plea: We have so little to give, it is hardly worth while to pass it over. This precedent to-day certainly disposes of that excuse;

and all experience teaches, that those who have but little they can give, are the truly generous givers, giving far more in proportion to what they have. It is they who make the sacrifices; they, mainly, who feed the swelling streams of beneficence. It is they especially whose gifts bring down the Lord's benediction. Then there is that other plea, far more common and unworthy; namely, We cannot give, because we have met with losses: these persons not considering that they have something left, — the fruit and preservation of God's goodness; not considering, too, how appropriate it would be, and how beautiful, how savory to heaven, to make an offering to the Lord out of what his goodness has spared to them. This also is said: The Lord has not prospered me of late as I hoped and expected, so I must be excused. Has he not prospered you before? Yes; and that pile you call your own is the monumental evidence. Shall we stop and reprove such a plea as this against generosity? That silent example before us does it as I cannot. Your pile, with that great heart of hers behind it, would scatter, in angel fragments, the world over. There is this plea against giving at the present, found among those on whom God has sent prosperity: I have other uses for my money, crowding it into business, choosing to employ it all in various gainful enterprises for the present. I have met cases like this, yea, this specific case, the man who said sometimes to God, I have nothing to spare just now; but I will give by hundreds, perhaps thousands, provided this scheme I am prosecuting, or this adventure I have made, turns out well. Have not other schemes turned out well? Yes: I know they have: I know how God has blessed him, blessed him with an estate burdening for its bigness; but of this not a dollar, not a dollar. If the Lord has a mind so to order things in his Providence as to make money out of that scheme I have set a-going, then he may have some. Need we bring for correction and reproof such a case as this, to the example and standard now before us? If you were to do it, yea, if you were to bring such a person to the spot where that blessed woman was buried, to utter over her ashes this plea and purpose, I almost think that the dust, which has been still for nearly twenty centuries, would be moved and agitated by the profanation.

These, and such like excuses, are but the grim fallacies of a hateful selfishness; all wrong tracks, which hurt our souls by leading us off from the privilege of giving. And it is a privilege, — so this example teaches us; felt to be a privilege when the heart is in it; especially when we take into account the attribute of indestructibleness, that may pertain to what we give; made indestructible by this heart-quality; made, too, eternally our own, — never to reach a fixed and final dimension in the slide and the roll of that immortality. What you do not give, what you selfishly hoard and finally keep, you eternally alienate. What you thus leave behind, so far as you are concerned, will be as if buried in the grave that buries you. But what you give, what your heart gives, you eternally appropriate as your own, link it indissolubly with your name, and make it the wealth and the joy of your spirit. What a treasure, when you shall meet it on the other shore. When, too, you shall meet the souls, your sacrifice and toil have saved, meet your neighbors, your spirit and life have won; meet your children, your example and prayers have led in the same beneficent path; what a reward, what a blessedness, shall be yours.

# XI.

## THE MORAL DISCIPLINE OF GIVING.

*But rather give alms of such things as ye have; and, behold, all things are clean unto you.* — LUKE xi. 41.

CHRIST, being invited, went in to dine with a Pharisee. His host marvelled that he sat down to meat without first washing; whereupon the Lord addressed him and other Pharisees gathered with him: *Now do ye Pharisees make clean the outside of the cup and platter, but your inward part is full of ravening and wickedness. Did not he that made that which is without, make that which is within also?* Did not he who created the body, create the soul also? And is it not at least equally proper and important that the inner part, the soul, partake of the cleansing and the purity?

Assuming that it is important, our Lord proceeds to prescribe a mode by which the moral cleansing, the purity, may be obtained: *But rather give alms of such things as ye have; and, behold, all things are clean unto you.* These words present somewhat of difficulty, when we consider that they were addressed to a company of Pharisees, inasmuch as the Pharisees were notoriously given to the performance of these outward acts of charity. They did these outward things and remained all vile within. An outward injunction, in their case, could hardly touch the infected spot.

Some suppose that the Saviour spake in an ironical strain. As it regards your inward parts, all you have to do is to go on with your tithing system of mint and rue, anise and cummin, and all is clean to you; yours a perfect purity down to the bottom of your hearts. This view we cannot admit. The Lord, we think, spoke seriously; uttered before them a great truth, not a stinging sarcasm.

If we suppose that the company of Pharisees gathered on that occasion were, as many were, exceedingly avaricious, given to the getting of gains by the closest and hardest means, and were also given so to hold on upon their possessions that they could not, by any means, be brought to devote them in charity, in any worthy measure, then the Saviour's words, which struck at their pockets, would have also a deeper aim, and strike and enter their hearts.

The difficulty abiding in these words comes from the fact that so much efficacy is assigned to an outward performance. A great commentator, however, remarks, in mitigation of this, that it was the manner of the Saviour to command an outward act as a sign of the disposition, instead of enjoining the disposition itself. But here the giving act is put in a somewhat different relation. It seems to be put as an antecedent, a means to an end — cause to an effect. Giving according to the right standard and mode, is promotive of the soul's discipline — its growth in moral purity, holiness.

I come to this, then, as the main topic of my discourse: Giving of what God may have given us as the means of disciplining, purifying, elevating, the character. And I might speak of this discipline as both retrospective and prospective.

In regard to the retrospective action, a few words will suffice; and these are suggested by the context. It is clearly implied that those addressed by the Saviour were given to injustice. They had sought extortions and wrongful gains. In the strong phrase of Christ, *Your inward part is full of ravening and wickedness;* all there greedy, rapacious, grasping. What now follows as duty in such a case? This, first, and without delay: Repent and return from such ways. From being injurious, rapacious men, become generous men; do justly, deal kindly. Then, farther, the gospel enjoins this: Redress past wrongs; make reparation, restitution, as far as it can be done. But there are cases where it cannot be done. Those who were the subjects of the wrong, and all their representatives, have passed away, and can no more be found. Or the wrong is so complex, so woven into the web of other things, that it cannot be separated and acted upon, so as to be set right directly and specifically. Where this is the condition of things, what then? Here let charity apply her corrective: *Give alms of such things as ye have, and all things are clean unto you.* This disposition and distribution of the estate got by hard means, indicate a softening of the character, even the genuineness of the repentance. At once the conscience is relieved, and the heart is made better by the course taken. The possessions which the individual feels are not his and cannot be put back whence they were wrongfully taken, he chooses to make over to the Great Proprietor of all, by devoting them to his service in the welfare of his creatures. This is the most natural dictate of the heart, once base and wrong, into which the spirit of religion and reform has entered. So was it in the case of Zaccheus. Half of his goods he gave to the poor; then the most generous restitution to all whom he had defrauded. Who can doubt the integrity, the moral purity, of that heart henceforth? Who doubt that all the residue of his estate was clean unto him? Who doubt that from that time he began truly to possess and enjoy his own?

This is what we may call the backward correction, the retrospective discipline of benevolence. It is not the giving of a portion of ill-gotten wealth to sanctify the rest, also and equally ill-gotten. The principle does not touch such a case. Such a case is only and intensely atrocious and abominable. This is simply a case both of generousness and justice where the opposites of these had been.

We suggest whether this backward correction, this retrospective discipline, should not be matter of thought and consideration now: whether the Lord's cause and the welfare of men would not receive means for their promotion, if there were more inquiring and acting in this direction; the Lord's treasury receiving numberless fragments, and some huge masses, which are now in hands that would be better off without them. Let each take the candle of the Lord and pass through his own premises, — its rays penetrating all the tortuous intricacies of the past, — and then let him do what this revealing light shall teach him to do; and he will be likely to do both generously and well; certainly, be likely to improve his standing for this world and the world to come.

But I pass now to what is more generally applicable and practical, — the present and prospective discipline of the spirit and habit of giving, — giving as a means of spiritual advance, of growth in moral purity; all within, and all pertaining to one becoming clean, pure. The word used here is the same used by Christ in that other place: *Blessed are the pure in heart.*

In order to make a man clean, pure, particularly a character like that contemplated by Christ in the text, certain evil and corrupting things are to be removed out of him. There is to be an ejectment of the corrupt and corrupting, in the process of attaining to the clean, the pure. And one in the category of the corrupt and the corrupting — and this a main one, abiding at the fountain, a grand promoter and feeder in the wrong direction — is the love of money. So Paul names it, and then attaches to it this primal and terrible potency, *root* of all evil, — pronouncing the love of money the root of all evil. He means that love of it which leads the individual harboring this passion to address himself to the work of getting it — accumulating, heaping it together; this his end, his great object in living. The Apostle shows this to be his meaning, in the verse immediately preceding, where he uses another phraseology, — *They that will be rich,* — this is the working and the end of the passion. It resolves itself into the will to be rich. Christ's word chosen to describe it, yields the same idea on being subjected to an analysis; his word is covetousness, which means, etymologically, have more, — the desire to have more. This, as a very common desire or passion in the human soul, is quite obvious, showing itself on every hand in the schemes and the toils to get more. This, as being an evil desire, most fruitful of mischief, Paul portrays in that flaming sketch: *They that will be rich fall into temptation and a snare, and into many foolish and hurtful lusts, which drown men in destruction and perdition.* This passion, how sure to grow. If the person dare indulge it, it will grow and get stronger than he; increasing still in capacity, in greediness, in clamor; ever ringing the repetitious cry, "Give, give." The already vast quantity of possession only adds vehemence to the cry, "More, yet more."

And under its influence, what wrongs, oppressions, crimes, are enacted. And what follies, too. This rage for more, in its height and intensity, seems not only to blind the eyes, but strangely to abate the brains. The Saviour, in addressing one of the sort, — a representative man, doubtless, to resort to the modern parlance, — used upon him the rather curt term, *Thou fool.* Sometimes it is one by himself, "Thou fool." Sometimes — and have we not seen something of the kind? — large masses are frenzied together. There stands forth pretty much a whole generation of fools, inciting and inflaming one another, expanding and spreading out, till there comes a crash and a conclusion; and the whole surface is seen strewn with wrecks of character and fortune. There follows a wholesome pause; and one would suppose that some abiding wisdom would be derived from the meditations and amazements of the compulsory silence; certainly, suppose that such a course and result never could be repeated by the same individuals, or their immediate successors. But it is repeated. The same ones, with the smart of the old chastisement in their skins, and the indented bruise of it in their bones, will spring forth, eager to re-enact the same old fury. So it is that this desire grows when allowed, and maddens men, and ruins characters, fortunes, and souls.

It is plain, as I have already intimated, that in the course or process of becoming clean and pure, this evil desire must be repressed, and even put out. We come now to hint the way of doing it.

One way, a most legitimate and summary way, — may I not say *the* way, no other being wanted? — is this; namely, by giving. Let a person give alms of such things as he has, and he will be cleansed of this foul and ever-defiling desire or passion. But, in order to the achievement of so great an end, there must be conditions to the giving. It must be principled, the result and flow of principles, — principles in this Holy Book laid down, and by the heart cordially embraced; not impulsive, giving as the fit takes, as the sympathies happen to be stirred. Based on principle, uniform and habitual, it bears a just relation to the means God has put into our hands. This is one of the principles or laws in this matter, that the giving bear a fixed and just relation or proportion to the means placed at our disposal. And what is the proportion? or what the principle, the rule to be made?

This principle, that every one at stated times lay by him in store for this purpose, according as God has prospered him, would be sufficient, if we may suppose in him the thoroughly Christian heart. To add this, namely, Let him lay by for charity a generous proportion, is leaving it still quite too indefinite. To say a tenth of all that comes in, is greatly unequal. There is neither justice nor benevolence in this as the universal law of giving. For the object I have in view this statement may be an approximate; at least, may stand preparatory to one more definite; namely, That a person give in measure and continuity sufficient to feel it. How little, probably, is given in the church of God where this is the effect. How very few, probably, from the measure they give, have any, even the least, sensation of inconvenience. Of self-denial, and real sacrifice from giving, I suppose the great majority of Christian givers know nothing. In all such cases, of course, the entire personal benefit and discipline from giving, is lost. According to the statement now in hand, the sensation-principle, the tithe system, or the law of tenth, can be no general rule; for, in very many cases, the amount dictated by this rule would hardly be enough to throw any, even the smallest, twinges, into the soul's cleaving selfishness. A tenth can be given, and the man never know, by any appreciable diminution, that he has given any thing; of course, he can give all that, and vastly more, without beginning to feel it. What is done, is but shelling off some of the loose outer scales of one of these leviathans of wealth. The giving, to be effectual as a discipline, must be on a principle that shall reach and restrict the desire for getting, the intent to have more; for all the mischief and meanness and smallness lie in that, emanate from that. On that it is, all Scripture pours its intense and concentrated exprobration.

What principle and measure of giving, then, will administer to this the repressive, yea, the annihilating blow? That principle which says, "By the grace of God, I will no more lay up treasure for myself;" the person at once and for ever renouncing the purpose, even crucifying the desire, to be rich. Then, that measure or amount of giving which accrues from giving the whole beyond a certain prescribed boundary. No accumulation of property, does this mean? No: not that. Accumulation there may be, and should be; and the amount, the extent of it is to be settled in the best moments of Christian experience, under the most decisive action of the Christian spirit and principle; a definite amount fixed under the felt meaning of that great vow of an entire consecration to Him. It may be thousands, or tens of thousands, or hundreds of thousands. More or less, this is its solemn condition and quality; it is a Christian amount, religiously retained as the means to still larger deeds of giving and blessing. Here we have the man, all he has, and all his power of getting, possessing, diffusing, devoted to God. With him accumulation has this purpose, — it is for God. It has this limitation, — nothing for self; nothing beyond a solemnly prescribed amount; no indefinite laying up. It is a great step for a person to come to this point; costing a mighty wrestle, and the bloody sweat of the soul, probably, to renounce the purpose of personal and selfish getting, the intent of property, wealth. It is something every one will profoundly feel in the conflict, the actual doing it. Some have succeeded in the doing, and have stood forth noble examples of character, and prodigies in the line of giving.

We are sure that, in this repression and restriction just indicated, the course, the action, is right. There can be no mistake at this point. If this thirst for money, this purpose and practice of indefinite getting, — all one can, to the end, — if this is wrong, has on its face the indignant brand of Almighty God, then is it right for the disciple, made his duty by the law and spirit of his religion, to fix a limit, to build a Christian boundary somewhere to this fiery and rampant lust of humanity,—desire of possession, to have more. This terrible lust, you cannot pet it, play with it, and say, you will keep it under. No man can. No man can serve two masters. It will be one, a single allegiance; one up, and the other under. Hence the right, the necessity absolute, that there be ordained the broad line of demarcation; that there be dug in the soul a deep and impassable trench between God and Mammon.

Let us see now what is accomplished in the way of discipline — moral cleansing and keeping clean, — by the action thus far. This first at the fountain — that great, generic, base, cloven-footed, all-defiling thing, the selfish, self-seeking love of money, will to get it, — this, in the case supposed, is pretty much wiped from the heart by the one broad, introductory stroke, by that soul's counter and higher purpose, in that soul's true consecration. This purpose, once enthroned in the soul, summarily subordinates and drives out the whole litter of mean and craven lusts. I knew one for years, and loved him, and learned of him, though officially his teacher, and deemed him the model giver of the State of Maine. This was his principle, — his purpose. Early and with a true Christian heart, he marked off the sum to be retained, and fixed the boundary; and he made over all the rest, freely and broadly scattering it as it came. The love of money, the desire of holding, he often said, and more often showed, that he knew nothing of it. The faintest breath or motion from this source never, so far as he was conscious, stirred the outer surface of his soul. In the eight years of my connection with him, he gave away probably twice the sum which he reserved as the capital of his business and his beneficence. He is now in heaven ; and can we suppose that he there regrets that measure of consecration and sacrifice?

Another thing : the central and despotic lust extinct, at least brought under, then the wrong deeds so apt to be perpetrated in the eagerness for gain, in the rage for yet more, — no such deeds will ever be done. All business, all labors for the world, are sanctified by the soul's good purpose ; are a part of the man's Christianity, the dictate of rectitude and benevolence. Never does such an one overreach and craftily haul in huge gains upon an already overgrown stock ; never take advantage when he can, and grind the necessitous ; never throw blight upon others' fortunes, that he may add brightness to his own. Not a dollar comes into his coffer dimmed and stained by his manner of obtaining it. It is all clean money. From all the temptations of business his comes forth an unsullied and honorable name. The great and kingly affection of religion, the love of the heart, abides unquestioned in the supremacy. The other graces take their proportion and place ; all the impulses of a pure and genial nature blend to produce a character whose descriptive is goodness ; its form, a winning, admirable symmetry.

Of such a character we find that generousness is a prominent, practical attribute. Let us, then, pass on and see how naturally and infallibly the principle I have indicated produces it ; how surely it grows and benignly spreads under the soul's high purpose of restriction upon the world, and the purpose to be "rich toward God." We have already noted the fact, that it abolishes, at once crushes out, the leading cause of closeness, stinginess in a man, — this cause, the desire of getting, the fascination of accumulating. I want here the Greek's terser tongue, and the privilege to cry, *pleonexia*, — have more. Henry Rogers, in a late work, speaks of a man who always gave a guinea to each of certain good objects. This person at length received a bequest which, he says, "might be made the basis of a fine estate." He caught the idea of increasing, — rather, that caught him. When asked the next time for his donation to an object approved, though more was justly expected, nothing was received; not a penny would he give: but a reason he gave; and the sum of it was, that now he had something considerable in hand, and there was a satisfaction in making it more. Before, there was no such object in keeping, so he freely gave: now, there was an object, and every little he kept, told on the result. So he kept it, and so he would not give. Just here we have the secret why men, prospered in the world, perpetually swelling their gains, are proportionally slender givers, often the most grudging and stinted in their giving; while those who eat up their income, and not enough at that, those who have made up their mind to do good in the land, and trust God to be fed, are among the foremost in generous deeds. On the one side it is the purpose, the desire to get and to add, that dwarfs the soul so ignominiously; on the other, it is the purpose, all for God, which fashions the soul to that largeness and generous doing. And in the latter case, not only is the measure made over admirable; the manner of it, the freeness and heartiness, make it still more so. Such an one has not, on every presentation of charity, to wage a bitter warfare with the base and servile part of himself; has not to debate and contend with and wring at length a few reluctant driblets out of a dry, hard, tyrant passion, who is allowed the keys; has not to go and pound and importune, as it were, at the tight door of a gloomy iron box, constructed for a smooth passage in, but a most rubbing passage out. Behold,—see how pitiably poor the little creature is. How dreadfully hard it comes. Taking from him his money, is very much as if you tore off the flakes of his flesh; and we can seem to see the wry face he twists into, under the agony of the parting. To the man of the other sort, with the heat and lust for more summarily quelled,—the great purpose, all for God and human welfare, kept dominant; to him, it is the sweetest and best of all privileges to give. He welcomes every authentic application; even searches for the opportunity, and blesses the man who furnishes him with one. He finds the words of the Lord Jesus true, when he said, It is more blessed to give than to receive. All is turned to a pure heart—comfort—a fresh fountain of happiness.

We see how important it is, that one have, at the bottom and the beginning, right principle. It is a grand regulator. One right principle at the head and fountain of conduct, puts and keeps every thing in the region of it, and resulting therefrom, right also. And a principle like the one we have now stated, thus generic and summary in the prevention of evil and the production of good, has herein a proof that it is right, and is of God. Just see what it does. This one word, giving, carried through on this principle, succeeds to blot out those other traitorous and engulfing words, will to be rich, among the most tainting and deadly in all the human vocabulary. Planted here, doing this, no taint shall ever touch you: no ill-gotten gain shall ever sear your conscience or burn your palm. The clustering graces of holiness, the rather, will gather around and adorn your character. All that is given will go with freeness and joy; and the result, the amount imparted, shall stand in the end as a noble monument, not of merit, but of grace,—the soul's treasure passed over, laid up on the other side, its own inalienable possession, the glory and wealth of its immortality.

Not only shall you be blest in your character and deed, but those connected with and dependent upon you shall be blest through you, as your intent and prosperous hoarding never could have blessed them. Hence, in another sense, all things are clean unto you. By this standard and course of beneficence, by this example of piety, by the prayers which go up from a heart thus pervaded and consecrated, by such large outgoes of charity as shall keep down the hope of inherited wealth in those coming after, you help form an atmosphere of purity for children to breathe and grow up in. The property which, fast held and to the last skilfully rolled up, would have been a snare to them, an omnipresent temptation, as it commonly is, and would have taken away their manly strength and salient aspiration and achieving enterprise, as it commonly does, dooming them, and passing them, with rare exceptions, to the shades of insignificance and blank nothingness in creation, as is most obtrusively and painfully the case, — this property, dealt with and disbursed on the other principle, is charged with no such perils, is changed wholly to another, a vital element and issue. The carnal and corrupting given, the spiritual is received, and so the treasures of your home become vastly greater and richer. The crowning good is, that all is clean; your hands clean; your reputation clean; your soul, through grace, clean; your children, through the same grace, clean; all these clean to you.

We should love to commend, could we do it, this principle of repressed selfishness and of enthroned benevolence to that great company of disciples, who have recently been brought into the kingdom of Christ. How remarkable have been God's dealings with the people since this Board held its last Annual Meeting: * the business of the world, by a sudden stroke and shock, thrown into confusion, into complex and prostrating disaster; men's hearts failing them, distress and ruin settling down upon all ranks and conditions; then, directly upon this, almost simultaneous with it, the heavens opened and poured down righteousness, and myriads have been made rich in the inalienable possession. How fitting, that those who have come in, and are still coming, we trust, amid circumstances so significant, and outpourings of the Spirit so indicative of the grandeur of prophecy, should join to inaugurate a new order of piety; rather to bring back again the primitive order and type. We would beg of this com-

---

* This sermon was preached at Detroit, Sept. 7, 1858, at the Annual Meeting of the American Board of Commissioners for Foreign Missions.

pany of new disciples, could we speak to them, to take their stand for Christ; resolved to live a life of singleness and generousness to the Master and the race he is redeeming. Only let it be so; this elect company coming along to be such givers and workers, and still rising higher in this divine scale, then shall they inspire even veteran breasts with fresh assurances of success, bring light and cheer amid worldly depression and gloom. Then will they be an honor to Christianity, a new argument of its verity, and an added force to send it to the remote, and apply it to those near. We have reason to take courage from this living accession God is making to us. We may not repine at the great secular catastrophe and revulsion, but accept it as a just discipline, and be thankful even for those quick-working breaks in the invisible enginery of God's providence, which bring men to a stop in season not to leap the precipice. We welcome these fresh co-workers, because, coming in as they do, we expect that they come to be whole men, — altogether on one side, — that they come by that singular sort of consecration which gives up all to the Lord, — body and soul, the man and the money, — not trying to stand somewhere between, as if adjusting and connecting those great antagonisms, God and Mammon; just where any quantity of professing Christians seem to be standing, — I mean, *are* standing; and what they are doing; doing nothing as they ought to do, nothing largely and worthily for the Master; cankered, eaten all through with the rust of selfishness; spoiled for any noble, Christian work. To any persons remotely meditating the hopes or the profession of Christianity, we say, neither the Church nor the world wants any more such Christians. These anomalies of discipleship, these abnormals of the kingdom, who lay down a part of the price, — give their carcasses and keep back their coffers; they bring neither power nor credit nor a blessing.

Is it not an astounding fact, when there is so much created in order to be given, and when there are so many professed servants, new-created of God, who hold it, and are bound to give it; the oath of consecration most solemnly upon them; a world needing it; the world all thrown open to receive it, or the gospel it might send; its millions upon millions brought into vicinage; and when we may come directly to them, and impress them, and mould them, and put them in the way to heaven; and yet that the Church fails most frequently and decisively in meeting the cost, as though she could not afford to set her dollars against the redemption of these souls. I fear she hardly puts down annually a dime against a soul. The men to go are oftener on hand,—it is the money that lags. It does seem often as though the worst, the most cruel, form of selfishness, is this which links itself with religion and religious people. Oh this selfishness of the new man, this Christian worldliness, this baptized carnality, this holy greed of gain; what a demoniac heart thou hast! Accursed shape! hellish thing! away from our temples and our hearts! Let the Master come, if he must, with his scourge of cords, and drive him out of our temples and our hearts; and himself possess us, and fill us with his own good spirit.

But the blessed Master has another and a better way to purge out the evil, and take the possession; namely, by his truth and grace. This is the doctrine of the text, and of all his gospel. The Christian character is benevolence, — the spirit of sacrifice and of work for a lost world. A missionary spirit is the measure of it; a giving spirit, at once the measure and the promoter of it.

Giving, then, is one of the means of grace, — one of the best means of spiritual growth. If no good externally is done by the gifts, the charities, still a vital and immeasurable good is done to the giving soul; enough, and vastly more than enough, to justify the deed. The sordid taunt so often thrown, "Why all this waste?" it comes of the sordidness that is equal to the sale of the Lord himself, — the thirty pieces in the pocket better than He. I repeat, if no other good is done, there is no waste; no matter what the amount given, be it only enough, and given with the Christian motive, then the character is set forward, and the Church is brought up higher and nearer to the millennial state. The Church must pass through the work and the sacrifice of establishing the millennium abroad, in order to make one in her own pale. Those final words of her Lord, then, which lay upon her this amazing responsibility, — "Go, preach the gospel, evangelize all nations," — are to her an untold heritage of blessings and of blessedness. They embody the corrective and expulsion of her deadliest foes; they are to her the necessary means of the victory, and the kingdom and the crown; I mean on this ground of attainment, — personal, separate fitness, reached by the culture and through the conflict of beneficent giving and doing. The question before us is, Will we meet these conditions, and have the millennium at home, the kingdom within us, — not forgetting the one condition our Lord so significantly marks, giving alms of such things as we have?

To very many, this, as a means of grace, of spiritual advance, stands in the first place, and is indispensable; stands, in a sense, even before prayer; they being ahead in prayer, behind in giving. To all those, then, who have given leanly and grudgingly, we say, Arise and give, — give bountifully — give heartily — give wilfully, — just because something within resists and says, I won't. Give the more, and still more, from the very teeth and grip of the old retaining passion. Give with the measure and intent to crucify it, — that hundred the nail, that thousand the spike, that ten thousand the spear, — and so proceed and persist till the base and slimy thing is wholly dead.

And, in our dealings with others, the minister, in his appeals to his people, must come to them with some authority, with a worthy object, and with a sizable claim. A small matter will not do the business with men, taking them as they rise. The heart of the majority is so snugly shut up, — the orifice not unfrequently all tight and twisted and gnarled, — if you would come upon it with any likelihood, it must be, not merely with a sharp tool, but with some bulk and weight. Pry at it with a massive lever; some little local appeal will not make a passage. The field is the world, — the instrument also. Then make the big world into a wedge, and drive that in, and so you shall succeed, and they and the world shall be the better for it.

Giving, doing, sacrificing, on the right scale, is not only the means of grace to ourselves: it is the secret of power in what we do for the needy or perishing.

Money so given that it does us good in the giving, does, we believe, vastly more good in its going forth. It takes, so to speak, an embalming and vitalizing from the heart it leaves, which gives it, or the truth it commissions, an imbedding in the hearts it goes to. A thorough victory over selfishness, achieved and shown on the part of Christians and the Church, becomes the miracle of the gospel, — its moral sign, which opens a path for it to the souls of sceptical or idolatrous men. What economy appears in the arrangement of means, and what responsibility it imposes, that our condition of power toward the world is simply that the gospel, by our whole reception of it, has become a power upon us, — first, a power upon us, then a power within, and a power emanant. The gospel living in us, and working out, is its own witness. In this condition, we need spend no time in preliminaries, none in philosophizing or proving. Filled full of it ourselves, that is the argument; and overflowing, that the argument; and giving bountifully, and intently working for the good of others, that the argument. So was it with the apostle Paul. Mighty as he was in the tread of his logic when he chose, in the main he was his own argument, — moved over lands and seas, himself a colossal demonstration. The same with the Christians then, — their character, the reign of love throughout, their total conquest of selfishness, no man calling any thing he possessed his own; that their argument. What they did, history tells us, and we shall repeat the achievement when we repeat the character, and not till then. Our first responsibility is to be what we ought to be, and what we may be. The path is all open to the attainment; the divine Helper open to our access:

to him let us come, with hearts open and longing to receive the replenishments of good which shall eject the evil; those enrichments of grace, those treasured gifts of salvation, that repletion of the love divine, which shall make us ready, eager even, for any work or sacrifice fitted to advance the kingdom and the glory of the Master.

# XII.

## DOERS OF THE WORD, AND NOT HEARERS ONLY.

*But be ye doers of the word, and not hearers only, deceiving your own selves.* — JAMES i. 22.

THE following classification, I suppose, would embrace the entire human family: First, those who never hear the gospel; second, those who only hear it; third, those who hear and do. The most numerous class is made up of those who never hear, — taking in the entire world, immeasurably the greater portion; the next larger class, I take to be those who are hearers only; the smallest of the three, those who hear and do. As to the first class, it will be of no avail to appropriate to them a portion of this discourse, for the simple reason, that they will not hear it if we do. We come, then, to the second class, the hearers only, with the exhortation of this practical apostle, *Be ye doers of the word, and not hearers only.* It would not be very strange, if some of the last named were present to-day, hearers only: they are those who hear, with no intent of any thing further; hear, with the calculation that the ear function will be the last of it. If I were to name some subordinate sections of this large general class, —

1. One might be made up of those who happen to be, at a particular time, in the place of hearing; mere in-

cidental hearers of the gospel, brought in by some curiosity, or by following in the wake of others. Such are pretty apt to sit through, as hearers only. There are those who are hardly hearers at all. They came with no such design. They came rather to see than to hear; and some, more especially, to be seen. They have no thought of worship, or desire for the heavenly good and place. Vacant are they, vagrant, unthinking; hardly lifted to the respect of hearers at all. If at all, hearers only.

2. There are those who hear to cavil; to take some exception to the system or the gospel of God, and so to find out some way of escape from the terrible bearing of this gospel upon them in their worldliness and their wicked rejection of it. They see difficulties, mysteries, inconsistencies, they think; contradictions, even, in the system; certainly and flagitiously, inconsistencies on the part of the Church and its members. They hear, if perchance they may detect something of the kind; for they are sure they shall feel somewhat better for it. If they can by any means get their Maker, the great God, into a corner, they hope to be able to keep their own souls out of hell. Such are hearers, nervously awake, and dissectingly sharp; and amid the heavy drowsiness which is sometimes the condition of things in this place, there is a sort of satisfaction in having a few such as these. They do us this honor,—they hear us. But we have to retort back upon them the charge of being hearers only.

3. There are those who hear with the mere critical ear. They are not so much cavillers at the gospel message, as judges upon the merits of the preacher; and they are keen at seeing blemishes, quick and fruit-

ful in the line of fault-finding. Style, argument, figures, manner, here and there awry,—so they pronounce. We would commend this thought to such,—that this spirit of depreciating criticism indicates a limited and shoal mind; one not having attained to know, nor having the breadth to see, the difficulties of a right performance. This also holds,—they are hearers only.

4. There are those, and this is a growing class, who hear as matter of present satisfaction; hear the preaching of the gospel mainly to be pleased by it; to be gratified by some accomplishments of rhetoric, or rapt away by some feats of oratory. If these are not here, they go yonder for them. They want the pleasing performance. They do not want any stiff, rough truth; they want nothing that shall task their attention, lay any load on their consciences, or wake any terror in their souls. If they have succeeded in hearing some fine music and some charming preaching, their end in coming to the church is wholly answered. Certainly, and most flagrantly, are they hearers only.

The apostle advises, yea, commands, us, *Be not hearers only, deceiving your own selves.* And this is the reason he suggests for not being hearers only,—that such deceive their own selves. They deceive themselves, doubtless, with the idea that they are growing better by a course of hearing merely. Some are uniform and respectful: storms and foul-going may keep Christians away, but not them; always are they in their place, and outwardly so reverent and attentive, that the deceiving heart whispers to each one, Now, some good will come to me, who sit here thus respectfully and patiently, fetching in twice every Sunday my lump of clay for the divine Potter to take and fashion into a vessel to honor; submissively ready am I, if he only will; and I cannot but hope that after, on his part, looking upon the same lump so long, he will be induced to take hold of, and, for variety's sake, make a change in it. My respected and passive friend, you deceive yourself in the thought, that coming and sitting and hearing only will bring to pass any such work of sovereign grace upon or within you.

There is another way in which this class deceive themselves, not merely by the long and reverent continuity of hearing; but also by certain complacent experiences, which overtake them as they sit and hear such truths as are frequently addressed to them. They have sensibilities, and now and then these are touched; under some pathetic description, are moved, even to the shedding of tears. Beneath certain grand revealings of truth, as they sit and listen, and are rapt above, there come to them moments in which illusion drops, and reality lifts up its head; then, as they catch a glimpse of themselves in God's glass, they say, Oh, the emptiness of these pleasures, and the folly and shame of living on as we do! Now, as these little spots or passages of something better heave up in their natures, these momentary self-reproachings and upward aspirings, they deceive themselves by supposing, as they are pretty sure to suppose, that they are growing better in consequence of them; when the fact is, as our faithful apostle lays it down, they go directly out from one of these most melting occasions, or entertainments, — for all such are entertained when some pulpit enchanter makes them sob religiously, — though seeming angels in their trance of goodness, they go out, and straightway forget what manner of men they were. The world, which they thought was lifted away for a little season, comes back with redoubled force, absolutely whelming and burying them; and they forget all about the higher life and the blessed land. Instead of being made better by the fascinating process, they are made worse, hardened, by it; are farther removed from any likelihood of any thing valid or abiding in religious experience; a sort of sentimental sinners, but moving on to a veritable and a terrible damnation.

Our reason, then, against being hearers only, sums up in this: that hearing only brings guilt and peril to the soul so practising. Observe, the sin is not in the hearing, but the hearing only. The sin may be even greater, where one can hear, but indolently, in the spirit of rebellion refuses to hear. I can conceive that his offence is the greater who proudly and purposely separates himself from the gospel of God. Still, the offence is great of him who hears, and that only; and the retribution is certain, first, deceiving, and then bringing destruction upon himself.

1. The deception. How great the deception, to suppose that hearing a way pointed out will bring one on in that way. As if one who is sick should conclude that hearing the prescription of the physician will make him well again; or the worldling, that hearing the road to wealth pointed out will load him with riches. Just so great the deception that the hearers only practise on themselves in the matter of religion.

2. Not only great is the deception; great will be the destruction: on the principle that he that knew his Master's will, and did it not, shall be beaten with many stripes. What an anomaly will he be, as viewed in the

light of those coming scenes, standing there as one who came from the presence of such truths, the proffer of such gifts, and the pressure of such motives; hearing the unmeasured in grace and goodness, and moral grandeur even, and not condescending to have what only the Infinite One can give, and he give only through an infinite sacrifice, and what he stands ready to give to every receiving soul. Who of us would care to encounter the doom incurred by folly and guilt such as that? Who care to go from these flooding beams of truth and mercy, and there be awarded as one who lived and moved amid them, only to disregard and despise all? We had better not, any of us. We shall be piteously sorry for it at the end; mourning then with unavailing and consuming regrets, and saying, *How have I hated instruction, and my heart despised reproof; and have not obeyed the voice of my teachers, nor inclined mine ear to them that instructed me.* Woe unto thee, Capernaum; unto you, ye inhabitants of Capernaum. Ye hearers of the words, ye beholders of the works, of Jesus, who are now exalted to heaven, lifted though ye be to the highest pinnacle of privilege, ye shall be brought down to hell.

This defective character of the hearer only, so profoundly doomed and sunk in its conclusion, let us proceed, in the next place, to supplement it according to the teaching of our apostle; and this is done by the adding of a single word, — Doers. *Be ye doers of the Word, and not hearers only.* There is a vast reach and potency of meaning in this little word, standing in this relation, — hearing and doing, — hearing, with the heart to do, with the purpose to do. The hearing most favorable will be the hearing affected by the purpose to do. Then it will be candid hearing: nothing of the exceptional or the critical hearing we have referred to, but open, candid, — a desire to know just what this word means; ready to admit whatever God has declared. Exhaustive hearing: drawing to the largest extent the substance, the nutriment, out of the Word, that it may minister strength and growth to the soul. Comprehensive hearing: ready to hear all the sides and contrasts of truth, the fearful as well as the gentle, the fiery doom as well as the radiant mercy. Courageous hearing: having attained to possess the doing heart, he is at once a man with a brave heart; no terror of God can disturb a single fibre of his frame; he is calm, peaceful, blessed; alike before law and before gospel, the threatening or the comforting strain.

It is apt to prove, also, understanding hearing. If heard with the purpose to do it, it is commonly with an instinct rightly to understand it. This doing frame abates in him all prejudices against, and the particular truth stands before him precisely as God intended it should. There is nothing of the wheeling or breaking it into the direct contrary of what it says. He perceives it and receives it just as it comes from the mouth of God, *He that. believeth and is baptized, shall be saved; and he that believeth not, shall be damned.* Every creature with the obedient frame, the world over, will join in this understanding, that the believer shall be saved; the unbeliever shall perish. The fault not at all in God's putting, — all clear as the sun on his part. It is the twisting, distorting heart of disobedience, in its refracting prejudices, that puts all into crookedness and contraries, where God has put all in clear beauty and harmony.

God's own great principle of interpreting the grand maxim of his kingdom is, He that doeth the will of God shall know of the doctrine. This holds ever, because nearly all essential religious truth is practical truth; it is truth to be done; and the doing of it is an expounding of it. Hence the shortest way, commonly, to clear away the difficulties and the mysteries pertaining to it, is to proceed and enact it, adopt it into the life. Take prayer, for instance: what a mystery or wonder, — the creature approaching into the presence of the Infinite Creator, to address and influence him. How can it be? How can I presume to do it? You may read libraries and never know how, till you proceed in the spirit of a child and do it; till you actually commence speaking to him. Thus begin, and you will find help in every preliminary; some new light, it may be, at every step, as you go alone, and reverently kneel, and audibly speak, and say, *Our Father which art in heaven.*

Or the word you hear calls you to Christ, saying, Come to me and find rest to your soul; but the way is all dark, and so nothing is adventured or attempted. But try, attempt it, by entering on some service Christ enjoins. Do that duty cheerfully, as well as you can, because Christ asks it of you: for the sake of pleasing him, attempt it, with all humility and self-renouncing; with the desire and the prayer that you may be enabled to lay over your soul and all its interests into Jesus' hands to be blessed for Jesus' sake; and I should not be surprised, if you were to find the way opening, the difficulty diminishing, and the darkness clearing. The duty attempted in all sincerity, because Christ commands it, and for the sake of pleasing and honoring him, will prove, pretty likely, a step toward him, if not a step clean to him.

It is very obvious how it comes to pass that there is no more profit in the hearing of God's truth. It is because of the practice, so common, of letting it slip, — hearing and then dropping it. It is because there is no wakeful, active response to the great summons of God; because in these premises no resolved putting forth to gain the mighty boon held out to us by the generous goodness of our God. Men grow perversely orthodox; become sticklers for grace; choose to sit and see and receive the salvation, wholly by grace, in no sense by work; they cannot bear to have God's sovereign grace dishonored by the creature's working. True, God the Father works always; this they know: and the Son works also; and these very persons work for every thing else they have, or hope to have; still, notwithstanding the God of nature, and all the beings and forces of nature, and themselves, too, are thus alert and operative, these persons persist in being saved by stubbornly doing nothing. Some of you are not saved because so untrustful, because you will have no confidence in the Blessed Master. When he calls for some of your doing, as when he says, Go wash, you refuse: you do not go. When he says, Stretch forth thy hand, you reply, Absurd; all the way down it is flaccid and dead with palsy. It is not absurd; because with his word goes the vital power. The instant you begin obediently to raise that arm, that arm is up and out. So in all. When you begin to do in loving, trusting obedience, help and life divine begin to circulate through and fill you.

My unconverted friends, let me close by saying to

you this one thing, — that there is not much mystery in being saved ; yea, none at all. It is all plain matter of fact. There is a perfectly plain letter about it. You know the letter, are full of it, are reeking and running over with it. Will you do it? This one work of God, will you do it? Believe on Jesus Christ, whom God has sent.

## XIII.

### JUSTIFICATION BY WORKS.

*Ye see then how that by works a man is justified, and not by faith only.* — JAMES ii. 24.

WE have in the New Testament the great subject or doctrine of man's justification before God, presented under two aspects: one made prominent by Paul; the other by James. And on account of the different aspects, or parts of the doctrine they severally had their eye upon, some have maintained that they held conflicting views; Paul's language being, *That a man is justified by faith, without the deeds of the law;* James's language being, *That by works a man is justified, and not by faith only.*

1. Let us examine, now, into these utterances, and see if they be at all conflicting.

The subject we are introduced to by James from his stand-point is, the importance, yea, the necessity, of works in our justification; and thus he seems to teach that justification is by works, works taking the precedence of faith, when he says, *By works a man is justified.*

The first question which arises is this; namely, Is it true that a man is justified wholly by works? We answer, No. There is not a declaration to this effect in the Bible; not a passage that reads, A man is justified by the deeds of the law without the faith which works by love. All Scripture unites in condemning such a sentiment; even this passage from James condemns it indirectly; his words, *By works a man is justified, and not by faith only*, implying clearly that faith has an important function in the soul's justification.

This leads to another question; namely, Is a man justified partly by faith, and partly by works? This seems to be the doctrine James favors in certain of his statements. If it is the doctrine of the New Testament, it stands. If another doctrine is taught by the whole tenor of Scripture, and this decisively contradicted, then it cannot stand, and we must seek for another as the true interpretation. I know not where the doctrine is taught, know not the text which unequivocally affirms that justification is partly by faith, and partly by works, as its primal ground and meritorious cause. If no such doctrine is clearly taught, then, further, we ask, Is there any thing in Scripture which cuts short such a doctrine, clearly condemning it, and as clearly teaching another doctrine? We think there is. It is denied in this Book that a man is justified partly by faith, and partly by works; denied, we say, inasmuch as it is here taught, in repeated instances, and in language which admits of no double interpretation, *That a man is justified by faith without the deeds of the law.* This is Paul's great proposition in his epistle to the Romans. He states it in different forms: he proves it by various arguments; shows that, by the deeds of the law, no flesh can be justified before God, because all have sinned, and come under the condemning sentence of the law. To such, justi fication comes freely by his grace. It is God's work, by him given. It is by faith, that it might be by grace. *Where is boasting then? It is excluded. By what law? Of works? Nay; but by the law of faith. Therefore,* says Paul, giving to the sentiment all the weight of a grand conclusion, *therefore we conclude, that a man is justified by faith without the deeds of the law.* And James, also, in the text, really teaches the same thing. He indeed asks, *Was not Abraham our father justified by works, when he had offered Isaac his son upon the altar?* But he immediately adds, *And the Scripture was fulfilled which saith, Abraham believed God, and it* — that is, this faith — *was imputed unto him for righteousness;* in other words, for his justification. Just take notice here, that, according to our apostle James, Abraham was justified by an act of faith; an act which was exercised some twenty years before he offered up Isaac upon the altar. James, then, teaches that it was by faith alone, and so not partly by faith and partly by works.

And, in this, reason concurs with the teaching of inspiration. We do not suppose that reason would have thought of the way of justifying sinners through faith in a vicarious sufferer. It was above reason, the device of God; the plan, the offspring of his wisdom; the sacrifice, the gift of his goodness. But reason approves of this mode, and says, If at all, it must be by faith alone. Justification, when it takes place, must be at some time, some instant, and be complete, when at all. But this cannot be, if it is partly by works. In that case, when the sinner believes, he is but half justified, when he has performed a few works, he is little more than half; and not till the close of a long life of good works is he wholly justified. He who should die between believing, and performing works, having no time allowed him for works, would belong neither to the righteous nor the wicked. The dying believer, believing then for the first time, could have no title for a place in heaven. Christ erred when he said to such an one, *To-day shalt thou be with me in Paradise.* Christ did not err. The dying penitent's *faith* was imputed to him for righteousness. The justification was complete the moment he believed, and the next moment he was in glory.

The question then returns, If a man is justified, without the deeds of the law or works of personal righteousness, by faith alone; justified before he has time to perform external works, so that they could have no part nor influence in the matter, — in what sense is a man said to be justified by works? What the meaning of the apostle James in his somewhat startling and seemingly dissentient language? The meaning is evidently this, That a man is justified by a faith which will produce works, and not by faith only; that is, not by a faith which is only faith; a faith which stands alone, because it has no power to connect with itself good works; no power to produce such works; no power, because it is dead. This what this apostle means, and all that he means; just what Paul means, and each of the evangelical writers. They all mean to say, that where there is faith to justify the soul, there will be works to justify the faith, to show that it is a living faith, working by love; so has power, productiveness. In this way faith is made perfect, complete. The good tree bringeth forth good fruit.

The justifying faith leads to acts of holy living; to

deeds of beneficence. As the fruit is part of the tree, intimately and vitally connected with it, so the benevolent and holy acts are a part of the faith: they spring right out of it, and can never fail to be where the faith is found. There is no justification, then, where there are bad works, a bad life ; no justification where there is a failure, after opportunity granted, to perform good works, because the faith is wanting. And, there being justification where there are the works that spring from the living faith, we see how it is, in what sense, a man is justified by works, and not by faith only. James's doctrine stands clearly forth in the following words or formula: A man is justified by a living, loving, working faith, and not by a dead faith. This is also Paul's doctrine, and John's and Peter's, and that of the Lord himself.

Faith and works, — how difficult a matter rightly to balance. And how bold are the Scripture statements on either side. The object, doubtless, is to place each in the strongest relief, that each may be duly considered ; that neither may be neglected by the soul honest and earnest to find the way to heaven. And yet it is a fact, that this very strength, fulness, and completeness of statement has even been the occasion of practical error ; not necessarily, but on account of the obtuseness of some heads, and the blindness of more hearts. The two features or aspects of the one doctrine lie apart in the Bible ; and some cannot and others will not put them together in one structure of symmetry and beauty. The part that is congenial is taken ; a part for the whole. Some take to the side of faith, and will have it dishonored by no works ; justified by faith, without any works of righteousness.

Such say, We believe, that is enough; believing, heaven cannot be missed. These claim to think a great deal of Paul and his teachings. Others prefer to go independently to heaven, if they go at all; not be beholden to another for their character and their title to the place. These profess to get their light from James. In the former case, the indolence of the heart operates, its love of ease, of self-indulgence: in the latter, its pride is at work; and, between the two, — the self-indulgent tendency, and the self-justifying tendency, — it is to be feared a great many souls come short and perish.

2. But, leaving its clearness and boldness of instruction, let me call your attention, in the next place, to the vast weight of motive the gospel brings to bear against these two false tendencies of our nature.

Take, first, the self-justifying tendency. How strong is this, often, and how common. The heart naturally is full of self-righteousness. It is the doctrine of the depravity of the world. It is the doctrine of most of the religions of the world. Far the greater part of the visible Church is resting to-day upon a foundation of works. And there is nothing men will not submit to, to gain heaven as matter of merit. They will give any thing; will sacrifice any thing; will suffer any thing. They will walk to heaven in their own blood, if they can get there in their own way. Such the strength of the self-justifying tendency. And how is it met? It is met and rebuked by the cross of Christ; God giving his Son; God manifest in the flesh. Why was this? It was that sinful men might be justified. It was because they could be justified in no other way. Paul has it put most conclusively, *If righteousness come by the law, then Christ is dead in vain.* It is an enormous absurdity to suppose that the Son of God, co-equal with the Father, would come down from heaven, and, by dying, do for men what every one by a little painstaking could do for himself. This one great and mysterious act, the wonder of heaven, and ever since the theme of its songs, admits of no such petty and contemptible partnership. The voice of this event, like the sound of eternal waters, proclaims through the universe, *Look unto me, and be ye saved, all the ends of the earth.* If Christ's death has any efficacy, it is a justifying efficacy; and, if men have any reason, they will bow before such a fact, the suffering Son of God, shedding cleansing blood for them; admit the truth that he is the only justifier, he the all-sufficient justifier, and consent to be justified, and beg to be justified alone by faith in him; by the efficacy of his obedience, and to the glory of his grace.

Pass now to the self-indulgent tendency; this, too, not infrequent or feeble, because fostered by the indolence of our nature. The plan here is to go to heaven on the strength of the atonement. Christ does all; we are simply to trust: there is no call for effort, or resistance to sin, or spiritual discipline. It must be acknowledged here, that, in a free salvation, it is exceedingly difficult wholly to avoid the licentious tendency. Where the pardon comes so cheaply to ourselves, the sin often will not be decisively dealt with; nor the offence cut short off; nor the duty, at all hazards, be done. The short argument is, If we sin, *we have an advocate with the Father, Jesus Christ the righteous.* If we have faith, we shall reach heaven; we have no concern about any thing else. A short argument indeed, and a very short-sighted one; for we can hardly read a single book of Scripture, not even a book of Paul, the great apostle of faith, without finding ourselves cut off from hope, unless we do works meet for repentance. We are even justified by works; cannot be justified by a faith which produces no works; are as really condemned without right living as we should be, were right living the meritorious ground of our acceptance. Thus at the first symptom of perversion in this quarter, we are met by all the weight of motive which can be made out of God's authority, and heaven's glories, and hell's wailings.

2. Let me, in another remark, ask your attention to this practical point, that the test God appoints is not the hidden feeling, but the outward, visible act. God not only requires us to have, but to show that we have, religion; his love in our hearts. Indeed, this matter, in a sense, takes care of itself. Where the vital principle is, there will be a manifestation. If here within, you cannot hide it. It goes forth, and will go forth. It is light, and you cannot make it dark. You may, indeed, light your candle and put it under a bushel; but if you put it on a candlestick it will give light to all that are in the house. It follows, that, if a man is a Christian, the world will find it out. If he has true faith in his heart, this faith will cause him to do something by which he will be exposed and known as having it. There is no such thing as having Christ's religion to ourselves; no going masked to heaven; no night passage there; no tunnelled underground road to the place. I know there are many who love to talk about religion as something between their own souls and God, — nobody's else business. If it be so, al-

ways and everywhere a hidden thing, we tell you it is a dead thing. If you keep it thus a secret, it is because you are ashamed of it. Its nature is to come out; the teaching of its great Author is, that we confess him before men. Here the test: if you have it, you do show it. If you show it not, you have it not. If there is nothing seen, there is nothing inside.

And it is worthy of notice how simple and palpable this test is for the believing soul itself. Every one can apply it, and settle the matter with a good degree of assurance whether he is a Christian or no. Some may not have the power of going into a thorough analysis of their feelings, their love, faith, penitence, and deciding upon the genuineness of these affections. But they can decide whether they love to do good; whether the inward affection breaks spontaneously forth, in deeds of self-denial, acts of kindness; whether theirs is a life of piety, because they love such a life, its holy fellowships and occupations. One would think it easy to determine whether the heart, in the tide of its affections, flows easily in this direction. If so, can there be any mistake as to what is the character in God's sight? We may hesitate upon the quality of a tree, from the soil it grows in, from its form, the beauty or fragrance of its blossoms, or even from analyzing the sap that circulates through it. But when we see the fruit, handle and taste it, and thus prove it to be unquestionably good fruit, we at once exclaim, It is a good tree.

3. Another remark, suggested by the principle we are considering, is, that the religion of Christ, the religion of faith, holds a vast pre-eminence over all other systems or associations, as a religion of beneficence.

It exceeds every thing else in the mode of its operation. The good deed springs from, and is a part of, the good principle; the life of beneficence flows right out of the heart made right, and it will flow, if the heart continues to beat. In this way, there is certainty to the beneficence. God implants the faith and love; these impel to the labor of doing good, and make the labor a pleasure; and this labor of doing good, re-acting, makes still better the heart that gives the beneficent impulse. There are ways of doing good from the force of example upon us; out of a regard to our reputation, or fearing the imputation of meanness if we do not do; by agreements, associations, and organizations. God's way, the way of faith, is to do it right out of the character, whose light will spread, its pure fountain send out some refreshing stream. God's way is the better way for the greater extent which is reached by it. All other ways are limited, local, being founded on some form of selfishness. They mostly proceed upon the old heathen plan of loving those that love us, and of lending with the hope that we shall receive as much again. The law of faith contemplates no clan nor class nor reciprocity; but says, *Let us do good unto all men.* To the narrow, niggardly question, *And who is my neighbor?* it points, in reply, to a world in ruins, and says, To these distant and spreading millions all, are ye debtors. God's way by faith is better, too, for its tried character, its age and perpetuity. There have been other modes and styles and fashions, — now this way, now that; now this object, now that. Plans and schemes and clubs have risen and flourished and passed away; but this way by faith and love is the same yesterday, to-day, and through all time; perfectly simple and mightily powerful. It is doing good because the heart has faith, and therefore will make us, and we cannot help it, because our blessedness is in it. It has ever been the way of the faithful. Nearly all the good to lost and suffering men has been done thus; and all yet to be done, will be in the same way, through the same law and principle, and urgency of faith living in the heart.

4. I remark, further, that it is not easy to exaggerate the importance of works in religion, their importance as being the test of its genuineness. They are the proof that we have the living power; and proof, also, that it is a power from God. Good works authenticate the inward power, demonstrate its divinity; they crown it with honor; compel for it the respect, the homage even, of wicked men; they clothe it with influence and power over such men. Works, too, the just character and life, give power to the individual Christian; they give him a right to speak, and give an efficacy to his words. His words, backed by his deeds, and made living by his heart's love, become weighty, often, on other hearts that hear them. And then, the works not only give confirmation to the character: they are themselves angels of mercy; blessings wherever they fall; eyes to the blind, feet to the lame, life to the dead. They spread the light, and help bring down the power; and the dead in sin spring to a new and an endless life.

Well for us all would it be, my Christian friends, well for the cause of our Master, well for the world we live in, could we say, By works are we justified, and not by faith only. It is too much by faith only; the cold, dead faith, the demons' faith, which believes and trembles; just enough to disturb the soul, not enough to give it rest; not only no comfort in it, but no good will be done by it. But get the true kind, and you cannot have too much of it. Nor can you make too much of it. Faith is first and essential; faith before, and far greater than works. Faith constitutes the power, — power to conquer the world and conquer sin and conquer death itself. For this power, go to the right source. Such a light and flame can come from no spark of your own kindling. It must come from heaven's altar; it is the gift of God, to be sought by the importunities of a soul that hungers and cries and clings and wrestles, till the blessing comes, till the faith is given. This, given, will administer support and comfort: no comfort in works, but as the sign and fruit of faith. Faith and faith's objects, all in all. Simple faith and trust, — Christ's blood and righteousness, — these the soul's stay in its final exigency. The past life, the best deeds of it, afford no place of rest; all dark and drear till the soul come back to these; flies as a bird to the mountain. Comfort only here, comfort, support all-sufficient, all-sustaining here.

Thou man appointed to die, begin with this faith; let it enter you; make it your possession; receive it as the work and gift of God, and you will find, that, having this in its vital fulness, you have every thing for triumph in life's encounters, — for peace and joy at its close.

## XIV.

### CONFESSION OF SIN.

*But if we walk in the light, as he is in the light, we have fellowship one with another; and the blood of Jesus Christ his Son cleanseth us from all sin. If we say that we have no sin, we deceive ourselves, and the truth is not in us. If we confess our sins, he is faithful and just to forgive us our sins, and to cleanse us from all unrighteousness. If we say that we have not sinned, we make him a liar, and his word is not in us.* — 1 JOHN i. 7–10.

THIS passage of Scripture brings to view the duty of confession of sins, and the blessed consequences of that confession. It seems to be a very simple, practical exhibition of the way of being delivered from our sins. For this reason I have chosen it as the subject of my discourse, at this time: and if there are some before me to-day, who feel any measure of interest in this matter of being delivered from sin, and saved through the gospel, if they will attend to me, I will try to be intelligible and profitable to them.

Let me say, in the first place, that confession implies sin, because sin is the matter confessed, if we confess. According to this scripture, our condition is that of sinners. Do any doubt this, and so make it necessary to go into the proof of it? We say, in a word, God declares the doctrine or the fact, with great explicitness in his holy word. He testifies against his creature man, every man, that he is a sinner.

Men testify in regard to one another that they are sinners. Every man in the world believes, or acts on the belief, that every other man in the world is a sinner. Not only this, every man knows in his own case, in his own breast, that he is a sinner. His own heart tells him so; and God, who is greater than his heart and knows all things, tells him so. Well may we say in the phrase of the Apostle, that if any one says he has not sinned, he deceives himself, he speaks against the voice of his own conscience and consciousness. If any one says he has not sinned, and is not morally depraved, he contradicts the opinion which all the rest of the world have of him. If any one says he has not sinned, he charges Christ with impertinence and folly in coming to save him, and save the world, when there are none needing to be saved. One step more: if any say they have not sinned, they make God a liar. When men have done these two things, namely, made Christ inane and God a liar, it would seem that such, at least, might be set down in the class of transgressors, wrong-doers. The fact is, as God in his word declares, and Christ in his humiliation and painful death affirms, and every person, in the deep place of his own bosom, knows, that man is a sinner; all have gone astray; the whole race lies guilty before God.

Such being the unquestioned state of the case, it is the wisdom of all to acknowledge it. And this brings me to speak of the duty of confession. Much is said of this, great stress is laid upon it, in the Scriptures. It seems to be made one of the conditions of salvation; put, indeed, on the same footing with repentance. *If we confess our sins, he is faithful and just to forgive us our sins. He that covereth his sins shall not prosper; but whoso confesseth and forsaketh them shall have mercy.*

A duty or exercise which is related to such important results, it is well to understand; and, understanding it, that we truly and betimes perform it.

What is the confession here spoken of? Confession of sin. To whom is it made? All sin is to be confessed to God, because all sin is committed against God. *Against thee, thee only, have I sinned*, is the heart's language, when the heart speaks rightly of its sin. But this statement, though it seems to be, is not, inconsistent with another, that some sins are to be confessed to men. We mean here no auricular confession, confession of sins to the priest, for this practice can minister only to immeasurable evil, as it has done in the priest-ridden church which enjoins the practice. We mean that men are to confess to others those sins in which they have wronged them; the confession to be in part a reparation. But these sins, and all others, as I have intimated, are to be confessed to God. How confessed to him? What are the marks of a true and accepted confession? I answer, when genuine, it is not merely a service of the lips, but also of the heart; a service of the lips and the heart. Those err greatly who make confession and prayer a mere matter of silent, unuttered meditation. Such do not half do their duty; it is but a flimsy pretence, a putting off our Maker with a shadow of our duty. Confession implies a distinct, verbal mention and utterance of our sins, proceeding from a clear perception and feeling of the fact and guilt of our sins. This distinct, vocal utterance of our sin is essential to a proper confession. Another thing embraced in the idea of confession is a separate, and often minute statement, of the sins. The statute is, when an individual shall be guilty in one of these things, he shall confess that he has sinned in that thing. This particularity is important as a test whether there be in the heart the true spirit of confession. Is there not, sometimes, discoverable in people, may we not sometimes find in ourselves, a readiness to acknowledge in the general that we are sinners and utterly inexcusable; but the admission and the confession that we have sinned in this and that and the other, cannot be brooked for a moment? The soul most meekly lying under the generic doctrine and charge of sin, most proudly and fiercely repelling all specific allegations of sin, need we say, there can be no sincerity there. The hatefullest of all the forms and exhibitions of depravity is there.

Confession implies, furthermore, self-condemnation, and a full justification of the law and the administration of God. Its language is, *Against thee, thee only, have I sinned, and done this evil in thy sight: that thou mightest be justified when thou speakest, and be clear when thou judgest.* The confessor, seeing his sins to be great, aggravated, unreasonable, and inexcusable, he confesses, in view of his guilty course, that God would be just in cutting him off, and consigning him to the place where the bitter fruits of sin are reaped without end. In the act of confession he lays himself prostrate and submissive at the foot of the throne and yields himself to the righteous disposal of his Maker.

This implies that in true confession there is also an acknowledgment of the soul's helplessness, and consequent dependence. The language is, and it is truly felt, and fervently uttered, 'I have destroyed myself; my help is in thee.' I owe ten thousand thousand talents, and have nothing to pay. I have no works of merit, no untarnished righteousness, to present. If my debt is ever removed, it must be remitted; if I ever possess any available righteousness, it must be the gift of God.

There is one idea more, and this is a crowning attribute, altogether indispensable to acceptable confession; namely, the forsaking of sin. *Whoso confesseth and forsaketh them shall find mercy.* The purpose to abandon sin pervades and impregnates all the words of the confession. The purpose is an honest one, and begins to be accomplished, is more than half accomplished, in the act of confession. He, then, who sincerely confesses his sins, does it with a thorough conviction of the evil of sin and of the extent of his own depravity; with a deep sense of his utter helplessness and dependence, and a decisive readiness, an achieving resolution, to forsake all known transgression. These three things are fundamental qualities, inseparable elements in all genuine acknowledgment of our sins before God.

Such is the duty. The question arises, Why is such prominence assigned to it in the Bible? such importance attached to its performance? I speak of it, now, not as involving repentance, but solely with reference to this idea, this form of duty, implied in the word confession. What are the reasons for the considerations in favor of the confession of our sin? the motives, if you please, which, if you admit them, would lead you to practise it?

Let me state two or three points in this connection, and say, —

1. That when true confession is entered upon, evidence is furnished, that a course of serious dealing is begun with the soul. It is manifest that that person has taken up the matter of his salvation in sober earnest, as though he meant to bring something to pass in the premises. The way of confession is the way of thoroughness, involves the essential idea of thoroughness, inasmuch as it is a separating, analyzing process, taking up the parts, going through the books, item by item. The man goes about it very much as the merchant does when he would know surely just how he stands. A rough lumping and guess will afford no satisfaction to a creditor of his. But when he enters into the details, then it appears that he means to know, and that those concerned shall know, all about it.

2. I say, further, by this accuracy of detail, involved in the idea of confession, this separating and looking at the items and parts of our sinning, we gain the most vivid conception or realization of the amount of our sinning, the enormous bulk and magnitude which grows up from the sum total of our sinning. By entering into the minuteness of our sinning, we sooner come to understand how great sinners we are: just as going over, and causing separately to pass before the mind, the parts which go to make up some enormous material bulk, brings us nearest to an adequate conception of that bulk. How imperfect, for example, our idea of the size of the earth from reading the figures, noting that it is twenty-five thousand miles around it. But when we begin and survey in detail, with the number and dimension of each, the continents, islands, peninsulas, oceans, seas, lakes,

rivers, which go to make up the earth's size, we have then, impressively mapped to our vision, the greatness of the world we inhabit. Just so it is we approximate, in thought, toward the bulk, the vast aggregation, of our sinning.

3. There is another important service this confession of sin does. The particularity which we have seen to be essential to it, affects the heart. It is a law of our nature, that particulars move us, stir the sensibilities; whilst general views are distant, cold, unmeaning. On this principle it is, that confession leads directly to a melted, subdued, penitent frame of mind. By confessing sin, the heart becomes more sensibly affected with the evil, the hatefulness, of sin. It is the remark of a preacher of the olden time, "That while sin sits close in the heart, its baseness is hid; we cannot see it till we cast it forth by confession, as a man cannot see the corruption that is in his stomach till he spits it out." In this way, by a course of thorough, faithful confession, he attains to utter, and is constrained to utter, the patriarch's self-abhorring formula, *Behold, I am vile.*

I remark, in this connection, that we now see, in part, why it is that so much in the Bible is made to depend upon confession. Where the spirit of confession exists, there is great frankness, openness of character, — a trait which the religion of the gospel everywhere insists on, and greatly commends. Where there is true confession, God is honored. In this way do we especially give him the glory of his omniscience. Confession tends to abase the sinner before God, and bring him into a right state, — a humble, penitent, submitting state of mind. He comes into a state to receive the great remedy for sin provided. The confession does not procure the pardon, the cleansing, spoken of. It only puts the vessel into an attitude, a condition, to receive the washing, the cleansing. True, the promise is, *If we confess our sins, he is faithful and just to forgive us our sins, and to cleanse us from all unrighteousness.* But in a preceding verse we are told what it is that does the cleansing: *The blood of Jesus Christ his Son cleanseth us from all sin.* And all the sin that is ever cleansed away, is cleansed by the blood of Jesus. As another apostle teaches, *Without shedding of blood is no remission.* I will not here go into the argument, to show, that, according to the Scriptures, the blood, the atonement, of Christ, and not the confession, is the ground, the procuring cause, of the pardon and the cleansing. The confession is connected as a condition: a fit and reasonable one, but still only a condition. It is the blood of Jesus Christ his Son which cleanses us from sin. And when we come in the spirit of humiliation and confession, this blood of the Son of God does cleanse us from all sin. To the sin-sick, the sin-burdened soul, this is a most precious declaration. To the man lying beneath the revealing light of a near eternity, made serious by the contact, almost, of its mighty scenes, these words, if he can take hold of them, are words of solid comfort. "These words," said one, lying in these circumstances, — a man great both in intellect and heart, as great as this age has seen, — "these words, *The blood of Christ his Son cleanseth us from all sin*, I would not part with for all the world." So he felt and said at that hour: they were all his help and hope. And yet, this their power of comfort to the needy soul in its hardest strait, is alleged sometimes, in scorn, against them. The late distinguished Robert Hall tells us, that, immediately after preaching to his people in Cambridge a sermon on the doctrine of the atonement, salvation alone through the blood of Jesus Christ, a member of the congregation, some polished Greek, probably, came up to him, very much excited, and said, "Mr. Hall, this preaching won't do for us,—it won't do for us. It is fit only for a congregation of old women."—"Do you mean my sermon, sir, or the doctrine?"—"Your doctrine, sir."—"And why is it that the doctrine is fit only for a congregation of old women?"—"Because it is just what will suit the musings of people tottering upon the brink of the grave, and who are eagerly seeking support."—"Thank you, sir, for your concession," said Mr. Hall. And well might he thank him; for conceding that, was really acknowledging the doctrine to be of God. The doctrine that suits the soul, the provision that meets its wants, gives it comfort and support in that illumined place and most honest hour, and does this, not once, but always, when the sincere application is made, is unquestionably from heaven.

And we say here, in all seriousness, let no man be in any haste to reject it. Let him wait till he has got through with these two great chapters of experience, the checkered chapter of living, and the briefer and more sombre chapter of dying; and when he has felt the successive billows of sorrow, and the sharp pangs of conviction, the wearying burden of his sin as it lies heavy upon his soul; has known what it is to come with this burden to the outer edge of life, and bear it when the last sickness has wasted the energies, and where eternity sends back some flashes of its light;

let him wait till then, and, if he finds he has no occasion for this, his Maker's remedy for the ruin of his soul, then let him cast it from him, and go before his God without the garment his God provided for him. Let him wait till then, and I do not say he will be a believer, but, I say this, he will try hard to be one, and would give worlds, had he them, if he were a believer in the doctrine of Christ's blood and righteousness.

I have brought this subject before you, mainly, for its intelligible and most practical character. We here open to you, as it were, one of the outer doors into the kingdom of God. Enter that door, and you at once strike upon another; and, the moment you pass that other, you are safely and joyfully in. To the more interior and fundamental announcement the preacher makes, such as Repent of sin, Trust in the atonement, you reply, We do not understand: we do not know how: we cannot. We say, to-day, Confess your sins to God. Go into the secret place; take the proper attitude; with seriousness, with distinct vocal utterance, confess your sins to God. You say, perhaps, It will do no good. It will be only a lip service, the heart having no part in it, and so nothing will be accomplished. Perhaps so.

Let me tell you another thing: It is certain nothing will be accomplished, no redemption will come to your soul, if you do not confess your sins. But if you begin, where God enjoins you to begin, in the act of confession, you cannot tell but all the rest will follow. If by one step you enter the outer door, by another, if not by the same step, whilst in the act and attitude of confession, you may, by the Spirit's help, enter the inner, and stand, a redeemed worshipper in the temple of God's grace. You must enter the outer first. And this first thing or step is clear, simple, intelligible, practicable. God here says to your soul, This do, confess, — begin there. He seems to make salvation turn upon some visible, tangible thing. He said to the young man, Go, sell. This, first; then, follow me. Go, sell all. That enough? That save him? No. But in doing this, actually selling in obedience to Christ, the grace of God would meet him, his heart would come right, the Saviour be loved, and his treasure be in heaven. Here is the philosophy of being saved. It is God's order and philosophy. We ask you to try it. Where God says, Do, there do. Sell, sell. Make confession, make confession. For this there is the material. Sins enough you have, and a vivid memory of them; a tongue to utter them, a conscience to condemn them, a heart to feel them. Confess them till your heart shall loathe them, and your will shall abandon and cast them out; till the grace and the balm, and blood of Jesus, come with a cleansing and healing and all-blessing efficacy.

# XV.

## AND YE WILL NOT COME TO ME.

*And ye will not come to me, that ye might have life.*— John v. 40.

THIS our Saviour said to the Jews, as descriptive of their case. The fact with them was that they were not willing to come to Christ that they might have life. The fact, or the reason of the fact, applies equally to all who do not come to Christ; the reason is, they are not willing to come to him. To come to Christ, means to be a Christian. The text teaches that men, in their natural state, are not willing to become Christians, and through this course to be saved. My object in this discourse is to show the sinner that he is not willing; that these words of Christ are indeed true.

And my line of argument is simply this; namely, to point out some of the preventives, the difficulties, the hindrances, in the way of coming to Christ, selecting such as all will confess may be removed, and then show that where there is no attempt to remove even these, there is evidently no serious wish to become a Christian, and, as such, to be saved. To enter at once upon the process, —

1. One difficulty, and that a prominent one in the way, is the settled spirit of inattention. People do

not, as a general thing, give their thoughts, their practical attention, to the subject of religion. That this spirit of inattention is a difficulty, a barrier, where it prevails, I need not stop to prove. It is self-evident, that, in order to become religious, men must feel, repent, trust, love. But how can they, unless their minds are directed to those considerations which produce feeling. Right here, we affirm, is a grand difficulty in the way, — not giving heed to religious truths and interests. That this inattention prevails very extensively among all classes of the people, there need be no other proof than that found in the mind's absorption in other things; in this wide and deep engrossment in the seen and the temporal; an engrossment so absolute, that it leaves the mind free for nothing else, certainly not free for the pursuits of religion. The Bible, the Word of God, how rarely read and studied with the eagerness of a soul searching for truth and salvation. Then what neglects of the public worship of God, of the place where these great truths and claims are contemplated and enforced. What multitudes, who never go at all. How many others, who go as a mere form or fashion. How small an excuse will keep them away. Nothing will keep them from the mart of gain or the room of pleasure. They will go on hobbling limbs and with paralytic jerk, go through fire and flood, to reach the place of traffic. But the place of God's truth and worship, the will has no vigor at all in this direction. How often is the body only brought in; and that, perhaps, merely to take its hebdomadal nap. Or, if the soul comes in also, and keeps wakeful, how often is it that it may think of business, calculate the chances of success, count up the probable profits that will come along from this or that enterprise.

Let us now candidly and seriously bring the facts of the case before the mind. Do you believe the things which are spoken in the Word of God, — that you possess a soul; that that soul is defiled by sin, is justly condemned, and needs renewal and redemption; that faith and repentance are imperative duties; that the alternative is eternal ruin? Yes, you reply: we do believe these things. But when urged to this duty, and the other, to repentance and faith, you plead that you are unable; that you cannot repent, and so you cannot secure your salvation, if you would. If you would: very significant words these. Would you? Are you willing to be a Christian? Let me ask another question, which will help to answer this. You say you cannot do thus and so. We will admit it. But there are some things which you must confess you can do; and these God enjoins, as well as the others. Have you done, are you doing, these? You can give your attention, your thoughts, to the subject. You can put yourself in the way of being instructed, of being moved and aroused by expostulating truth and a striving spirit. The question returns, Have you done, are you doing, these? In other words, are you willing to give the subject of your salvation a thoughtful and earnest attention? This lies at the beginning, is the first step. The Psalmist says, *I thought on my ways, and turned my feet unto thy testimonies.* You say you cannot turn. But that is not the first thing in the order of the work. *I thought and turned.* You can think upon these matters. If you do not this, but steadfastly refuse all earnest attention to it, then the pretence that you would like to be a Christian is wholly insincere.

2. My next statement is, that sins, outward acts of disobedience, whilst those acts are persisted in, constitute an insuperable obstacle to the soul's coming to Christ. We do not say, that breaking off from outward sins is coming to Christ. But this we say, it always must and will be, that the person who truly comes to Christ breaks off from all overt acts of disobedience. Every thing which he knows to be wrong he is ready to give up, and does give up. And the casting off of these is ordinarily, and in a sense, an introductory step. There is a person, we will suppose, who is seriously thinking of becoming a Christian, has some desires that way. But he is an habitual sabbath-breaker. We say, not a step can he take, not an effectual inch can he move, toward the kingdom of Christ, till he ceases from that habitual sabbath-breaking. Or he is a profane swearer, and is seeking Christ, or pretends to be, and interchanges his oaths with his prayers. Can any one doubt that his first step is, to be done for ever with his swearing? Or he is persisting in a career of manifest fraud; or he is allowing some feature of decided immorality in the transaction of his business; or he is dealing out poison to his fellow-men, for the gains of the traffic; or he himself is indulging in the intoxicating cup; some practice is upon him, which God's law, and even the light of nature, condemns. And every person moved to thoughtfulness has some such things about him, habits, doings, which he knows to be wrong. We say, in no one of these, and we might indefinitely swell the catalogue of a similar kind, and still say, in no one of all these,

may the awakened, the interested person take the ground that he will persist in the admitted wrong till he has evidence that Christ has accepted him, and then break off. If he takes that ground, he probably will never have evidence that Christ has accepted him; because in that state and attitude he will never come and submit to Christ. But where there is a thorough procedure, from the very inception of the mind's interest, and a prompt acting, just so far as the mind has light, casting off the offensive thing, not as matter of self-righteousness, but from the force of ingenuous conviction, there is progress, and by the grace of God there will be greater progress. This, commonly, is the order, the process, the way, in coming to Christ.

The question before us is this: Are you willing to come to Christ? If you are, you are willing to abandon all known outward transgressions; for the abandoning of these is a part of the work in coming to Christ. The fact is, that a vast many are not willing to abandon these. They will acknowledge the importance of the matter, the necessity of the great preparation. They have a degree of solicitude on the subject. Still, there are certain wrong things they refuse to give up. We affirm, that it is wholly vain for them to plead inability to come to Christ, or to say they do not know how to come; for here is something they can do. It is a matter perfectly plain. They can see it, and they can do it. They can quit these wrong practices. There is not a particle or shred of mystery or impracticability in this whole region. We do not say, that quitting the wrong practices is the same as becoming a Christian; but that they must quit the wrong practices, if they ever do become Christians. This is a part of the work, ordinarily a precedent part. Inasmuch as this is a part they can do, if they are not willing to do this, then they stand convicted of unwillingness to come to Christ. The Saviour's words stand luminously, convictively true before our very eyes, *Ye will not come to me, that ye might have life.*

3. I remark, again, there are certain exterior duties which must be performed on coming to Christ; duties enjoined by the Saviour. I will name this one of Prayer. It is in part an external performance; and, when acceptable, it is accompanied with the desires of the heart. Persistent neglect of this duty is a matter standing in the way of a person's salvation; I mean by this, that, so long as there is persistence in the neglect, there can be no salvation.

The Saviour says, *When thou prayest, enter into thy closet, and when thou hast shut thy door, pray to thy Father which is in secret; and thy Father which seeth in secret, shall reward thee openly.* Here is the duty, having something external about it, something spiritual. The external part may be performed while the heart is wholly away from God. In that case, it is the form only. Still, the external is a part, and must be performed, in order to the complete and acceptable performance of the duty. Let the question our text suggests recur again, Do you desire salvation? Are you willing to come to Christ? Then listen to that voice, Enter into thy closet and shut thy door. Here is a duty. Are you willing to undertake it; to enter upon a course of stated, secret prayer; willing to go alone and prostrate your soul before God, and confess your sins, and implore his mercy, through his Son Jesus Christ, and persist in importunate pleas for this mercy upon that leprous soul of thine; and, if need be, continue long in that attitude, and those earnest beseechings for help? We seem to hear you confess the importance of salvation, and at times you sigh for the evidence of being in the possession of it. If I only could, how gladly would I take it. If I only knew what to do, how gladly would I do it. Well, here is something for you to do: will you do it? *Enter into thy closet.* I do not say that if you comply and do this duty externally, it will be enough; that if you enter into your closet, and remain there and are seemingly fervent there, you will assuredly find mercy, acceptance. I have no authority to say any such thing. But I have authority to say, Enter into thy closet, and when thou hast shut thy door, there pray, there humble thyself, there prostrate thy soul, as in the dust, before God. Are you willing to do this thing which Christ enjoins? You cannot interject the plea of incompetency, and say you do not understand, or have no strength to perform it. You do understand, and you can do it. You can go, for you can walk; and you can kneel, for you have joints. If you are not willing to do this, am I uncharitable in saying that you are not willing to be a Christian?

I might go on and introduce other plain and obvious duties, which are an indispensable and unquestioned part of the process and work of becoming a Christian, and make it appear that while you are unwilling to perform these, which you acknowledge to be obvious and practicable, you are unwilling to do the other part, the main thing, unwilling to come to Christ.

There comes not only the conviction of unwillingness from this process, but, as intimately connected, —

1. The fact of inexcusableness. It is clear that men have no good excuse for not coming to Christ. It is in vain for any one to say, I cannot repent, cannot make myself a Christian, whilst he has not done what he knows and confesses to be a duty, and also knows that he can do. It is in vain for him to say, I cannot pray aright, when he never attempts to pray at all. It is in vain for any one to say, I cannot feel, when he deliberately refuses to look at God's truth seriously, thoughtfully; to dwell upon the amazing facts and verities of his revelation.

2. I remark, further, that guilt comes as another ready inference from our subject and process. And the guilt in these premises is great, because it is the guilt of an almost entire neglect of those great matters. I am supposing, all along, that you admit their verity, and their unmeasured importance, as having to do with the weal or the woe of a coming, eternal state. The greatness of these things, their inconceivable worth and weight, we behold, as we can nowhere else see them, in the coming, the incarnation, the suffering, and the dying of the eternal Son of God. The things neglected are those which he, at such a cost, came to secure. The salvation, then, is a great salvation. This is what is neglected, this great salvation. And the allegation is, that you attempt nothing seriously for your soul's weal; and this, when you are ready to rise to any height or continuance of endeavor in the strife for mere worldly good. You do this, when Christ has done so much in the mighty promptings of his infinite heart, has poured forth the blood of that heart, has sent the Spirit, has given the Bible and the means and ordinances of grace. Yea, he stands and calls, *If*

*any man thirst, let him come unto me and drink:* the weary, come ye; the burdened, come all; *and him that cometh to me, I will in no wise cast out.* And then he is obliged to add, in grief, *And ye will not come to me, that ye might have life.* The life, it is there, and you can get it nowhere else, and yet you will not come to him for it. It is there in its fountain fulness and overflowing freeness; ye may have it by simply coming: *whosoever will, let him come,*—and ye will not come to him for the life. It is the supreme good, all-conceivable good, and good inconceivable, gathered and expressed in that one pregnant word, LIFE, the highest attribute and treasure of God himself, the light of the universe, the jewel of existence, a wealth infinitely transcending all the hidden gems in the world of matter,—and ye will not come to him, that ye might have life. Amazing and confounding in its mystery, that your will not should make the difficulty in such a case. When invited out of a dungeon of sin, from its filth and gloom, to rise and range in eternal day, and shine with seraphic purity, and swell with heavenly ecstasies, and reign as a king enthroned, is it so that ye will not come to Christ for this? Is it not, must it not be, something else? Some outward, despotic imposition it is; or some moral paralysis, which has entered and crept through my being, and touched every muscle and nerve and fibre with death; this, or something like it, which holds me inexorably. I would, but I cannot. My eager heart springs to be there, but these clogging chains will not let me. It is not so. If it were so, you would be comparatively an innocent man. As it is, you are a greatly guilty man; guilty, because Christ has come and spoken to you, done for you such deeds of love, uttered such words of kindness, wears to the eye and heart such winning traits and most benignant aspects, — and ye will not come to him.

I would ask each hearer to look at and consider his depravity, his moral state, from this stand-point; standing before this text, *Ye will not come to me*, to estimate the badness of his heart in this one thing, its stubborn bent through all to keep aloof from Christ. Only ruin and death can be reached by you in such a course: death in its consummation and hopelessness, irremediable and intolerable, carrying ever, as you will, a more than mortal sting in the thought that the ruin was all unnecessary; it was because you would have it so, because you would do nothing in earnest to have it different.

But I would charm you, rather, and draw your thoughts and your hearts to this Divine Helper. If I could, I would put on other attractions, new robes and aspects of glory, till they should prevail with you. Tell me what other stroke of the pencil will finish and array this Jesus to your liking. Really, is there any thing wanting? And as the case now is, as the Bible draws the heavenly portrait, is there any reason for not consenting to come to him? I remember once hearing a preacher say, that he had often put the question to thoughtful persons, those in a state of anxious inquiry, requesting them to ponder it and return a definite answer, What reason have you for not coming to Christ? And the result commonly was, an affecting conviction that they had no reason; and, often, they came at once, and were unspeakably blessed.

And have you, hesitating, halting hearer, have you

any reason for not at once coming to Christ? Do you discover in him an object of stern and frightful repulsion, behold a darkening brow, and eyes of flaming vengeance? See you a rod in that hand, to smite down the trembling and approaching suppliant? and as one and another draws near to his footstool, see you them meeting a cold, rejecting thrust, and turning back all disheartened? I, too, see Jesus, but I see nothing like this. I see a person resplendent with uncreated glories, an aspect most sweetly shining with heavenly compassion, a heart that heaves with the deep swellings of an infinite love, eyes that have wept over an obdurate world, saying, *If thou hadst known, even thou, at least in this thy day, the things which belong unto thy peace!* I see a golden sceptre in those divine hands; yea, a better assurance still, I see the scars of those wounds he received when he was smitten for our transgressions. I see one and another approaching him, some the very chief of sinners, some who had long despised that precious Name, all with a burden they do wearily bear; and, as they come, he smiles and takes them as his. Yes, thou blessed Jesus, even all that come, not one turned away unblessed; not one cast unnoticed out. That vast and shouting throng above say, Not one; and the wailing voices beneath respond, Not one. The archives of the universe have no such record to disclose. No, not one.

And what reason have you for not coming to Christ, that you might have life?

## XVI.

### ESCAPE FOR THY LIFE.

*And it came to pass, when they had brought them forth abroad, that he said, Escape for thy life; look not behind thee, neither stay thou in all the plain; escape to the mountain, lest thou be consumed.* — GEN. xix. 17.

WE have in this and the connected passage of Scripture the account of Lot's deliverance from an impending destruction, a destruction which came upon all in the doomed city but himself and those connected with him. These historical facts, embodying the account of this destruction and deliverance, run most instructively parallel with another class of facts,— those pertaining to the soul's deliverance from its exposure, its doom of sin. We are justified in this use of these facts, are led to it, not only by the striking resemblance between the cases, but also by our blessed Saviour's recurrence to them in a like use, where he warns us from the fatality which befell one who began to escape, but did not persist in following out the vehement direction.

Among the truths pertaining to the Christian scheme of redemption and its applications, forcibly suggested by this historic parallel, are the following: First, that we are parts of a place, portions of a race, condemned, doomed to be destroyed; and that, abiding with the condemned, as they are, we shall be destroyed with them.

Second, The fact, all but universally obtaining, that people are satisfied with this condition of condemned and exposed; contented to be with such, and to be such. Even after they are warned, and made to see the danger, they are held by a sort of enchantment to the doomed company and spot. So was it with Lot; when told that the destruction was just ready to fall, and urged to rise and flee, he lingered, so strangely hesitated and lingered, that he would have been whelmed with the rest, but for the gracious violence which those mysterious friends, those angels of mercy, used with him, laying hold of his hand and the hands of his family, and bringing them forth. Left to ourselves, not one of us would be delivered. By grace are we saved, by a divine interposition, a good power of God, by a gentle force which comes from without; not of ourselves, in no case of ourselves, ever is it the gift of God.

Then again, and especially, the refuge provided, this is the work and gift of God. That there is a refuge to souls exposed, is clearly brought out in this historic account. To Lot and his company the mount was designated, there they would be safe. For the world now, over which the desolating storm impends, there is a refuge. It is the mount where the incarnate, yet immaculate, One bled and died, — he the Refuge, he the Covert from the storm and the tempest. Fleeing thither, ye prisoners of hope, hiding in him, confiding in him as your Rock, your Fortress, you are safe. When the destruction comes, it shall not touch you. You shall behold the destruction of the wicked, but have no experience of it, except in vision. *There is therefore now no condemnation to them which are in Christ Jesus.* The curse of the law cannot reach them; for its blight and its burden, so far as they are concerned, came upon Him who stood in their place. He the believer's surety, the sure defence of all who flee and lay hold of him by faith. Who is he that condemneth? Christ that died for them, will he condemn them? He who has taken them into the shelter of his grace, will he hurl them back to be the food of the fire and the storm? His word is, a word written in blood, that he never will. *The name of the Lord is a strong tower: the righteous runneth into it, and is safe.* Who, then, can declare the greatness of the gospel provision, the goodness, the mercy, therein, such a refuge, so absolutely sure, and from such a destruction? We can only say, It is of God. He so loved the world. Greater love cannot be adduced. It is God's, whose thoughts, nor ways, nor works, are like ours.

But it is not enough that there is a refuge provided, and even proffered. The fact or mere existence of a refuge will protect no one. The fact, the mere provision of the gospel remedy, will save no one. We are, then, taught this further by the historic case before us, that not only must there be provision on the Divine part, there must also be effort on the human part. God provided the mountain and pointed the way; Lot's salvation could be secured only by his fleeing thither. God, in the gospel, lifts up to the eye of our faith Calvary and the cross. There we behold him, the great Sufferer for our sin; but all is nought to us unless we repair to him. There is laid upon all the responsibility of repairing to him. This responsibility, the actual doing of this, is necessary, if we would appropriate and make available for our deliverance his work of suffering that we might be delivered.

The indispensableness of this effort on our part I here take for granted. There is no time to adduce arguments for it: and it is strange that it should ever be necessary, a disgrace to any man who knows the toil and sacrifice of Jesus for him and the race, a disgrace to maintain, or even desire, a freedom from toil and solicitude on his own part, a shame to desire to escape ruin, and reach heaven without striving for it. He cannot thus reach heaven, whatever he may desire or think. It comes upon his soul, what the angel said to Lot, *Escape for thy life; look not behind thee, neither stay thou in all the plain; escape to the mountain, lest thou be consumed.* Assuming here the necessity of effort, let us turn our thoughts a moment to the kind, the tone, of effort which will bring us to the secure place, and finally to the blessed home.

There is one generic feature, implied in the words of the angel, one strong, bold character, impressed upon this toil which we are called upon to put forth in the saving of our souls, namely, this Earnestness, Decision, a measure of Endeavor which shall bring to the task all the might which is inherent in the soul or the sinews. If we analyze this generic wholeness, this full heartiness, this utmost mightiness of the effort enjoined, we shall find that it resolves itself into certain specific and very definite qualities.

One is immediateness, an effort to be made now. Those words, *Escape to the mountain*, are singularly imperative and instant. Do it now, off now. And the reason of the urgency is found in the close impending of the danger. Already the sound of the rushing wind is heard ; the heavens gather blackness ; the lightnings streak the clouds ; the sulphurous flames descend ; the city is just ready for a burial beneath the liquid destruction. With such a voice, and such signs crowding, could those in the peril admit any thought of lingering? Their endeavor for life, it must be at once; and those who found life, their effort was at once. On the same point gathers now the full weight and solemnity of all gospel warning and precept. It is to bring to pass, if possible, the rousing, the striving, the believing, now, — this now, which is the accepted time, and the day of salvation ; the next to come made lurid, perhaps, by the descent of threatened doom.

Not only immediate, also this : unfaltering, decisively and ever forward ; not a thought or a look or a desire backward to the region that has been left, to the portion that awaits destruction. *Look not behind thee.* What wisdom in those words, *not behind thee*, for there is enough before thee to fill thine eye and fire thy heart. The mountain is before thee ; security, peace, and all conceivable good are before thee. Look that way, and desire will strengthen ; and the purpose, the soul's resolve to be there, will take to itself solidity and firmness. Look not behind thee, for in that case your soul will begin to divide, little traitors begin to breed in its depths. Look not behind thee, for the good things there will flash their enticements upon you ; old habits, old companions, will wake the counter flame. The very thought, not to say act, of a look backward, is always ominous of failure. Such an one will fail for very feebleness, inasmuch as a thought or a look behind casts half the man behind, and the remaining half must be impotent for the contest which alone can reach the mountain. So all experience has shown; so the Lord pronounces, pronouncing him deficient, who, before obeying the call to be his disciple, asked that he might take one more look upon the scenes and friends at home. And the Lord put his seal of exprobration upon the whole retreating class, in those absolute words, *No man, having put his hand to the plough, and looking back, is fit for the kingdom of God.*

Another quality of the effort is, that it be continuous, persistent. If no faltering, then certainly there will be no stopping, no stay in all the plain. If there be the look back, there will be a pause in the progress, a hesitating whether it is best to proceed. On no possible account may there be this for a single moment. Though your eyes look right onward, and yet you cease to press ever straight on, on to the mark, on to the mountain, it will not avail you, will not save you. No imaginary soundness or integrity of internal condition will alone save any of us. Then, there was the outward condition to be complied with, the designated spot to be reached. And in the gospel there is no dropping down. If so, we on the plain, as well as the dwellers in the city, fall beneath the fiery ruin: *Remember Lot's wife.* To have made a beginning, done some things, parted with some sins; to have travelled far toward the mountain, bearing the marks of pilgrims, and in their good company; to have come clean up to the line; a pause there, brings down as heavy a perdition as a pause anywhere. We are nought till we are at the end. We must reach and embrace him by faith, be made one with him whose blood flowed on Calvary, then are we safe. No power in the universe then can harm us. This part of the counsel uttered by the angel let us receive and resolvedly heed it, stoutly pressing on, loitering for nothing, to pick up no gem, to pluck no flower, to breathe no fragrance by the way, ever showing, what it urges, earnestness, progress, indomitable persistence, an agony, if need be, to reach still ahead, to plant the feet on the protecting mount. And there is enough to justify all this instance and extreme of effort, to get beyond the pursuing fire, to the place of refuge and of rest.

It may be well here to turn back and refresh our memory with two or three thoughts sent to us from the mind of God. The great thoughts of his mind, and the great facts of his doing, if we will admit them upon our souls, will doubtless quicken us on the path to safety. I turn to these two things; let these stand before us; let them live in our faith, and come upon our souls as realities, — the Wrath, the Refuge.

God's justice pronounces its sentence of death eternal upon every man who is a sinner; and every man is a sinner. *The wrath of God is revealed from heaven against all unrighteousness and ungodliness of men.* The day of the Lord is coming with wrath, and his wrath shall burn like fire; a burning will it be which the Lord Jehovah shall kindle, a fire proceeding from the Lord out of heaven, and the earth shall feel it, and all the wicked be whelmed beneath it. Unto this the earth, with its dependencies, is reserved, *kept in store, reserved unto fire, against the day of judgment and perdition of ungodly men.* This is sure, that there is a literal and an awful meaning for us in those Old Testament retributions. The New Testament, for our warning, points its admonitory finger back to those scenes and days.

We look there, and behold the descending and engulfing flames of destruction. We open and read here of those wicked cities and the dwellers in them, as *set forth* to us *for an example, suffering the vengeance of eternal fire.* We may put between, or put on to quench it, our modern refinements and sentimentalism; but God will lay upon us the strength and terror of his consuming justice, and for our daring impiety in this matter, and in order to our final conviction of this his awful truth, will give us to know the *vengeance of eternal fire.* And do our souls shudder and shrink away from before that most appalling agent of doom? If the very thought unmans us, who can bear the reality? *Who among us shall dwell with the devouring fire? Who among us shall dwell with everlasting burnings?* I can conceive of no imagery more fearful than this, as the symbol of doom. I can think of no other phrase which suggests such measures and intensities of penal sorrow, so soul-startling, if by any possibility it may come down upon us. Oh, our God, thou art merciful, and yet thou hast writ it, *The vengeance of eternal fire.* If, now, there is such a storm pressing, and sure to overtake us, then have we an interest in that other fact presented, the mount of refuge, where we may go and be safe. If the storm is of such a character, hanging over, liable to come down ere we think, then there is reason in the cry, *Escape for thy life.* And if we felt it to be so, there would be quickness in our step and our press for the mountain. We could not lie down and sleep, for fear the storm would bury us in our sleep. We could not do any thing else till we had obeyed the momentous summons. Nor could we move our feet in any other direction till these feet stood upon the mountain. The first toil, and the mightiest, would be for the kingdom and the mountain. We must believe the penal fire as though we saw it, feel the touch of it on our sinews, and have a little taste of it in our souls; then let our souls' welfare fill full our souls' capacity of interest, press to the utmost our souls' extreme of endeavor, and make another stretch forward and escape for our life.

Not only the appalling awfulness, this as a motive to spur the activity to its extremity, not only this, but that other fact, the provision for escape. Escape you may, if you will. The path and the mountain are before you. Shall not this blessed truth also rouse us? We remember when our thoughts gathered darkly around the company on board that mysteriously delaying steamer. Perhaps friends were there of whom we thought as under the doom of a premature and oblivious death. And when the perils environed, and the death yawned to swallow them, can we doubt that all mortal strength or prowess could do, they together did, to ward off their awful fate? And when, at length, Providence revealed a refuge, lifted in the distance the land their feet might safely tread, and opened the way, and a voice, overtopping the storm, benignly shouted, Behold the way, *Escape for thy life*, can we doubt the desperateness of their endeavor at pump or oar? And when land was touched, can we doubt the devouring greediness of their feet, as they sped their way to the spot where life was assured to be theirs? It was not the peril alone, it was equally the deliverance looming up, which made them contest the odds with destiny itself. And if that for the life of the body, what shall it be for the life of the soul? And Christ, the soul's life, stands revealed, the way to him all high and open, and all terrors and all encouragements join to drive and to draw to him. Thoughtful one, will you linger? Anxious one, filled at times with fears; restless one, finding no peace, will you delay? Admonished one, who hast seen death's work at your side, that companion and friend stricken and laid away, this for your soul's quickening and saving, will you still hesitate and defer? It comes from heaven and earth and hell, *Escape for thy life.* The angelic and the glorified above, the voices of all the pure of earth, severity and goodness, the molten and treasured fires, and all benignant attractions and mercies, say, *Escape for thy life; look not behind thee; neither stay thou in all the plain; escape to the mountain, lest thou be consumed.*

# XVII.

## THE METHODS OF THE ADVERSARY.

*In whom the god of this world hath blinded the minds of them which believe not, lest the light of the glorious gospel of Christ, who is the image of God, should shine unto them.* — 2 Cor. iv. 4.

THERE are good influences in this world, at the head of which is God. There are also bad influences, at the head of which is the Devil. In preaching, we often speak of the good influences, and admonish men not to defeat them. It is equally proper that we speak of the bad influences emanating from the wicked agent referred to; apprise men of their reality and power, and urge them to a decisive resistance.

The wicked agent, who stands at the head of the bad influences, is called in the text *the god of this world*. We hesitate, at first, in applying a phrase of so broad and exalted meaning to any other than the Supreme Ruler, the rightful Lord of this and all worlds. But we find the Saviour alluding to the same agent, saying, *The prince of this world cometh, and hath nothing in me*. He is called *god of this world*, and *prince of this world*, on account of the sway which he exercises over the greater part of it, and on account of the service, the obedience, and homage, which are generally paid to him, rather than to Jehovah. Sometimes the agent in question is called *The Adversary*, as arrayed against all divine and human interests. The name *Satan*, which he more commonly bears in the Bible, signifies an adversary, an enemy, an accuser. In one passage (Rev. xx. 2) there are four terms by which he is designated: *He laid hold on the dragon, that old serpent, which is the devil, and Satan, and bound him a thousand years.*

I go into no argument to prove the existence of such a being as is described in the language just quoted, or the fact of his agency in our world. I take the doctrine as it stands revealed on the sacred page. It is revealed through the whole inspired volume; as variously and luminously as the doctrine of the divine existence and agency. The principles and style of interpretation which would blot out the doctrine of the existence of the Devil, would blot out, also, that of the divine existence. When I open and read the holy volume, I cannot be an atheist. I am compelled to believe in the existence of God, the universal Creator and moral Governor. At the same time, and with equal force, am I compelled to assent to the existence and agency, in our world, of Satan.

From the same book, the Bible, which teaches us the existence of this great fallen spirit, we learn also the character and style of his agency. Of these I propose to speak in the present discourse, namely, the character and methods of the Adversary's operation. While I shall not confine myself to the one main point, or power, brought to view in the text, that of blinding men, I intend to keep within the manifest teachings of the Bible respecting the agency in question. I mean to allege nothing against the wicked one to the support of which I cannot adduce the unqualified divine warrant.

I shall lead you to consider the agency of the Devil under the three following heads: —

I. — HIS INTENT TO DO EVIL.
II. — HIS POWER TO DO EVIL.
III. — HIS METHODS OF DOING EVIL.

I. The first point, his intent to do evil, we may soon dismiss. His nature is represented as essential malignancy. He is the implacable enemy of God and man. His warfare upon the human race is intense and universal; because they are the objects of redeeming regard; because God is meaning to raise up a great multitude from this fallen race to heaven, there to occupy, it may be, the very mansions out of which Satan and his hosts were thrust. We can easily conceive the bitterness of his hate against the whole scheme of redemption; especially against its Author, and all those who are in the process of being redeemed. His one rabid purpose, according to the Bible, is to defeat, as far as he can, the scheme of redemption, and secure as many as he can from earth for his own dominion of sin and death. Hence he is called *murderer from the beginning*, *destroyer*, *angel of the bottomless pit*. Hence his one great business of going about seeking whom he may devour.

II. Our second point is, The power of Satan to do mischief and destroy. His power, unquestionably, is very great, both from his own personal capabilities, and from the immense number of evil spirits subordinate to him as their leader. We are taught to conceive of Satan as the head of a spiritual empire of great extent, comprehending within itself innumerable subordinate agents. These, who were originally holy intelligences, swerved from their allegiance to the *blessed and only Potentate*, on which account they lost their first estate. Satan, as pre-eminent in rank and dignity, took the lead in the revolt; and, on account of this pre-eminence, continues to rule the rest, who are styled his angels. What their number may be, it is vain to conjecture; but when we reflect on the magnitude of the universe, and the extensive and complicated agency in which they are affirmed to be engaged, we shall probably be inclined to conjecture that their number far exceeds that of the human race.

In this view we easily account for the extent of his agency in tempting and destroying the human race. In the Bible there seems to be ascribed to him a sort of ubiquity, as though he were present in different parts of the world at the same time. We are not to understand that he himself is thus present. None but the divine Being has this power. The representation is based upon the fact that he has such immense numbers under him, executing his great schemes of wickedness, and that all their subordinate works are ascribed to the will and efficiency of the one controlling agent, the Devil. The power of Satan, as at the head of so vast an empire of wicked spirits, all ready to execute his crafty plans and malignant dictations, must be fearfully great. His own pre-eminence, his towering capabilities, which render him adequate to such a control, must be astonishing and complete.

How comprehensive and mighty the intellect of Satan. There is ground to suppose that, of created minds previous to the revolt in heaven, his was the most commanding, the greatest. This spirit, the highest of all the hosts of heaven, stood next to the uncreated mind; and from this very pre-eminence sprang the daring purpose of revolt, and the rearing of another standard in heaven. To this original and astonishing greatness of endowment, there is to be added the growth of many thousand years. This growth, considering how that mind has been tasked in its mighty schemes and conflicts, we must suppose has been prodigious. I might refer to the works of Satan as proof of the wonderful strength and scope of his intellect; but enough has been said to satisfy every believer in revelation, that the power of that being, who is warring on the theatre of this world with the Son of God,—his power to do evil, from his own intellectual endowments and attainments, and from the empire of wicked spirits which he governs,—is vastly, fearfully great.

III. We are now prepared to enter upon our third point, namely, his modes of doing evil, of bringing destruction upon men. "The methods of the Devil." This is a literal translation of one Scripture phrase, *τας μεθοδείας τοῦ Διαβόλου.* Here we open into a great field. We cannot go into minute description and detail. The time will allow us merely to indicate some of the general schemes and manœuvres resorted to by the Adversary for the corrupting and destroying of men. The great object of the Adversary manifestly is to prevent the effect of the gospel upon the minds of men. Truth is Christ's grand instrument in all his works of reformation and redemption. The Devil keeps it off and keeps it out as far as he can. The text so informs us. *If our gospel be hid, it is hid to them that are lost* (that is, lost in sin), *in whom the god of this world hath blinded the minds of them which believe not.* And why blinded? *Lest the light of the glorious gospel of Christ, who is the image of God, should shine unto them.* What the precise nature of this blinding is, and what the way in which it is effected, we are not informed by the inspired writer; nor is there time to go into any inquiries at this point. The fact (and with this we are chiefly concerned) that the Adversary does blind the minds of men is unequivocally asserted; and the effect is asserted with equal clearness. A man, or body of men, so blinded, do not see or apprehend the evidence, the reality, the force of truth. The first step being to get and keep the minds of men dispossessed of truth, a kindred and auxiliary measure is to keep those minds possessed of error. Error is the grand instrument of all the Devil's achievements, as truth is of Christ's; and his character and name are in perfect keeping with this instrument. For, says Christ, *he is a liar and the father of it.* In the Revelation it is said, *he deceiveth the whole world.* We have seen that he is god of this world, that he blinds men. His blinding, then, is on a large scale, by getting in false religions and systems of error. It is in this way, rather than by direct instigation, that he is represented as working in the children of disobedience. Here we see the strength and craft of that mighty intellect. By these comprehensive manœuvres, by extending and establishing false religions, by getting accepted great swaying superstitions in some sections; in others, the polluting and destroying doctrines and rites of paganism,—he is enabled, safely to his interest, to withdraw his solicitude from a very large majority of the human family. In those parts he knows that, without any special efforts or care, all will be allegiant to him while those great schemes of falsehood remain.

The next manœuvre or method is, where there must be Christianity in some form, to get in, if possible, a corrupt form. He introduces some great religious error, and it goes for Christianity, though there be not a particle of the spirit and power of religion in it. These various corrupt and fundamentally erroneous forms, suited to different orders of mind, tastes, and degrees of cultivation, are embraced; and just so far as the Adversary, by blinding, can establish men in these errors, all is deemed safe: he has no concern about those individuals so long as the errors are adhered to. Here let me add, it has been well remarked that religious error is at issue with religious truth at this point; namely, of the punishment of wicked, unregenerate men in the future world. God has declared, and placed it on record, *The soul that sinneth, it shall die.* The great Adversary early began to say, and has been busily saying all along down the line of time, *Ye shall not surely die.* Here we have the great, standing, stereotyped lie of the father of lies. Upon this one text, which he took in the garden of Eden, he has been discoursing ever since, and with it filling up his fiery dominions with spirits from earth. "Be prayerless men; be dishonest men; be profane men; Sabbath-breakers, thieves, liars, adulterers,—continue such, go out of the world such, ye shall not die; surely ye shall not be very gravely punished; it shall be well with you in the end." How comforting, but oh, how destroying.

For the sake of clearness of view and impression, let us come down to an individual case. The Devil, as a skilful, practised seducer, aims, in the first place, at the destruction of principle, right religious principle; if possible, to get truth out of the mind, and error in its place. If, by his deceptive, blinding power, he can only induce a person to deny the existence of God, or the inspiration and truth of the Bible, or the doctrine of atonement or regeneration, or of the future endless punishment of the wicked, and keep to that denial, he is satisfied. He knows that the irreligion, the impenitence, and the eternal ruin of that person comes along as a matter of course. But in regions where gospel truth is proclaimed, it cannot be kept out of the minds of many by all the diligence and blinding power of the Devil and his angels. Blessed be God, the great Promulgator and Patron of this truth is stronger than the patron of error. This gospel truth, where faithfully proclaimed, does enter the minds of some. Sharper than any two-edged sword, and backed by an almighty power, it cuts its way through the steel and the adamant. To change the figure, the incorruptible seed enters, is lodged in the soul, and begins slightly to work. The sinner begins to feel, to be alarmed, to be moved. At this juncture, the effort of the Devil is to catch it away. We have this, most explicitly, on the authority of Christ. Said he, not in figure, but in the literal explaining of figure, *Those by the wayside are they that hear; then cometh the Devil, and taketh away the word out of their hearts, lest they should believe and be saved.* In addition to the authority of Christ, we have the evidence of our observation. We see this thing done; we see men seriously impressed; they are under the incipient workings of truth, — when we are grieved and astonished to learn that it is all gone. They see something, or hear something, or think something, and their impressions go away with the suddenness almost of lightning. It is the Devil snatching away the word; and, beyond question, he is wonderfully busy in this way in seasons of religious revival. But he cannot always succeed in getting away the word. In the breasts of many it is inserted too deep; it adheres. Where this is the case, his next effort is to induce delusion. While the truth works, he manœuvres to conduct the process so that it shall terminate in a false hope. Here he comes forth in a new garb, even as an angel of light. By this we are to understand that he puts on the appearance of goodness; he is even religious; and helps others, if not in becoming so, at least in appearing so. He operates on the imagination; presents forms and visions which excite and exhilarate; injects passages of Scripture, such as *Thy sins be forgiven thee*, with the interpretation that they came right down from God, and are God's words to the burdened soul. The burdened soul believes it, and leaps forth with an assurance of forgiveness. The hope in these cases is built, not upon the fact of gracious exercises in view of divine truth, but upon the fact that some remarkable vision or dream, or some passage of Scripture, came suddenly and unsought to the mind. The Adversary, doubtless, has many methods of bringing about a false hope; and a great point is gained when he has done it; indeed, two or three points. He has succeeded in keeping another soul from Christ, when convinced of his need of Christ, and even feeling his way after him. By the delusion, the spurious experience, he has made the final destruction of that soul altogether more probable. Finally, he is enabled to show that his schemes of error will bring about conversions, and religious experience, about as well as what is called the truth. Thus he brings forward his own works, almost his own miracles sometimes, in order to give currency and permanence to his errors.

I should like to pause, and speak in this connection of the wonderful versatility of the Devil. We do not comprehend — certainly, we do not properly consider — the great variety of things he can do, or help men to do; and we ought to understand that he is just as ready to do religious things as wicked things, if he can as effectually accomplish his malignant purposes thereby. His borrowed form is manifestly his favorite one, and the most to be feared. I do believe he inflicts far deeper injuries upon the souls of men as an angel of light, than as an angel of darkness; destroys more effectually and more to his mind, as the fair-mouthed and still seducer, than as the open-mouthed and roaring lion.

But Satan cannot defeat all truth by catching it away, or by bringing it to a delusive result. The divine Power makes it end in the thorough conversion of many souls. They come forth into the light; they stand firm upon the rock. This brings us to another stage and field of the great Adversary's operations. His strongest and most definite efforts are made upon those who stand forth as professed Christians; even upon those whom he knows Christ stands pledged to protect. In this view, we behold the astonishing audacity of the Devil. We may be astonished at it, when we remember how he assailed in three artful modes, and tried to throw down, the Son of God himself. What disciple may hope to escape, when the Lord himself was the object of his wiles? It is very evident from the Bible, that the specific, individual, and very concentrated assaults of the Adversary are made upon those who are known to the world as Christians. Against these are employed his most ingenious devices; for these he spreads his most artful snares; at these are cast his *fiery darts;* by which we may understand the injecting of wicked, blasphemous thoughts, the inflaming of the imagination, the enkindling of the unholy passions, and making them burn as if set on fire of hell. He peeled and desolated Job, in order to compel him to curse his Maker. He incited David to number Israel, a crime which brought down the desolating sword of God. He desired to have Peter, that he might sift him as wheat; and but for the prayer of Christ, he would have had and sifted him. He entered into Judas, one of the chosen twelve, and, through the passion of avarice, persuaded him to sell Christ to his enemies. He put it into the heart of Ananias and Sapphira, disciples who probably had thus far run well, to lie to the Holy Ghost. These are specimens of the direct and fiery assaults of Satan upon the professed friends of Christ. His object is to overthrow Christians; to make them sin and fall, in order, first, that he may disgrace them individually, and, if possible, pluck them out of the hands of Christ, and destroy their souls. What a triumph, if he can only get one of Christ's little ones under his foul, cloven feet! His second and greater object is, that he may disgrace the cause of Christ; that he may bring discredit upon the truth of Christ. His name means calumniator. He is called in the Revelation, *the accuser of our brethren.* The sinning of his own subjects is done very much out of sight. The deeds of wicked men are deeds of darkness. He is willing that they should remain deeds of darkness. Not so when the Christian sins. The Adversary, unquestionably, often instigates the crime; and then he manages to have it brought out, and held up in mid-heaven for all men to look at. It is the sin of a Christian. "Don't you see," he says, "that this spiritual, praying religion makes people no better? They are all hypocrites, or nearly all. The soundest morality, the real practical goodness, after all, is with those who make no pretensions to this sort of experience." One or two such arguments in the hands of this arch deceiver are enough to satisfy multitudes, in every community, that spiritual religion is all a pretence; that men are just as good, and just as safe, without being born again, as with it. They lie down and sleep on the easy pillow of this delusion. It is so easy, and so many new opiates are administered, that they sleep quietly, brutishly almost, up to the hour of their sleeping in death, and their waking in eternity as deluded, unregenerate men, there to lie down under the dreadful wrath of God.

Such are some of the methods of the Devil. The object in all seems to be, to stand between the gospel and a world of lost souls; and, by blinding their minds and obscuring the truth, prevent, as far as possible, all salutary results. The subject we have been discussing suggests various topics of remark, on some of which we will dwell for a few moments. Though a dark subject, it sheds light on some points which otherwise seem nearly inexplicable.

1. In the first place, it furnishes an explanation of the fact, that men, capable of reasoning, often reason so strangely, and come to such unaccountable conclusions in matters of Christian faith and practice. The fact of such reasoning is frequent and notorious. We observe that clear-headed men, whose minds on all other subjects move straight and sure as a demonstration in geometry, when they come upon some great truth of God, involving unbounded interests, even their own interminable destiny, exhibit altogether another order and style of intellectual movement. They are not able to see the strongest points that ever stood forth in effulgent light for the mind's apprehension. They cannot walk without staggering and stumbling in the high, broad, illumined path which the Holy Ghost has marked out for our certain arrival at truth. How does it come to pass? Clear-headed, straight-minded everywhere else but within the precincts of religion, how is it that they move so here? I confess I am utterly confounded on this point, till I read in the Bible that *the god of this world hath blinded the minds of them which believe not.* This is the explanation which God gives of this matter; and, as we can get no other in any quarter, may we not be permitted to rest in this? This does account for the anomaly. It is owing to a blindness preternaturally induced upon the mind, keeping out *the light of the glorious gospel of Christ.*

Take, for instance, the doctrine of a retribution to

come, already referred to. God declares that there is a hell, and that it is the place where fallen angels and incorrigible men are to be for ever punished. In the clear and strong assertion of this truth, God has put human language to its utmost limit and energy of expression. If there has been any failure to express it, it is a failure in the power of language, not in the purpose of the speaker. Language, as employed in the Bible, we repeat, has again and again done its utmost on this subject. In addition, wicked beings, the Devil and his angels, have been permitted to come up thence in demonstration of the fact, that there is a place of torment, and that God is punishing, and will for ever punish, there his rebellious subjects. Yet, after all, multitudes will have it that there is no such place, no such thing. In accounting now for this very prevalent unbelief, on a point where testimony is so perfect, and evidence is so made to flame and to blaze, we are forced to admit the fact of a positive and thick blindness upon the minds of these men. It is not only a blindness: there seems in connection a contracting and depressing of the mind. There are men, we find, who can take large views on other subjects, can discourse admirably on human law and government: "There must be authority here, penalty here ; both inflexibly maintained ; no government, no order, no security without it." Very well: but these same persons of great and comprehensive minds, civilians, magistrates, who have just been reasoning so admirably on human law and government, the moment they touch on matters connected with divine government, change the entire style of argument: "Authority is nothing; penalty, no need of it." A wavering, womanish weakness is made to pervade the whole divine administration: it is represented as an administration conducted throughout on the most imbecile principles; principles so imbecile, that it would be impossible in the strength of them to govern successfully and progressively a community of half a dozen children. And yet these comprehensive minds seem to suppose that the great Monarch of the universe can, on these same principles, govern the literal immensity of his dominions. What does it mean? What means this childish, this inane logic, in connection with such minds? Only one thing solves the mystery: the blinding, narrowing, depressing influence of the god of this world. And thus he maintains his bad pre-eminence of god and destroyer of this world.

2. My second remark is to suggest a reason why the Devil disseminates so widely disbelief in his own existence and agency. It is remarkable to what an extent, even amongst those who receive the Bible, there is this disbelief. God's revelation is as clear on this subject as on any other. The doctrine of Satanic existence and agency is asserted in every variety of name and form. It is a tissue running most intimately clean through the Bible. According to the divine teaching, it is a terrible power and agency; and yet multitudes, who profess to believe the Bible, believe nothing about it. Others, who pretend to do so, do not more than half believe it. With the majority, the whole tremendous subject, on which God in his Word is so serious, is matter of jest and sport; something to be witty upon and laugh about. How can we account for these things? In this way: it is one of the devices of the Adversary; what he himself brings about; what he knows to be necessary to his most successful opera-

tions. He operates, we have seen, very much by stratagem. We read of the *wiles of the Devil*, of *the depths*—that is, the hidden plans—*of Satan*. We read repeatedly of *the snares of the Devil*. As a great fowler, spreading his net for the entrapping of souls, he knows, and so may we, that his success depends upon his keeping out of sight. The Bible says truly, *Surely in vain the net is spread in the sight of any bird*. The fowler conceals his person, and, on the same principle, the Devil conceals his. While men are not aware of his presence, while they are stoutly denying his existence, he is seizing upon them. While they are jeering at his name, and making themselves merry at his doings, he grapples them; and, ere they are aware, brings them to that world where the laughers now will weep and wail and gnash their teeth for ever.

3. It is obvious from our subject, and the whole teaching of the Bible, that the Christian has a great labor and duty to perform in order to stand. It is to the highest degree important that he do stand, both for his own sake and for the sake of Christ's cause and truth. But how shall he stand with such powers against him? He *wrestles not with flesh and blood* (not with merely human enemies), *but against principalities, against powers, against the rulers of the darkness of this world, against spiritual wickedness in high places*. They are evil angels, spiritual foes, the legions of darkness that are against him. They are malignantly determined in their onset. They mean, if possible, to overthrow him: they work by wile and craft: they mean to do it, before he is aware of danger. What can the Christian do? The apostle instructs him what to do. Let him take unto himself *the whole armor*

*of God, that he may be able to withstand in the evil day, and, having done all, to stand. Stand, therefore,* disciple of the Lord, *having your loins girt about with truth, and having on the breast-plate of righteousness; and your feet shod with the preparation of the gospel of peace; above all, taking the shield of faith, wherewith ye shall be able to quench all the fiery darts of the wicked. And take the helmet of salvation, and the sword of the Spirit, which is the word of God.* This last, Christ wielded to the utter discomfiture of the tempter. In each instance, the appeal, "it is written," silenced and confounded, and, in the end, drove him away. Let it be remembered, that this whole armor is to be worn, and employed with prayer, the weightiest consideration of all. Whoever does this, *praying always*, as he contends, *with all prayer and supplication in the spirit, and watching thereunto with all perseverance,* will be able to stand against the wiles of the Devil, especially if he keeps fast to Christ; upon Christ as his foundation, under Christ as his protector, he is perfectly safe from all this hostile array. Were it tenfold greater, he need not be disturbed. It would still be true, that more are they that be for him than they that be against him. We are sometimes astonished at the ease with which, according to the Bible, the Christian may turn back this terrible foe of his salvation. It is only, *Resist the Devil, and he will flee from you.* The efficacy is all in Christ: the power is there, before which the foe quails and recedes. One with that Saviour, faithful in the adherence, you shall abide in safety, you shall prevail over the arrogant and plotting enemy. Standing in Christ, you may strike a blow with your frail arm of dust, which shall stun and prostrate the Arch-fiend. But never forget, a single moment, that your entire safety and final triumph depend upon your abiding in Christ.

In view of the number and strength of the Christian's foes, it is no great marvel that he is sometimes overtaken and overthrown. The Adversary has only to take him when off his guard, when he has laid aside his armor, or when separate from his Lord, and he makes him comparatively an easy prey. This leads us to remark, in the fourth place,—

4. That the fact that some who are not Christians stand, while some by their side, who are known as Christians, fall, is no ground of special self-complacency on the part of the former. There are some, in almost every religious community, who, though not religious men, are exceedingly amiable in their spirit, and correct in their way of life. They appear even better outwardly, more sober and consistent, than some professors of religion, who, it is hoped, are Christians, though with many infirmities. These persons mean by their correct demeanor nothing further than to live as upright men and good citizens. But the Adversary, we may safely presume, has another design to accomplish by them; the same design, indeed, that he has in the fall of the professed Christian,—namely, to help on his great business of blinding; to give augmented strength and vividness to the impression that men can live correctly enough without religion; that they do, on the whole, live as well without as with it. The case standing thus, we ask, What possible inducement can the Adversary have to assault this fair man of the world? What is to be gained? Possession? He has that already. The fall of the individual? In that

there would be loss rather than gain. He knows better than to make an assault there. He makes it rather where he has lost possession, and where much is to be gained to his cause by an overthrow. Hence it is that the one is borne down upon by the prince of the power of the air, with the purpose of crushing him; the other is even upheld externally by the same power. The one is shot into with deadly and fiery weapons; the other is unmolested by any such missiles. The Adversary is interested in the overthrow of the one, that he may bring a soul into jeopardy, and Christ's truth into disrepute: he is interested in the upright standing of the other, that he may make it appear that men can live even better without religion than with it. Certainly, in this view, the worldly man has nothing to boast of. He stands externally, because the Devil is willing, even desirous, that he should. There never was a greater mistake than in supposing that the Adversary is interested in having his servants act with outward and abominable viciousness. It is not so: his devices are not so gross as that would imply. He cares not how correct and even grave the manners of unregenerate men; the graver the better, if the heart only remains unsubdued, still linked to his interest and kingdom. He cares not, we believe, how morally, how soberly, and even religiously, men go in the path to death, if they will only consent to go in that path. He will be satisfied with any order of belief or disbelief, any style of conduct, any subordinate arrangement, which will allow to him his usurped supremacy of god of this world.

5. Allow me, before closing, to dwell a moment on the dark picture before us, for the purpose of Christian

incitement. It is, indeed, a dark picture, and has been for successive centuries. Contemplate it. A world of minds, each of uncounted value, under the merciless and deadly despotism of the Adversary of God and man; a world, too, that has been marked with the feet and wet with the tears and the blood of the Son of God. It is Christ's by creation and preservation; Christ's, too, by the purchase of his own mysterious agony; and still the Adversary holds under his foul sway far the greater portion of it. We know, indeed, it is by sufferance on the part of Christ, and that good will be brought out of this evil. We know, also, that the ascendency is kept by craft and deception on the part of the Adversary. He manages to corrupt and obscure Christ's truth; to defeat, in a measure, its operation; even to blot it out and bury it up. He gives currency and efficacy to all kinds of monstrous superstition and falsehood; spreads, like huge and black palls, his blinding and damning systems over nations and continents. Let the Christian look at these facts,— almost an entire world lying in the Wicked One; the Devil with his thousands where Christ has his tens; and the vile way this vile ascendency is maintained,— and, it seems to me, the view cannot help to move his spirit, and give new intensity to his prayer, that God would come down and relieve an oppressed world, and give the kingdom to Him whose right it is to reign, and in whose sceptre there is life and peace. The deep wrong, the utter outrage of the case, as it now stands, is enough to awaken to indignation all holy feelings, and nerve to extremest exertion all sanctified energies, that truth may be more rapidly diffused, and more quickly do its work, and the darkness recede, and sin be done away, and the miserable captives of Satan become the freemen of the Lord. Can the Christian be satisfied, can he remain supine, when he beholds an overwhelming proportion of the race, for whom the Redeemer died, against the Redeemer, — on the side of, and doing service to, the Destroyer? No: not if there abide within him a single particle of the vivid, working, aggressive spirit of a Christian.

But it is not all gloom. There is hope to incite. We know the scene is to be changed. Complete redemption is decreed. The promise has been uttered, the power pledged. Christ is the wielder of that power. He has appeared for this one simple purpose, to destroy the works of the Devil. He has begun to destroy these works: he will complete what he has begun. And how will his glory shine forth in the final achievement of this destruction and of a world's deliverance. The Christian, then, labors in hope. Let hope warm his heart and wake up his energies, and let him do something worthily in this advancing enterprise of mercy. If he takes but one soul off from the empire of darkness, and sets it over to the empire of light and love, he does a noble work. Each disciple of the Lord may do more; may, if he will, win many from rebellion to allegiance. Then would Christ's kingdom rapidly spread: he would ere long come into possession of the world he made; and peace would pervade all its borders, and the voice of gladness and thanksgiving be heard in all its dwellings.

In conclusion, we ask all unconverted persons to consider the nature of their position. Let it be remembered, that there are but two standards in this world, but two great moral sides; that of Christ and that of the Devil. On one side or the other all mankind are arrayed; either with Christ or with Satan. It is an appalling consignment, I know, which thus sets all men, who are not at heart living Christians, over on the side of the Adversary. The Bible does it: we must do it, or go against the plainest teachings of this book. According to the voice that speaks here, no matter what the standing of unregenerate men, what their outward character and appearance, they are the subjects of the Wicked and Malignant One; they are doing his work; they are preparing to share his prison and torments. We ask the sinner, if he is contented with this relation? Is it a worthy position for an intelligent creature of God? Is it a fitting service for those noble powers? The Devil's drudgery is it not, rather, infinitely dishonorable and degrading? And the end, the award, who can look at it? The unquenchable fire, the horrid companionship. Who can meet and bear such a doom? Consider these things, and look away from all this infamy and woe, to that other side of truth and love which still invites your allegiance. Yield, this hour, to that attracting goodness; submit to that rightful authority; become a member of that kingdom which is destined, in its consummation, to fill the earth and the universe with glory and praise.

# XVIII.

## THE DEATH OF ELISHA.

*Now Elisha was fallen sick of his sickness whereof he died. And Joash the king of Israel came down unto him, and wept over his face, and said, O my father, my father! the chariot of Israel, and the horsemen thereof!* — 2 KINGS xiii. 14.

WE have here the dying scene of the prophet Elisha. Of the material surroundings nothing is said. They were doubtless humble; for the man here prostrated had no earthly possessions. As he lived and wrought for God, sheltered and sustained by charity, so, at the end, when arrested by disease, where he was taken, there he lay and was ministered unto. He was in extreme old age, having spent more than sixty years in the prophetic service; sixty years from the time when he left the plough in obedience to the call of Elijah. There was one mourner present, — Joash the king of Israel, now in the eleventh year of his reign, who came down and wept over him; a plaintive, but not a sincere mourner. He had received the stern reproofs of the man of God, but refused to hearken to his word; and his tears now are those of regret that he is to lose so powerful a defender of his kingdom. How often had the realm been saved by the counsel and the miraculous might of this now dying man. The king, doubtless, remembered the times when this prophet sent, not once nor twice, to his predecessor on the throne, word of the approach of the enemy, their exact position and design; remembered when he smote a whole army with blindness, then led them right into the midst of the whole Israelitish force, and there opened their eyes to see that they were all captives, and to suppose they were all dead men; and they would have been dead men but for the merciful overruling of the prophet. The king remembered, also, the time when Samaria was closely besieged, and famine and destruction seemed inevitable to all; when, by the counsel and the word of this prophet, complete deliverance came; one single night, and the foe was not. Again and again had this dying man been the savior of Israel. The cause of the king's sorrow in prospect of the prophet's departure was, evidently, that the great bulwark of defence was about to leave them. Hence those words he uttered, *My father, my father! the chariot of Israel and the horsemen thereof!* in which he acknowledges that the prophet had been a defence of Israel, equal to, yea, beyond, the defence of chariots and horsemen. It is noticeable that these are the same words which Elisha used when Elijah was visibly taken up in the chariot of fire and by the horses of fire. It may be that that visible appearance suggested to Elisha this symbolization of the prophet Elijah in the character of defender of his country; so that, as he saw his friend and father, who surpassed the might of kings, thus gorgeously passing away, he broke forth, *My father, my father!* and this phrase, so grandly expressive, passed into a proverb; and this king Joash seized, and uttered it as he hung over the dying bed of Elisha. It is possible, that he knew it as Elisha's utterance in witnessing the departure of Elijah, and thought, what more fitting words for him called to witness the departure of Elisha. This, certainly, is true, in the case of us who read the account of Elisha's death; they suggest to us the other departing scene, when Elijah went up. There is a resemblance between the two, or the same terse words could not have applied as descriptive of both. The resemblance is here: that, in each of the cases, it is the departure of a righteous man from the world; and that both were distinguished for their deeds, for the high office they bore, and the signal service they rendered to the church, the world.

There is also a difference in the cases, arising from the difference in God's treatment of the two at the end of their respective courses. Elijah did up rapidly his mighty and splendid deeds, and at once, on the close of them, went off by a rapt and luminous departure, was taken up living, in the fulness of his strength. Elisha performed his great and visible works in the first fifteen years of his appearance, during which time he was the observed, the honored, and the feared of kings, and of all the people. At the close of this magnificent series, of this visible and awful usefulness, he was not called up home, but was sent into obscurity, to pass, so far as the record declares, forty-five years in unnoted retirement. Then he is placed before us, that we may see the seemingly forgotten old man languish and die. And we see him going out of the world in the humbling and painful mode of other men. *He fell sick of his sickness whereof he died.* This phrase is descriptive, evidently, of a process of slow decay. Life, in his case, ebbed away and sunk from view, under the weight of infirmity and disease.

In view of these so notable facts, I wish to state the great truth or principle involved here; namely, God's sovereign hand in the adjustment of circumstances when his servants die. I say sovereign hand, because there are often comparative scenes in the death of his servants which cannot be explained by recurring to their lives. Often are there distinctions made, which we cannot account for as having their foundation in the character and career of usefulness. Had character and usefulness been made the basis for awarding the respective passages out of the world of these two men, there would not have been that sort of discrimination. There would not have been; for the man of the languishing and painful departure was, so far as the record shows, the greater achiever of the two. Elisha surpassed Elijah in the number and power of his miraculous works. His request to his ascending master was, that *a double portion of his spirit* might rest upon himself. A huge request; but it was to be so, if he should see his master when taken from the earth. He did see him, and the sign was fulfilled; the double portion was his, and appeared afterward in multiplied, if not in mightier, deeds. Then when we come to character in the two cases, Elisha seems to have a clear advantage. We discover a point of weakness in Elijah's character; a weakness at a vital point; for at one time his faith faltered, his confidence in God all but gave out. Nothing of the kind appears in Elisha. It might have been, and he spared the record; but not likely. If any omissions occur in the Bible, they are not of the faults of the men who figure on those pages; these are pretty certainly told: but none told of Elisha. Not only is there this cleanness of the record in his case: as we read the history, we feel him to be the most perfect character, feel our hearts won to him as not in the other case. It is fear in the other case; here it is love, a reverent and affectionate admiration. But, leaving the character and the conspicuous deeds, if we come to usefulness, — make a comparison between the two in this regard, — the later prophet rises the higher; from the fact that he, probably, exceeded even in mighty deeds, clearly in character, and very much in the term and the variety of service. It is a great mistake to suppose that a person's usefulness is in proportion to the conspicuity and remarkableness of his actions; that the great, the notable deeds, those that take the attention and call out the admiration, are the specially productive ones. So people are ever judging. The man that is cutting the figure, moving all tongues, and marshalling all type in comment, he is the man that is doing the good. Bringing all eyes to see, and all ears to hear, he is the man mightiest in influence; as was Elijah pretty much through his whole term; as was Elisha the first fifteen years of his term. These naturally come first in the order, the notable, the achieving. They did with Elisha. They did also with Christ. His ministry opened with the notable. Though there were miracles to the end, they were mainly near the beginning. The attesting came first. The teaching, the shining, the suffering, afterward. We say, emphatically, the course or the life that wants the quiet, teaching, shining, suffering part, wants the completeness, fails of the greatest measure of usefulness. What, in comparison, would Christ's have been with only the miraculous, the splendid public deeds; having done these, had he gone up in one of them, the nights of prayer, the sweat of Gethsemane, the blood of Calvary wanting? It is hard, indeed, to pass from the achieving and acclaimed publicity to the oblivious line of checks and sorrows. Not so was Elijah called, and therein was he wanting. It was so with Elisha; and herein his completeness, his advantage over his predecessor. And can we doubt that those forty-five years of unnoticed service were years of pre-eminent usefulness, though through all he was simply the holy liver, the retired teacher, the master of prophets? Such, now, were the respective courses of these two men, their characters, and probable usefulness: Elisha, at least on full equality, in some respects the superior. What ground find we for that difference in their departures, that God should grant to one a triumphant departure, without tasting death; the other made to traverse the entire path of weary and oppressive decay? How instructive, how suggestive the fact, that the prophet higher, completer in character and in service, met the slow languishments of the death.

The question forces itself upon us here, Are we sure that the first, the brilliantly ascending prophet, had all the advantage in the mode of his departure? This advantage, I think, had Elisha; his was the more useful departure from life, a lingering, Christian death, more impressive and influential than a translation. Do you say, the translation shows an instance of the spirit's life and of the body's rising? We reply, the ebbing, sinking breath of the dying prophet, taken in connection with that exultant hope within, rising above the decay, tells equally and more eloquently of death abolished, of the spirit's perpetual life; every ebb and pang is a fresh argument of the life. We call to mind those symbolic arrows shot from the window of this prophet's dying chamber; and we believe more convictive arrows went from this humble yet radiant death scene, convincing men of the truth, the life, the immortality, than from the pageant of the other prophet's ascension. There was not only power in his death, but also power in him as dead; life, a germ of life, even, in the dead and mouldering bones. These take down into the grave with them the pledge of the rising. The dead prophet taught this, the rising, as effectually as the translated prophet taught that there is life in the bones. He taught it by imparting life to a dead man suddenly cast into his sepulchre. The instant that dead man touched the inhumed prophet, he sprung back into vigorous life, a significant symbol and instance of the body's rising. Precious truth, the decree goes down into the grave with you, imbedded in your bones, that your body shall come up again; and *live* again, fashioned after Christ's *glorious body, according to the working whereby he is able even to subdue all things unto himself.*

But let us recur a moment to that resurrection scene in the cave, as setting forth the soul's life,—the Christian's power after death to give life, impart spiritual rising to the dead in sin. It has proved in the case of many a wicked man that the holy living and the peaceful dying of some Christian friend failed at the time to affect him; but afterward, as he remembered that life, that death, as the silent thought passed back to the scene, entered the place, and touched the now buried form, then came the searching, life-giving efficacy. So is it that the memory of the good man, years after he has gone, will operate to bring up souls from death. The honor, the privilege, the productiveness of the Christian life, who will not aspire to live it? And who desire to be excused from the lowly and the suffering close, when we see that the vitality and the efficacy lies very much in this part?

How forcibly is it set before us in these Scripture instances, that the manner of the dying is no sure criterion of the character and life. One may go off in rapture and shouts and songs; another hardly getting beyond the penitent moan,—God be merciful, oh, help mine unbelief; and the last shall stand at the judgment brighter and higher than the first.

We learn, also, that the pains and decays of death are not always appointed as a discipline. It doubtless holds elsewhere as here, that the lingering and the suffering way out of life is prescribed for the maturer and more perfect of the two. The weary and the sorrowing way being ordained in order to bring out a testimony, into this is taken the person who is so full of faith, so ripe in character, so unquestioned in his godliness, that the arrows will fly from his chamber, invisible but mighty, to convince and subdue the unbelievers. They see the argument in the dying, and confess there is an endless living for the righteous.

This, then, is clearly taught; namely, the reasonableness of submission, when ourselves or our friends are made to pass the ordeal of death, in peculiarly hard and trying circumstances. For the righteous there is a good in death, and a privilege, and an honor even, in the sharpest severities of dying. Behold, and consider; it is a loving hand that leads into the deep gloom and implants the terrible agony. Behold, consider this, and be still when the pang is laid on thee or thine.

Look to this instance and learn the certainty of death. Each of us may fix on this conclusion, death is sure to come to me. Its bitter experience I know I must traverse. For here is a man, this prophet of old, who succeeded to a translated master, as good, as useful, as eminent as he, and yet death became his lonely lot. Here a man whose breath breathed life into others, and his sepulchred bones were pregnant with life to one buried with him, yet death smote him down and held him fast.

This mortal certainty, then, admit it as awaiting you; though scores of years between, yet soon it will come. Try to live as one who realizes this doom of death, and that more awful fact, *After death comes the judgment.* All now and on, and then and for ever through the eternal ages, depends upon your being ready, that you prepare betimes to meet your God; depends upon your repentance, your faith in Christ, your righteous life. Do this, and it shall be well with you. Refuse, and you go the other way,—where the prophet did not go.

# XIX.

## THE SON OF MAN IS COME TO SEEK AND TO SAVE.

*For the Son of man is come to seek and to save that which was lost.* — LUKE xix. 10.

THE language of Scripture is very simple, yet full of meaning. What can be more simple than this language of the text: *For the Son of man is come to seek and to save that which was lost.* Here redemption is described. Redemption: a great work accomplished by a great Being; that Being, the Son of man. This is one of his humble titles, reminding us that the mode of his coming was by human descent, that he was the babe of Bethlehem, born of a woman; and yet the Lord himself, in the use of this humble phrase, utters a passage which most clearly and unequivocally declares his Divinity: *And no man hath ascended up to heaven but he that came down from heaven, even the Son of man which is in heaven.* This Son of man who came down from heaven, and was then speaking and acting in the seeming, yea, the reality of a man on the earth, was also, at the same instant, in heaven; a fact to be explained only thus: God alone is everywhere present; therefore Christ is God as well as man; as God, he was at the same instant in heaven and on earth.

*The Son of man is come;* we have here announced a great coming. He is *come to seek and to save that which was lost;* we have here a great object. It is reasonable to suppose that the two parts of the text are in keeping. A great coming, therefore a great object. It is legitimate to argue the greatness of the object from the greatness of the coming, and this I proceed to do. The first topic being, —

I. The greatness of his coming.

That it was a great and glorious coming appears from the fact that so much is said of it along the whole line, and in all the representations, of Scripture. It began to be spoken of four thousand years before it took place. It is the grand theme of prophets in every age. Not only the words, but all the types, of Scripture have a finger significantly pointing to the Being in whom they were all to find their realization. Poetry and song brought forward and tasked their highest conceivings, produced and arranged their divinest images, to honor the personage who, at the appointed time, was thus to appear. Language, in its largest capabilities, was tasked in the pregnant service. *Unto us a child is born, unto us a son is given: and the government shall be upon his shoulder: and his name shall be called Wonderful, Counsellor, The mighty God, The everlasting Father, The Prince of Peace.* Thus the expectation of the world for these four thousand years was stretched and held to Him who was to appear. And when the eventful moment arrived, and the predicted One came from heaven to assume our nature, heaven itself, for a little season, broke over the separating line, and threw its wondrous music on the air, giving forth words worthy of the angelic strains in which they were announced:

*Glory to God in the highest, and on earth peace, good-will to men.* How natural, now, to suppose that the Being who was to come, the Being to whom all this referred, was a notable being.

We legitimately make out, further, the greatness of Him who came, from the very language used in the text: *The Son of man is come to seek and to save.* This implies his pre-existence; not that he was created, that he might be a Saviour, but he came: implies not only pre-existence, but voluntariness. He came to be a servant; was not a servant in his original state, but equal with the Father. *He is come to seek and to save the lost.* In those plain words you really have the divinity of our Lord. You have pre-existence, which, if you will trace back, and follow up to its fountain, will bring you to Deity as its origin. Reasoning minds have found it so; hence reasoning minds, who have wished to run clear of our Lord's divinity, have in the majority of instances discarded his pre-existence, because they knew where the admission of this would lead them; namely, to the doctrine of the Son's equality with the Father, according to that most stubborn text, *In the beginning was the Word, and the Word was with God, and the Word was God.* The Word was God, and made all things that were made; *and the Word was made flesh, and dwelt among us.* Though equal originally, he voluntarily made the sacrifice: he emptied himself, and took the form of a servant. How justly now may we predicate greatness of that coming, in view of the elevation and glory of the Being who came; the glory inherent; the glory he had with the Father; the glory he laid off for a season; and, also, of the condescension of that coming; the depths to which he stooped, that he might touch us and take us up. It is all, indeed, a great proceeding; nothing finite, nothing human about it in the plan or the execution: it is all God-like, marked with the infinite. We feel it to be so: our souls so testify and say, as we read and ponder upon these things. And what was it for? We answer, it was for a great object. Here we reach our second point; namely, —

II. The greatness of the object, argued from the greatness of the coming. A greater coming could not be projected or conceived; the Being, the sacrifice, the suffering endurance, all having the mark and the measure of the infinite. Now, in God's scheme and workmanship, means are adjusted to ends with the exactest precision, so that there is no large, needless waste in the moral forces he appoints or the provisions he makes. This comes of his wisdom, and his economy of expenditure. When such a being as Christ, at such a labor and cost, comes into the world to save, then there were beings in the world to be saved. It is a fair inference, that there were and that there are sinners here. If a Divine Being, one intrinsically God as well as truly man, came to save sinners, then this work of saving was too great a work for mere created capabilities. A man, an angel, could not do it: if so, a man or an angel would have been appointed to do it. We thus reach the conclusion, that this work of saving men is a great work, from the fact that divine capabilities were assigned to accomplish it: and the process is a perfectly fair one. If it is fair, legitimate, to infer that we are a race of sinners, from the fact that the Son of man came to save the race, it is equally legitimate to infer from the fact that the Saviour is God incarnate, divine powers enlisted, that the condition of the sinner is a desperate one on any other supposition. And this is the meaning of this word *lost.* A vast compass and depth of dismal meaning is revealed in it, — lost. It is because man was past all possibility of self-recovery, fallen too low to be reached and restored by any created arm, that the term lost is made the descriptive of his condition. Because this is the right word for his case, his a completeness, a totality of ruin, so far as all created helpers are concerned, therefore the infinite Son came to save.

Not only the greatness of the Saviour, but the mode pursued to effect the salvation, also proves the completeness of the ruin. That the Son of God must suffer as he did, though the pureness of his character made only joy his soul's fit companion, yet that sorrow should overwhelm him; that that soul which knew no sin should be stricken, crushed, and buried in gloom; that this Being, in the hour of his conflict, should be a spectacle of suffering, surpassing all that had been seen or known elsewhere in the universe, — all this was strange, unless we consider for what it was. It was the great act and passion in the scheme of saving these lost. Does it not follow, then, that the setting of a right example, teaching them, giving them good instruction, were not sufficient to save them? Suffering and death came in. The suffering and death of the Son of God were demanded, or they would not have come in. They were necessary, on account of the obstructions to be got out of the way. That the dying of the infinite Son was the divinely appointed way to do it, satisfies me that it was the only way to do it. I could not, nor could any of you, nor all of us together, nor all the higher ranks of being,—nothing in might, in influence, in worth, below the Godhead,—could meet the case. I prove it thus, because one of the persons of the Godhead was set to do it. Shut out that Being and his work, and our case is a dark one, because we cannot cope with our ruin, have no strength; we are in fetters, bound, condemned; we are lost. Oh that you would, all of you, but let the full meaning of that term come in upon your souls, and feel the fact, the reigning sin, which makes it a fact. Then the preacher would want no other argument. And let me say, here is the place, after all, to begin, with the lowly heart; here, the true stand-point; here, the pregnant centre from which to reach all truth, all its fruits in the character, all its blessings in the soul's eternal redemption.

Having begun at the other end, and attempted to reason from the greatness, the infinite character, and measureless glory of Him who came and bled and died to save us, proving thereby the entireness of our ruin on account of our sin, let us now start from the depths we have reached, from the conviction of lost, and pass back on the ascending line to the character and person of Him who came to save. And, let me say, there is no difficulty in going this way; no mistakes are ever made in tracing this process. I do not believe the case has occurred since the glorious Advent, the case of the individual, whose heart received this doctrine of lost, who felt his sin and its irreparable mischief, who has not very soon admitted the doctrine, and rejoiced in the proffer of the infinite Repairer; simply because such an one sees the fitness in his own case, because on a lower theory, and with a human

Saviour, his prospects grow gloomy; for he has a work on hand, rather a work on his heart, which only the Maker of the heart can do. I wish you to mark this in God's Book when you read it; in all the characters and experiences you have an opportunity to read, your own and others, mark this,—that the equation is always run out, a perfect equation always made. In the Bible we find, on the side of the Redeemer, an infinity of greatness; on our side, totality of ruin. And when we come to the records of experience, to the heart where the Spirit has been, to write its letters and its lines, that heart understands that the Bible is no exaggeration. Sin is all through me: *lost* is the word. The heavy heart moans in the night watches, Oh, my sin, my ruin, height, vastness, oppressive burden. Who shall deliver me? The Deliverer comes, the Saviour saves that lost one; and that delivered soul is not long in telling you he is a great Saviour. His heart sings it in its first swelling emotions. All through life, till the wave of death touches his feet, he testifies still, Mine is a mighty strength and measure of sin, mine a great and a mighty Redeemer. And when those feet are planted on the other side, the equation still remains; the soul in its retrospect beholds more clearly the compass and the aggravation of its guilt, and more loftily and transportingly the might and majesty of its Redeemer.

Pass now to an opposite page of experience; to a class who have not much belief in human sin, their own or anybody's else. They view sin as a trifle, easily managed; but little of it, and that little they can dispose of, or keep in check, at their pleasure. A little sin, a like Saviour. There you have the equation; the quantity of sin, and the quantity of Christ wanted, in exact proportion to each other. Oh that God would make us to know ourselves; and, from this knowledge of ourselves, lead us up to an acknowledgment of redemption in the mystery of its doctrines, in the unmeasured resources of its grace, in the boundless might of the agents pledged to conduct it to its grand consummation.

III. I come now to the third and last step. The first is the greatness of that coming; the second, the greatness of the object in that coming, namely, to retrieve and save from an utter ruin; the third is the duty and the privilege, on our part, of receiving this great Saviour: this argued also from the greatness of that coming, and the greatness of our necessity. The greatness of that coming, the more we meditate upon it, the more it will amaze us. The mystery of love in that coming is beyond our fathoming. *God was manifest in the flesh.* He came, he stooped to the condition of a servant, that he might make us kings hereafter. And for this he ought to have all our hearts; but, in fact, for this he commonly receives the treatment of a servant. Because, in the godlike workings of his love, he laid aside his divine glory for a season, there are those who refuse to give it back to him; deny, henceforth, his right to that glory. The Jews were satisfied to crucify Christ in his humanity. These crucify him in his divinity, making his very kindness an argument against his prerogative. It is an argument all the other way. That wondrous laying off, that condescension, establishes the validity of the prerogative, and demonstrates the fulness and reliableness of his resources, the strength of his purpose, the readiness of his heart to save. *He is come to save:* those words are only winning, most tenderly persuasive. But to whom do they apply? Where do they reach, and receive the warm and gushing interest? *The lost,*— the hearts that have that feeling of lost are the hearts to respond. Christ did not come to save everybody; to save those who have no wish to be saved; no thought nor belief that they need to be saved; not to save rocks, or the senseless things colder and harder than the rocks. As the argument of the text is so adjusted and balanced as to play back and forth,—a great Saviour, therefore a great ruin to be repaired; a great ruin existing, therefore only a great Saviour could be adequate,—so in the appeal growing out of the text, it plays both ways. If any can do without him, it will appear that he can do without them. That matter stands even. But the hearts that know and confess that they are lost, the sinners, coming to him as such, he will not pass such by. Those that bend and incline toward him, he bends and inclines toward them. Between that soul all sensible of its need, oppressed with its unfitness and unworthiness, and the blessed, boundless heart of the Saviour, there is a quick and eager affinity. Christ has a purpose in that direction, there is the specific errand he came for,—to save that lost soul. A whisper, methinks, comes up here, and another rises there, It cannot be I, It cannot be I. Yes, you, if you lie within the circle of the lost, in the number of the stripped, helpless, perishing ones; if you are willing to be saved, are truly wanting to be saved, saved in that Saviour's way, from your sin,—you will hardly get out of this place to-day without being saved, your sins forgiven, the blessed work begun in your soul. Your unconsenting heart out of the way, there is nothing more in the way. For Christ is willing; and why will you doubt it? when this is what he came into the world to do, to save; his sole object, business here, to save. His name is Saviour. This his chosen descriptive; Saviour, — his whole mind and heart and being filled and glowing with this work and enterprise of saving. His soul's desire and passion are to save, all eager to engage, the moment he can find a subject, find a sinner, a soul sick of its sin and willing to be saved from and out of its sin. Wherever there are such souls, in a Hottentot's kraal or the jungles of India, or beneath Afric's palms; whoever they are, the refined, the erudite, the enriched, or the debased, the poorest and obscurest of earth, — Christ is there on his work of saving. There is not one such soul on this earth, but Christ knows it and is there. If there is one such here, Christ is here. And he has at this moment a deeper interest in that one than in all the rest of us, and he will do in him his blessing, saving work. What a work when finished, — *Saved*. What a contrast to the former state, — *Lost*. Gloom and misery your oft companions; now, peace, hope, and soon to be heaven. The work of saving finished; the work of praising never finished.

# XX.

## THE GLORY OF CHRIST.

*And the Word was made flesh, and dwelt among us (and we beheld his glory, the glory as of the only begotten of the Father), full of grace and truth.*—John i. 14.

CAN we do better, in meditating on these words, than try to bring before our minds a few gleams of the glory of Christ? I go into no discussion, no studied profoundness; but, mainly assuming the truth we hold, I shall touch in a rapid, discursive way some of the items which go to make up the completeness, the infinity, of the glory of Christ. To sum up all in single words, they would be Greatness, Mystery, Condescension, Love, Wealth, Power, Achievement. All these we find in him.

Christ has the glory which comes of Greatness; greatness of being, underived, unending being. *I am Alpha and Omega, the beginning and the end, the first and the last.* His an existence before any created thing, and holding on amid all the mutations of beings and worlds finite and dependent, sublimely unchanging,—*the same yesterday and to-day and for ever.* His presence everywhere that his people are, to protect and bless. His knowledge, like his presence, commensurate with all breadth; knowledge reaching to all the secrecies and depths, declaring himself to the churches as *He that searcheth the reins and the hearts.* Such the character of his attributes all through. In his higher nature not finite, but underived, independent, infinite, possessing the glory which comes of greatness.

Then, most intimately connected is the glory of Mystery. Christ, in his wonderful qualities and constitution, is a subject not easily mastered. Questions arise about him not readily answered; bounds are there, if any, our scope cannot reach; depths we cannot fathom. *Great is the mystery of godliness; God was manifest in the flesh.* God and man, two natures: this a fact revealed. One person: this, too, a fact revealed. The facts we can see and receive. The mystery connected we cannot explore. But we can bow and confess that there is something greater than we; something for tasking the advanced powers, for subsequent revelations. It is folly to be offended at the mystery, for the mystery arises from the greatness and the glory of these truths. The glory of our Lord is greatly advanced by the mystery of his person. His the glory of mystery; and his glory shall heighten as these mysteries shall unfold; and the mysteries shall still remain, we believe, to re-act, and new ones arise, perhaps, to heighten yet more the glory of the Lord.

Then, further, intimately connected with the glory which comes of the mystery is the glory of his Condescension. And there is a glory in condescension. We feel it when we see it in a human character; one great in endowments and station, yet ever spontaneously coming down, ready, rejoicing to bend in order to confer a benefit; no hauteur or arrogant assuming, but everywhere the gentle, the condescending bearing. We pronounce this a crown of glory in a character that has any just claim to greatness.

But the condescension of Christ, we will let Paul tell you it. How great the condescension, when he who was in the form of God, and who thought it no robbery to be equal with God, yielding the claim of equality, made himself of no reputation, and took upon him the form of a servant, and was made in the likeness of men, and in that form became obedient unto death. That great act of condescension was followed by an unbroken series of touching and humble ministries, ever bending to the lot of all the smallest, the obscurest, and most despised. Such was he ever when on earth. The same, exalted back into heaven.

Another item, quite kindred with the preceding, is the glory of his Intention. The glory here lies in the generous love of it; and the height and strength of the love appears in this, that it goes forward and accomplishes its blessing purpose through difficulties, over obstructions; a love that no barriers could arrest; a love that many waters could not quench, nor floods drown. The sentiment which reigned in his heart was compassion for us in our lost condition. The object to be accomplished, our rescue from condemnation, our justification, sanctification, restoration to God's favor and presence. The obstruction was the justice, truth, holiness of God; to be maintained only by God's maintaining his law, the penalty of which we had incurred; a difficulty Christ could take out of the way only by putting himself in our stead, taking the penalty upon himself, himself made a curse for us. He bearing it for us, we believing in him, accepting what he has done for us, are made free from the curse, through faith in him. Is it not love in its height and perfection, that would do that for such as we; that would make such a sacrifice, endure such an agony, surpassing, doubtless, all that had been witnessed on earth before; a suffering the sun refused to see, and that brought inanimate nature into shrouded and convulsive sympathy, — this for enemies? How exceeding in glory; and how much more admirable and glorious as a love that discriminated; that would not tread down principle to gain its end; and, while it would save if it could, would not and will not save to the dishonor of God, or the weakening of his government, or the obliterating of the distinction between holy and unholy; not that weak, loose, profligate love that pities, but cares not for integrity and purity, as though happiness were the great ultimate good, not righteousness. And whilst the glory of this love is the fact that it discriminates, it is not, we add, narrow nor partial; that death of the Son was borne for all; the provision made for all; the inviting voice sounds forth to all, *Ho, every one that thirsteth, come ye to the waters.* Such the strength of his love, and the breadth of his kindly intention.

Then his Resource. This another item in the glory of Christ, — his fulness, and exhaustless means and material for blessing, the glory which comes of possession; this, in part, the glory of Christ. We make no reference here to outward possession, material wealth. This, indeed, is all his; for he made it. Men are mad after this; but he has what is vastly higher, without which the outward is a mere nullity. Men gain wealth, but lose life; and what shall it profit a man if he gain the world, and lose his life? This possession is Christ's, — Life. He has life in himself; life, physical and spiritual. He is the Life, the eternal life. Such as this has he in his power, such to give. Just think what a stock of life, what quantity, what power of life resident in him; so great that he concedes to all the successive and countless millions of earth the privilege of drawing upon him, drawing from him the boon of life, knowing that he has in himself, as the joint creation of his power and the purchase of his death, enough to honor, even to the end, every draft of faith, every want of true humility, every demand of believing prayers. We may, perhaps, gain our best idea of the quantity of possession, the compass and glory of wealth in him, by looking at, or conceiving, as best we can, the process and items of dispensation on his part.

In this comprehensive gift of life to a soul doomed, a soul dead in sin, there is the pardon, the release of the soul from the sentence of death eternal; this done by an efficacy resident in him through his sufferings; an efficacy, an influence he has abundantly, namely, the power to forgive sins; a fund of merit which shall fill the enormous vacuity made by the sinner's demerit, and which makes him, all wanting as he is, perfect in righteousness, rich in the treasures of an obedience not his own and yet made his own, and the fruits of it and the mighty awards laid upon his worthless and naked soul.

Not only the pardon, the justification, but the sustenance also. First, the life, an implantation from him, he the author of it; then, perpetually after, he the feeder, the sustainer of it. In this comprehensive gift of life, himself the bread, the flesh to nourish and support it. The great declaration is, *Without me, ye can do nothing*, are nothing, and come to nothing. Broken from that stock, the vital, transmitting connection sundered, the disciple droops and dies. It follows that every thing which contributes to the Christian's vigor and prosperity comes directly out of the fulness in Christ; Christ always giving, the disciple always receiving. And all that he wants, and more than he dare think, or could think till he received, he does profusely receive.

It is wonderful in his single case: a glory of Possession is it that can thus give and do for one needy soul, making it thus rich in present experience, rich in assured and boundless hopes. And he is only one. When we take into consideration the numbers, past numbering, that have thus drawn upon him, and are now drawing, and the vastly greater numbers that shall yet draw life and sustenance and boundless enrichment from him, what then shall we think of the repleteness of the fountain, the glory of his wealth, that can thus give, and not be diminished; with whom is no fear of exhaustion; no possibility of a balance against him; no compulsory protest there of crowded and beseeching claims; enough there to make them all princes and kings, royal in wealth, and to have thrones and crowns at length? We may exclaim in the phrase of that blessed confessor, Samuel Rutherford, of Scotland, who had as long a line as any other man to sink into this profound of Christ's treasured wealth and good, "Who can fathom, who tell, how far it is to the bottom of our Christ? Who hath ever grasped the foldings and the piles and the heights and the depths of that grace and glory which is in him, and freely made over to us?"

With this glory of possession there is connected in

our Lord the glory of Achievement. And here we keep on moral grounds. His higher glory comes of his moral deeds. We admit that it was great to speak a world from nought. This our Christ has done. But it was greater to redeem. This our Christ is now doing. Redemption — I speak of redemption applied — is, in every instance, a conquest; the now happy subject of it, once a resisting rebel, Christ subdued him, conquered him. Hence, Christ appears as a conqueror; and the world has ever resounded with the glory of conquerors. Christ's, pre-eminently, is the glory of a conqueror; using for his purpose, however, only the weapons of truth and goodness; never the carnal, ever the spiritual and mighty. The glory lies partly in the power displayed in the doing; a power to transform infuriate rage to gentleness and peace; arrogant pride to meekness and humility; the lust of gain to the love of giving; the hateful and hating qualities changed as by one stroke of that power into the fervors of gratitude and the kindliest sympathy; the will that would not bend, but refused, and stiffened itself more stoutly, ere it thought, bending cheerfully, it knew not how, but knew how blessed it was thus to be made willing. Such the power shown in Christ's conquests, — glorious for this. And then, his design therein, — glorious for this, too, — not to make the conquered a slave, but a freeman; his a conquest into liberty; from Egypt and all its durance vile into Canaan, where rest is found, and sweet refreshment and all good experiences. Thus far there has been not a little of this sort of achievement. This glory of conquest on the part of our Lord has been witnessed more or less in every nation and tribe where the gospel has been carried. Cases innumerable have occurred of the most exciting interest, marvellous, glorious; and for them the heavens give him glory, crying, *Great and marvellous are thy works.* And could all the cases that have transpired, yea, all now on the stage, some, the most remarkable, hidden in India and the islands of the sea,—could all be brought together and brought under human view, as they are under angelic, men would join and equal in fervor the acclaim of angels, saying, *Great and marvellous are thy works, Lord God Almighty;* great the glory of thy conquests, *thou King of saints.*

And yet this glory is now mainly prospective, the glory of works to be done; what he has done demonstrating his fitness and ability yet to do. He still lives and works the conqueror; and will work, with none to let, till the world shall be submissive at his feet. We choose to stand by and maintain the competency of Christ, enthroned above, for the enterprise on his hands; to be consummated as a moral enterprise, by his truth and Spirit. So shall the glory of it be greater, moral, not of force, not of a re-appearing king. We have faith that it will be. By faith, even now, we behold it as done; the blessed Comforter descending, according to the promise, and a world transformed, a world redeemed.

Then, perhaps, another scene should be added. These, even all his trophies of every age, by the glorious Leader and Conqueror conducted into heaven; the resurrection and the judgment passed, all gathered safe in heaven. They all belonged originally to another place, and were on their way to it. All owe it to him that they are at length in heaven; saying and singing, that all they have, their treasures of character and affection, the beginning, the progress, the holiness, the peace, the victory, the triumph, the crowning, — all, the gift and achievement of Christ. Will these not shine forth in him an unapproached glory of achievement? And will he not then be worthy of the many crowns that shall be placed on his head?

But the subject is too vast for our hearts. It comes with a greatness and opulence that hold us, at times, in a species of confused, abstract admiration. And yet it is something which concerns us, something set before us, and which we ought to see, so far as we can, *the glory of the only begotten of the Father.* It is not a subject to be wrought up, and then ended in strains of rhapsody. It is directly and solidly practical. It has its substantial Christian uses. I can name but two or three.

1. If such is Christ, such the qualities which constitute his character, it follows that he is worth seeing. The sight of Christ, if our heart should go with our eyes, would contribute to make us like him; beholding, though imperfectly, the glory, we should be *changed into the same image from glory to glory, even as by the Spirit of the Lord.*

2. Again, the sight will contribute to make the soul more blessed, gazing, and perceiving more and more what a Saviour he is, and what a Saviour it has. This view, by faith, of that amazing glory will make scenes and moments of heaven here upon earth. And this it is, we believe, in open vision hereafter, which will wake and sustain in heaven itself its most heavenly rapture, when that memorable prayer of the Lord,

presented just before his passion, shall be answered, *Father, I will that they also whom thou hast given me, be with me where I am; that they may behold my glory.* Wonderful words, *that they may behold my glory;* a glory in its brightness which only a celestial vision can meet; a succession of glories ever rising upon the soul, rising and unfolding new matters of entrancing interest, deeper mysteries of knowledge and of wealth; fresher the longer seen; and the more intently seen the more of treasure gained, and the higher the experience of blessedness.

3. To be, indeed, the disciple of such a Master, the relation is a privilege and an honor, a fountain of wealth and of all possible good. If you are his, such the largess of the covenant, that all his is yours. His own words are, *Ye shall ask what ye will, and it shall be done unto you.* Draw to the extent of your heart, and it shall be given you. Thus he maintains his glory, by his divine style of giving. So many Christians have found it, and more will, as more shall come, as the Lord loves to have them come, in a way that shall make it consistent on his part, like himself, to give; his glory and happiness lying in the line of unceasing and unmeasured giving. And the Christian's happiness, too, like the Master's, consists very much in giving, not merely in receiving the opulent blessings, but more in giving back the heart's gratitude and praise.

4. I remark, further, that it is very evident what is incumbent upon Christians, in order to advance and make still more manifest the glory of the Master. This is done, his glory made manifest, just so far as they invite or promote, on his part, dispensation. Infinite

treasures of grace and glory are resident in him; but restrained, held back, it is a glory concealed. And what restrains? What binds and holds, ingloriously confined, those exhaustless resources? What, when on earth, ignobly cramped, that divinely beneficent Power, who would, but could not, could not do his mighty works there, because of their unbelief? Worthless and weak as we are, yet, astounding fact, we do stand at the gate of such outgoings as these, and succeed in holding back, or more copiously inviting, the enriching floods. Unbelief shuts back all outflow from the infinite fountains. Faith and the prayer of faith brings him forth in prodigal dispensation; and the world brightens under his beneficence, and new ones spring forth to praise him. His glory then shines; shines just in proportion as his friends get out of the way; rather prepare the way for him to do his redeeming works, and scatter his princely gifts. And they, too, in this state and mood, themselves begin to shine and to reflect that glory. Thus we ought ever to do, that men may behold in the church the glory of Christ. So our blessed Lord would have us, even like him in character. And then this, I suppose, is what our Lord would have us do; namely, put him upon achievement. And such deeds as belong to him to do, this tortured world now begs to witness, and receive at his hands.

Oh, Lord, how long? In wailing cries it comes repeated to our ears, How long? We here bow before the glory of mystery; and there is no mystery profounder than this delay on his part to work and to save. Let not our faith falter for this. Let it ride still that ocean of grace gathered in Christ; safely and confidently ride, because anchored on the unfailing bottom of eternal promise.

Let us come to-day where our souls may be filled, and ask others to come that they may be blest. Come, ye who have not yet known him. If you feel the burden of your sin, lay your soul in penitence and faith at his feet, and he will give you rest; will replenish you with all good, and bring you to behold his glory.

## XXI.

### SEEK FIRST THE KINGDOM OF GOD AND HIS RIGHTEOUSNESS.

*But seek ye first the kingdom of God, and his righteousness; and all these things shall be added unto you.* — MATTHEW vi. 33.

HERE is something to be sought. *The kingdom of God, and his righteousness.*

*The kingdom of God.* What is this? We may conceive of it as a place, or realm, where the dwellers are the subjects, yea, the sons, of God; in character, substantially right; in destiny, eternally secure. Seek to enter the door of that kingdom, and become one of that privileged company. *The kingdom of God.* We may conceive of it as a condition, or state; a state of submission to the reign of God. Seek to put yourself, your heart, in that reverent and becoming attitude. *The kingdom of God.* We may conceive of it as a possession. In that case, *the kingdom of God is within you, not in word, but in power.* It is the authority, the truth, the love of God, abiding within, as the ruling principle of the soul. But there is another phrase in the text, *The kingdom of God, and his righteousness.* God's righteousness. What is that? It embodies this idea, a righteousness like God's. *Be ye therefore perfect, even as your Father which is in heaven is perfect.* Again, a righteousness which is the gift of God. While this moral quality is to be sought by the creature, there is a sense in which it is the work or gift of the Creator. We are commanded to seek it, do it, be it. *Make you a new heart;* and, in immediate connection, we read the promise, *and I will give them one heart, and I will put a new spirit within you.* There is another idea: it is not merely God's sanctifying grace, and the moral element, the holiness, the sanctified state produced thereby; it is also his justifying grace. The person that has entered this divine realm, that has the loyal, obedient heart, God's love enthroned therein, stands there, and will stand, at the last, before the judgment-seat of God, as righteous, as completely so, as if the guilt of sin had never been on him; and it is the righteousness of God he then wears; God's righteousness, as being the result of his saving plan, by his wisdom devised, by that great sacrifice, the incarnation and death of his Son Jesus Christ, wrought out. Whoever enters the door, and has within him the principle, the spirit, the power called righteousness, has about him, also, the perfect robe righteousness; has both the character and clothing of righteousness; within and without, righteousness, — a good in life, a support in death, a treasure and a crown in eternity. This is Christianity, true religion, the spirit and the power of it in the soul.

Thus far we have the object to be sought. This religion of Christ and the heart is made, by the authority of Christ, an object of human seeking. There is a sense and a mode in which men are to seek it. Still, I admit that what is called seeking religion is a phrase and a practice which has been greatly abused. But no abuse and no injury can accrue when it is sought according to the direction of this great precept, which says, *Seek first the kingdom of God, and his righteousness.* And what does this imply? That I may describe clearly, let me describe concretely, introducing a person, one who may be said to practise obediently, and *seek first the kingdom of God, and his righteousness.* We say, then, of such an one, —

That religion is put first by him in his soul's estimation. He looks all about him, and finds nothing in the depths or the heights that, for substantial worth, will compare with this righteousness, the character and the clothing which assures to him the approval of God and the inheritance of eternity.

I remark, further, that, in his seeking, he puts it first in the order of time. This before any thing else; this in the first of life; or, if life has somewhat advanced before he comes to the just, the ascendant estimation, then this as the first thing he does after his eyes begin to open, and his heart to be moved; the first of all that remains of time; the first, the best, the freshest hours of every day of time, and so all through time. This suggests another idea.

Seeking with this great interest in the ascendency, he seeks with all other things brought into subordination. Seeking this first, whatever puts back his success he is prepared to put aside or put down. With this principle we may go on, and sweep the entire field of minor and conflicting claims, demanding a sacrifice of the less to the greater, and whatever it is that lifts its head or its arm as an obstruction, it is put out of the way, simply because the first, the ascendant seeking, is the seeking of the soul's right character, and eternal interest and destiny. Another thing is, —

He seeks with a resolved and inflexible will. There has been in the preliminary, as we have seen, a canvassing, an estimate, and a decision. He has intelligently erected this as the great end; has planted himself on this basis, and put his eye off yonder upon the eternal; and his living now is to be for that. He has satisfied himself that it ought to be, and has resolved it shall be for that. It is the position, the fixture, of an inflexible soul. If it is not, if he is half decided and half in doubt, — perhaps, to-day strong in his purpose, to-morrow shaking, hesitating in his place, the next day, not there, but somewhere else, — he is not the man I am trying to put before you, and commend to your imitation. The resolved and inflexible will, firm as adamant, stiff as steel, is indispensable to this character and style of seeking. In that case the desires and affections of the heart are toward it; and the judgments of the reason, the decisions of the will, and the persistent strivings of the whole man are for the gaining of it. So much for the mode, as involved in the terse phrase, *Seek ye first the kingdom of God.*

The considerations which make it reasonable and proper to seek this kingdom and righteousness, after this mode, may be soon stated. Indeed, they have already been implied. The chief reason lies here; namely, in the fact, that the estimate we have spoken of, which places religion in a supremacy of importance, is a true estimate. It is so. I cannot formally argue the matter, because too plain for argument. Written here within, as our soul's intuition, men feel the handwriting, the engraved truth on the living tablets, that they are in fault, that there is disorder, derangement within; that sinning has brought them into great difficulty and peril; that they have a great preparation to make, a solemn account to settle with their Maker. Now that is the thing ye are to seek first, that something which puts all right with you; the germ within, pregnant and deathless, of right character, that righteousness which will give you a kingly seat hard by the radiance of the ineffable throne, to shine with the lustre of that heavenly shining. It is the best, the highest in worth, the richest in the true wealth, infinitely above and beyond any thing the world has to offer.

Furthermore, this religion of Christ, this principle of life in the soul, is not only the highest good in itself considered: there is this idea also, that all subordinate good comes in the train of this. *Seek first the kingdom of God, and his righteousness; and all these things* — all the necessary things of life — *shall be added unto you.* The point is, secure the supreme good, then all other real good will come as a consequence to this. The possession of this places in your hand God's certificate, the written promise and bond of his hand, that you shall have all the other; that all worthy good, just so far as, in the divine judgment, it will prove a good to you, shall follow the chief and great possession. There is to be industry, providence. There may be sometimes want even, where the recumbent on straw lies there with his roll, and on it is written, heir of all things; seemingly very destitute, dependent on charity, when, in a little, the weary feet shall stand on the golden pavement, and the pauper soul range as proprietor of heavenly magnificence. There are some dark spots and some dark days, now and then mysterious conflictings between the severity of God's dealings and the breadth of the promise made unto his own. But let there be faith. Let God be trusted while he works: his compass of wisdom and resource is very great. It will come out according to the promise. Indeed, so far as the darkness lifts, we see it so coming out; *all these things shall be added unto you.*

The supreme good, the life of God in the soul, his kingdom and righteousness made yours, so that you are a son and heir of his, all that is truly desirable or profitable to you, in the things, comforts, possessions of this present world, shall come to you. How absolutely conclusive and clenching the argument that this is the true way of seeking; the possession of the primal, the greater, makes sure the possession of the rest. Thus grand and sure is the march of this divine process. Allow me now to recapitulate and consummate it. Religion in the heart, Christ's kingdom and righteousness, is the all in all. No soul that is enlightened but knows it to be so. This gained, every thing is gained. Well, then, what next? When? The time, the manner? How seek it? First, the very next thing you do; thoroughly, even to the end, allowing no faltering, no hesitating, nor backing down; life or death; through life, on to death's blighting touch. And the reason for this is, it is so great a matter; and possession will be so glorious, and defeat so disastrous. This, the reason for this style and tone of seeking. It is that the objects demand such seeking. It is that this spirit and mode of seeking will be followed with success. It is a principle God has laid down, and I suppose he will never depart from it, that if we would do our great work, if we would get these souls of ours through their mighty exigency, with the favoring aid of God's Spirit, we must proceed according to the ordering of his promise. But I will leave the reasons in favor of this order and spirit of seeking, and come to a few practical uses of the subject.

1. And, first, let me say, the subject has a voice of instruction and appeal for the Christian. Your work is not finished on becoming a Christian. It is only begun. The consecration of your soul, coming with that to the cross, and laying it there, was the first introductory stroke of service done for Christ. Your Master's interest is now your object. Seek first the growth, the progress of his kingdom. This your end of life. Be it yours; and let every thing you do have this end; all desires, solicitudes, enterprises, terminate here. This thing I am about to do, how will it affect the kingdom of God? These gains reached after, they are first for the kingdom of God. Gold has its more than golden preciousness in its power to help on the kingdom of God. This everywhere uppermost in your heart; this the great bent of your soul, the marked trait in your character, everywhere a studying and an acting for the kingdom of God. Let it be so with any Christian: there is an efficacy in that character the world will feel; an integrity and consistency in it even wicked men will honor. Let it be so with the church generally, and all her depressing and defiling sordidness will be done away, and her clogs thrown off, and her bright shining blaze out, and her achieving triumphs signally open. The kingdom and the righteousness, this is first with the Christian. If not, then there is no Christian there. If first for yourself, then you will seek it for your children. Make it appear

all through your plans that you have no wish they should figure in the world, be great or rich or honorable; but that the burden of desire all presses at this point, that they may be good. No matter what else, if only Christians, with hearts to do Christian work. No matter where they labor, or how much they suffer, or how obscurely they die; it is enough if they did, faithfully, Christian work; and died, peacefully, the Christian death. That parent is infinitely satisfied; is ready for the final prayer, *Now lettest thou thy servant depart in peace, for mine eyes have seen thy salvation.*

2. I remark, once more, that Christ's great principle, or law of human enterprise as announced in the text, comes with a tone of reproof to the engrossed worldling. It reproves him for the bold daring found in his procedure, fetching clean about the divinely authorized schedule of affairs, putting that last which God puts first; and this, most evidently, done without reason, done in violent counteraction of reason. What else is this than blind and passionate audacity? It is something deeper and deadlier than this; proof undeniable of a monstrous, yea, a despotic depravity; despotic for its power of degrading and crushing, bringing what is truly great and noble to do beneath a menial work in servile chains. We do find here the marks of a violent depravity in this inverted order of things. Your souls, as God made them, are deathless and great; made with capacities for the infinite and eternal; capacities which reach upward and outward, and which time and the world can never fill. You cannot satisfy them here. You know you cannot. So far as you have made trial, you have failed; and all have failed who have tried. All experience and all testimony

come, in emphatic harmony, to this point; God's and man's, that of the living and the dead, all agree. And yet you go right in for this: by your conduct saying, This first; the freshness of my youth on this; the fountain and vigor of my manhood on this; the feculence of my age, God, and the things of God, may have that; my dried heart and shaking bones, God and his kingdom may have those. It is not the insult virtually offered; that is not the worst of it. It is the violence, the mortal injury done to the nobler powers. It is that, with the greatness God made you with, you will not go first, foremost, for the greatness he made you for; first, and all through, for that greatness of possession which so sublimely answers to this greatness of capacity.

Let me touch, in closing, upon the practicableness of putting this matter as it should be. The reasonableness, we have seen, shines as the cloudless noon. The practicableness is just as clear. It is to do the bidding of reason, and just put the great thing first: God's first, put it your first. Put it thus, intelligently, decisively, resolvedly, and rivet it there. Inasmuch as it is first, say it shall be first. Young man, say you this. All ye in the opening of life, the same. I know what your reason says, and what your conscience says; but your will, your soul's executive purpose, does this say first?

Would that some among us might be moved thus to say, writing it deep and clear, where nothing shall ever bury or blot it, First, *the kingdom of God.* Yes, henceforth I will. Though I go long without light or cheer; no matter; it is fixed, this first. Companions may taunt, the world may frown: I care not; it is written, this first. My friends, you see I have got your duty all into a word. That word: will you do it? If you will, you are made for two worlds. That word is the gem in a passage which together makes a clustering and weighty treasure, and leads the soul into possession of all the weightier treasures of God and eternity. Follow it. Do it. The pith and gist of all do not forget. Now, on to the end, for ever, with the whole gathered and expended powers of my being, FIRST, *the kingdom of God, and his righteousness.*

# XXII.

## CHRIST'S BODILY AND SPIRITUAL HEALINGS.

*And again he entered into Capernaum after some days; and it was noised that he was in the house. And straightway many were gathered together, insomuch that there was no room to receive them, no, not so much as about the door: and he preached the word unto them. And they come unto him, bringing one sick of the palsy, which was borne of four. And when they could not come nigh unto him for the press, they uncovered the roof where he was: and when they had broken it up, they let down the bed wherein the sick of the palsy lay. When Jesus saw their faith, he said unto the sick of the palsy, Son, thy sins be forgiven thee. But there were certain of the scribes sitting there, and reasoning in their hearts, Why doth this man thus speak blasphemies? Who can forgive sins but God only? And immediately, when Jesus perceived in his spirit that they so reasoned within themselves, he said unto them, Why reason ye these things in your hearts? Whether is it easier to say to the sick of the palsy, Thy sins be forgiven thee: or to say, Arise, and take up thy bed, and walk? But that ye may know that the Son of man hath power on earth to forgive sins (he saith to the sick of the palsy), I say unto thee, Arise, and take up thy bed, and go thy way into thine house. And immediately he arose, took up the bed, and went forth before them all; insomuch that they were all amazed, and glorified God, saying, We never saw it on this fashion.* — MARK ii. 1–12.

MARK, in his gospel, makes a selection from the miracles of our Lord; his object being to illustrate the two great functions of his prophetic office,— his teaching and his miracles. And he, in part, chooses those that gave rise to some of his pregnant occasions of teaching. Christ was evidently engaged in the work of teaching when the palsied man was thrust before him, to engage the interposition of his healing power. We have here an instance of the wonderful effect of his miraculous healings in drawing the crowd together. Such was the fame that attached to him from his words and deeds in Galilee, that, so soon as it was known he was in a certain house in Capernaum, immediately a great throng pressed, and those not able to enter stood without, and the Lord preached the word unto them. Here occurred the miracle of healing the man sick of palsy. Mark, probably, selected this and drew it out in such detail, inasmuch as it furnished the occasion of the first hostile manifestation toward Christ. Here we hear the first mutter of that enmity which grew by feeding on his goodness, taking to itself new and sharper exasperations from every new deed of mercy, till, at length, it satiated its greed of hate in his death and blood. The subject of this healing was a man made helpless by palsy, probably, suffering in his body from the disease; and also, doubtless, suffering a keener anguish in his mind; his disease, as it is conjectured, having been caused by sinful excesses, it so stirred within him the sense of guilt, that he felt it to be in punishment for his sins. Be this as it may, the disease of his body and the disease of his soul seem to have been closely connected, so that each re-acted upon and aggravated the other.

*He was borne of four.* But the diseased and helpless man, we think, was the most earnest of the four to find or force a way to Jesus. It was he that begged of them to persist; very likely that devised the plan of breaking a passage through the roof. It was his twofold anguish, the torment without, and the far more fearful within, at the very core and life of his soul, that urged him on. His faith, too, urged him on; and he urged them on. It is said that the four had faith; for *Jesus saw their faith.* He, too, we must think, had faith in the Lord's ability to relieve him of his trouble. The Lord, in his power of insight, penetrating to the man's inmost soul, seeing the primal and deeper trouble there, and the strong desire for relief, and the silent and pleading faith, began, in his process of cure, with his soul; knowing that no cure could satisfy him that was only external, giving life to the dead and withered muscles, leaving dead, unforgiven, unrelieved, the burdened, anguished spirit. Hence the Lord's abrupt and profounder utterance, even before he or they had spoken: *Son, thy sins be forgiven thee.* This word, which brought relief and cheer to that suffering spirit, operated to quicken the cavilling malice of certain religionists in attendance. No satisfaction to them that one had come, purporting to lift some of the ills so heavy upon our sinning race; such sticklers were they for the honor of God; so jealous of any encroachment upon the divine prerogatives; but really and only jealous lest the rising prophet of Galilee should overshadow them, seated and fattening, as they were, in their prescriptive place.

These scribes silently brooded their grave accusings. But these their injurious thoughts were assailing words in the Lord's ear. And he turned at once upon them in a track of reasoning which summarily confounded, and, as antagonists, annihilated them. Their suppressed charge was that he was guilty of blasphemy, because he assumed the right or power to forgive sins, which belonged only to God. In that they were right, that it belongs only to God. In the charge that Christ wrongfully assumed this, and was guilty of the crime of arrogating to himself God's prerogative, they were in fault. His argument, of overthrow to them and of vindication to himself, was a word and a work. In this argument of our Lord, he does not ask which is easier, namely, to forgive sins, or instantly to cure a man of the palsy; but, which is the *easier to say, Thy sins be forgiven thee; or to say, Arise, and take up thy bed, and walk?* Certainly the former: to say, *Thy sins be forgiven thee;* for if the words do not produce the result, the failure would not appear; the impostor might go unexposed. But to say to a palsied man, *Arise, and take up thy bed, and walk,* — if his words do not reach and vivify the flaccid muscles, and set coursing afresh the stagnant currents of life, then the pretender's falseness and impotence are patent to everybody. The fact that a restoring, and even a re-creating, power went with Jesus' words, proved to all that he had power to forgive sins, and also to waken the soul dead in sin to a new spiritual life. Christ virtually says in this, By doing that which is capable of being put to the proof,

I vindicate my right and power to do that which is incapable of being proved. *That ye may know that the Son of man hath power on earth to forgive sins (he saith to the sick of the palsy), I say unto thee, Arise, and take up thy bed, and go thy way into thine house. And immediately he arose, took up the bed, and went forth before them all;* went through the before densely packed throng. This man, who could not get through this mass-gathering when on his way to Christ, but had to approach him by stealth and violence, now, the cure, the redemption being wrought upon him, finds the same crowd ready to open and let him forth; and he walks through them in a sort of triumph, amid the acclaim of voices, ascribing glory to God, and saying, *We never saw it on this fashion;* whilst these whipped and sanctimonious trappers doubtless sneaked away in the shame of their defeat, and in the deeper infamy of their utterly craven spirit and purpose. And then there stood forth from this instance of healing, demonstrated by it to the faith and even the senses of people, the glorious doctrine, that there is forgiveness with God, and Christ, as God, has power to forgive sins. The ground of forgiveness, the sufferings of the mysterious Victim by which the forgiveness was made possible, is here not at all touched; only the fact is given, that Jesus has power to forgive sins.

Most intimate, in this instance, find we the connection between our Lord's work of bodily healing and his greater and ultimate work of spiritual healing, of forgiving and redeeming souls. It is very obvious here to state, that the connection or relation between the two is that of an analogy; and most striking, instructive, encouraging, inspiriting even, are these analogies. This, doubtless, was one main intent of our Lord in these manifold cases and diversities of healing, to impress upon the minds of the people at once the great doctrine, and also the subordinate processes, of redemption through Jesus Christ.

My object in what remains is to suggest some lessons that come to us from the analogy of certain diseases, and from the fact and process of their cure; lessons which bear on the fact and cure of our great spiritual disease. The first lesson suggested is, —

1. That the main thing now wanting is, that the people everywhere be made sensible that they are spiritually diseased. This must be if the people, to any extent, are to be saved. It was a grand maxim our Lord uttered, on one of his healing occasions, *They that be whole need not a physician, but they that are sick.* The people then crowded upon him as they did, because they knew that they were sick. They could not help knowing it, when the evidence that pierced and distressed them so was in every nerve and fibre a ceaseless throb of agony. Hence, in the pressure of the literal malady, they sought out the physician. They could not stay at home; were carried to him, if they could not go. But, though a physician still of undiminished efficacy, the people now, except here and there one, do not repair to him. They are sick, mortal disease is working in them; but they do not know it, have no sense of it; and the most terrible and fatal feature of their case is, that they do not admit it, that they will not come to the light, where their deeds shall be reproved. And we fear they never will, many of them. Indeed, we know they never will, till the Holy

Spirit comes down and fills their souls with the convictive light and influence. To-day, my brethren, this is our great necessity, the presence of the convictive Spirit; this the great duty of Christians, to bring down the Holy Spirit by the strength and persistence of their praying.

2. We learn from the analogies of our subject, not only that men are diseased, but also the fearful depth, the type and tenacious hold, of this disease of sin in the human soul. The outer or bodily diseases, those our Lord dealt with when he moved amongst men, seem to have been chosen by him as symbols or descriptives of the inner and spiritual. For example, the blind, even those born thus, came to Jesus and were healed. Here the counterpart of one of sin's terrible qualities or powers, — that of blinding the soul, and making men choose the darkness, and love to live and even riot in the darkness, and refuse to come to the light, *lest their deeds should be reproved*. Another example was the palsy. In this we have set forth to us the impotence of death itself diffused all through the body. This, the symbol of the soul's utter weakness and dependence on God. Another and repeated case in the Lord's healings was that of the leper. This, so to speak, a religious disease, a singularly symbolic disease, visibly representing more of the real properties of sin than any other, was singled out as a type to the Jew of the shocking direfulness of sin; that it might ever be before their eyes how loathsome sin is; how contagious it is; touching it is taking it; and taking it is having it for ever, unless God interpose and help. The leper, he was put apart, in gloom and hopelessness, to be and to suffer, as a sign of corrup-

tion and certain death. The brooding despair of the leper from his immemorial exclusion comes out in the faltering speech of that first one who ventured upon Christ, *Lord, if thou wilt, thou canst.* The man doubted if he would. No other being would. Even the civilities and the humanities of religion were all against him. No wonder his mind drooped, even before the compassionate Jesus, where all others had found help. And oh, how that recognizing word must have permeated and thrilled him when Jesus said, *I will.* And not only the word, but the touch was added. Though against the law, he touched him, and the separating wall fell; and the disease, the most vivid, the sacramental type of all woe and sin, instantly left him.

Still another of the typifying cases of suffering was the demoniac. These cases are given in order to set forth the madness of sin. So the divine word says of the sinner, *Madness is in their heart while they live, and after that they go to the dead.* The Lord of all, in constructing this symbol, in making a fit and adequate representation of the madness of sin, availed himself of help from hell itself; made use of spirits from beneath, who were acting through the organisms of this manhood. We read the inspired descriptions of these wretched men, and in this we see a type of the madness of sin. How dreadful the case, as we behold it in that wild man of Gadara, who took up his abode in the tombs, there to live with the dead, and stretch his tortured frame on ghastly bones and skeletons. In the paroxysms of his huge woe, he tore apart the massive fetters as though mere flaxen strings, and then ranged abroad in a horrid freedom, uttering shrieks and yells, that reverberated among the mountains and echoed over the sea, so that no one dared pass that way; thus infuriate was he with the demons and the hell within, and bloody all over with the gashing stones. There was no extravagance in this symbol the Lord raised up and put forth. All was done to teach men everywhere the madness of their sin. We behold, and cry, Oh, the madness of sin. For all this there is a cure. So our blessed Lord demonstrated by his actual and oft-repeated curing; curing, as he did, every malignant type and form of sin. The power is his. But there is a responsibility upon all who would draw that power to their own help and redemption.

3. This is another of the unquestioned teachings of our subject; namely, that those who would have part in this soul-healing, be saved themselves, must also take part in the process by which the Lord reaches the benign result. In almost every instance, the Lord required faith, on the part of the sufferer, as the condition of his recovering power. *Believe ye that I am able to do this?* How reasonable, when we bring our ruined souls to him, that we believe him able to wash out the stain and break the chain. If we go to Jesus aright, it is with two ruling ideas: First, I know I cannot, second, I am sure he can, do it all; and do it, if he chooses to do, without any intervening or subsidiary duties. Yet this is not his way. He said, rather, *Stretch forth thine hand. Take up thy bed, and walk.* Wear, for the time, this plaster of clay. *Go, wash in the pool of Siloam.* The moment the sufferer did these things prescribed, Christ did the rest. If any applicant had not done the prescribed thing, Christ, on his part, would have wrought no relief.

Christ, in the soul's cure, now says, Adjust your quarrel with that neighbor or friend. Set right that defrauding act. Go, sell that idol, property. Relax the sordid grasp. Go, enter into thy closet. Bow in audible prayer, in humble confession. How many things to be done crowd upon the sinner. If at all awakened, how hard they press. And whatever this word of God, or God's word within, enjoins to do, though it may seem a trivial thing, a mere outward matter, still, let him do that thing; not say, It can be done only after I am converted: I will wait till I am converted, then do it. No, not so. It is a thing on the way to be converted; a thing often of the very article and instance of conversion; the very pivot on which every thing in conversion turns. Doing the outward duty because Christ enjoins it, and because you have a waking confidence in him, is the receiving from him a heart to do the whole. This, the outward, done, the light breaks; this done, the chain parts; this done, the heart melts; this done, the soul's joy and praise leap forth.

4. I remark again, that we learn from these outer cures of the Lord somewhat of the true tone and spirit of application when we apply to Jesus for the spiritual cure. When these sick and crushed ones came, or when friends came and asked for them, it was with a wonderful brevity of praying; the intenseness at the heart compelling the briefness at the lips. That mother, it was a single word by which she relieved her heart at its point of breaking: Lord, help me, oh, help me. That father, it was by a single sentence he conquered: *Lord, I believe; help thou mine unbelief.* The great want they came with was, as it

were, hove rudely right into the face of the blessed Master. This I want, that I may receive my sight. *Lord, if thou canst*, do it, oh, do it. By this heart and style of praying, they brought the Infinite under, brought all his love and power into subserviency to their welfare.

And have not we an errand there? These souls are sick, are dead in sin; and he, the all-sufficient Saviour; and life is fleeting; the present, the only opportunity; soon, soon it must be done, or all is lost; now the accepted time, the day of salvation. And have we not, too, all this history to encourage us? These great promises given; these mighty works of his, done to put strength into our faith; that divine heart, once pierced for us; that tenderness, and that quickness to heal, shown through all the earthly path he trod; those boundless riches and efficacies of grace and of life, all free, — we have the whole, simply by asking. Here, now, we are; and that Christ is here. Is he not here? The sinners, are they here? Your sin, is it upon you? Do you feel it? And are you ready to confess it, and to go to him that he may help you? Go; go, friend; and let your heart say, as you go, —

"Just as I am, without one plea,
But that thy blood was shed for me,
And that thou bidst me come to thee,
O Lamb of God, I come."

# XXIII.

## HELP THOU MINE UNBELIEF.

*And straightway the father of the child cried out, and said with tears, Lord, I believe; help thou mine unbelief.*—Mark ix. 24.

THESE are the words of a father who brought his son to Christ, that he might be delivered from a sore visitation. The son was a great sufferer, and the parent was greatly afflicted. He presents to Jesus a strong case. He pleads with great earnestness: *If thou canst do any thing, have compassion.* The Saviour's reply was, *If thou canst believe,* I can do. Then came the words of the text, they came with tears: *Lord, I believe; help thou mine unbelief;* and they have struck a responsive chord in unnumbered hearts since. No form of words, perhaps, has been so frequently adopted by those who have come in sincere prayer to Christ as these: *Lord I believe*; *help thou mine unbelief.*

I shall take the words out of tho particular connection in which they occur, and consider them in their general application and use. So considered, the following points may be regarded as involved: —

First, A true faith. Second, An imperfect faith. Third, The deep feeling that it was an imperfect faith. Fourth, The feeling of the imperfection, as conducive to the success of the application.

I. What is a true faith, or the faith that is made the condition of the soul's acceptance? Faith is one simple, intelligible thing or exercise. If presented as a single, simple exercise, it may be understood; it can hardly fail to be understood. Sometimes we resort to a complexity in our description, which may lead to some perplexity in the apprehensions of our hearers; as when we split faith minutely into various kinds, such as speculative faith, historic faith, evangelical faith, the latter only true saving faith. The confusion arises just here, that while there may be an intellectual faith, or an historic faith, which is not saving, there cannot be a saving faith, which is not both intellectual and historical. Saving faith is all the rest. It takes in all the kinds and varieties of faith. You have true faith, we will suppose, that which will save your soul. When the proposition, and the evidence thereof, that *God created the heaven and the earth*, or, that he overthrew the Egyptians in the Red Sea, comes before your mind, you believe those historic statements; and your belief is based on your confidence in the divine testimony. That God overthrew Babylon requires only an intellectual assent. The proposition that he is the Supreme God, over all, God blessed for ever, demands of you, as a moral being, something more than the assent of the intellect. To believe that proposition is to believe in God. If the faith in God is genuine, it is attended and followed with reverence, submission, love, obedience. If Christ be the object of faith, and the faith is genuine, it regards him as a Saviour; it defines and grasps the whole doctrine and mode of saving through Christ. It is attended and followed with trust in that person and in the mode of saving by him; and there is the yielding up of the soul to be saved in that way, desiring no other; and there is not only the trust, but the love of the soul, and the obedience of the life. The faith in that object calls for these, and they are given; and they become the fruit and evidence of the faith.

We may go on and make the entire circle of the objects of religious faith, and we shall find that genuine faith is a perfect unity and simplicity, embracing more or less, according to the demands of the object of it; the object now demanding a mere and an easy intellectual assent; again, demanding a difficult and profound submission of the intellect; still again, demanding the heart's full affection; but, all through, the same principle may be operating, a true faith. I have gone into this sort of description of faith, as preparatory to the next statement.

II. That there may be a true faith with defects. And my aim here is, not so much to show the fact of defect, as the character of the defects. That there may be, yea, must be, defects in this particular, no one having any knowledge or experience in human infirmity will be disposed to question. And the character of the defects, the parts in which they may or do inhere, is equally plain. The defect may be in the intellectual apprehension, or in the knowledge which is the basis of that apprehension. Suppose the object of the faith to be Christ as a Saviour, the Saviour of my soul. Christ the Being who is to do that great work for me, if it ever be done, I may be measurably ignorant of; for the case in the text does not admit of wilfulness. I do not know, do not apprehend fully, the attributes of greatness and of power which reside in the person of that Deliverer. My intellectual apprehension does not bring him up in competency for the work I hope for, at his hands. Or the faith may be defective, not at the point of the Deliverer's ability, but of his benevolence, his willingness to save; a defect in not taking hold of him as one who, having the power, has also the heart to do, and who will do, the needed thing. Here we strike a defect which pertains to the heart, the feelings, the affections. There is not the confidence, the trust, the reliance, there should be. Sometimes the feelings are dull, because the intellectual perception is very dim. They must be so, in such a case. If I come to Christ for help, and do not clearly perceive his ability to help me, my faith cannot be very lively; the emotional part cannot be very vivid, or fruitfully expectant. So, too, the head may be clear in its perception of the object, whilst the heart fails to grasp, to lay hold of, the object. The affections, the feelings of desire, confidence, trust, are in this case wanting: the defect is very often in this part.

The objects of faith may be invisible realities, the things of the soul and eternity; all clear, grand, overshadowing, to the mind's view; but the heart's interest lags behind. The head says, the spiritual, the eternal interest ought to be first and uppermost; but the heart suffers the world to be in the lead. Having shown, thus far, that there may be a true faith, and yet a defect of faith, the next statement is, —

III. That in all cases of genuine faith, the defects of the faith, so far as they exist or are discovered, will be matters of quick acknowledgment, and of deep and humble feeling. This is only the statement of a specific truth, which comes under the general principle, that the instant any thing truly good, right, holy, is introduced into the character by the grace of God, all that is wrong in that character becomes visible and painful in its wrongness, as it was not before. Before, all was dark and all was hidden; the leprous skin then passed for fair as any. But the moment the light of truth and grace was introduced, the odious taint appeared. All that was foul stood hatefully forth. On this principle, the moment the gleam of faith enters the soul, the darkness and the baseness of unbelief glooms forth. Hence it follows that, just so soon as one has faith, he feels and laments the presence or the prevalence of the opposite quality, that there is so much of unbelief in him; so unreasonable is it, and so obstructing to all the purposes and achievements of the Christian life. Especially does he feel the defects, the imperfection, and feebleness of his faith, when the greatness of the objects of his faith, and the interests affected by the prayer of his faith, come clearly before his mind. So was it with the father who brought his suffering son to Christ. The case of dreadful distortion and agony, in the person of his son, was right before this father's eyes; the demoniac spirits waked to new wrenching and violence, as though they knew the Deliverer was by, and their time was short. It was the mighty urgency of the case, pressing on this father's heart the importance of the request he came to Christ to make, at the moment, all-important to him, that his son have help,— this it was, that drove him to that form of prayer: *If thou canst do any thing*, Oh, do it; help, help us. This, too, it was, which made him feel the inadequacy of his faith. So poorly did it compare with the great object of his heart, he seemed to fear to trust it, and fell back upon the defect; the defect which stared upon him. While his great necessity crowded upon him, his faith seemed as nothing in the exigency, so faint as to seem unbelief; hence that peculiar, persuasive cry, *Lord, I believe; help thou mine unbelief.*

When we pass into the region of still vaster objects and higher interests, where it is not the life of the body, but of the soul, — the soul, its eternal state, as affected by our measure of faith, and the prayer of our faith; when the Christian is favored with a glimpse into this realm of greatness, all objects and interests there partaking, as they do, of a species of infinity, soon to be won, or to be lost, by each and by all, and then turns and considers how meagre the faith where faith is so influential; especially himself, how little moved by the faith which takes hold of such things, — then, if ever, does he feel the cardinal defect; and fears, lest with him it prove all defect and pretence. His own soul, perhaps, suddenly called to go into eternity now trembles on the border, the mighty issue hanging in doubt and just ready to be determined. Only faith can save it. Is there any true faith there; enough there to save it? He falters before that question; he feels the fearful defect in that comparison; and he fortifies the doubtful case by retreating, and seeking refuge in the lowly cry, *Lord, I believe; help thou mine unbelief.*

IV. I am now prepared to show — indeed, I have somewhat anticipated the argument — how it is, that the realized deficiency of the faith stands related to the success of the prayer. Allow me a measure of re-statement, that I may exhibit together the parts of the brief and very simple process.

1. First, it brings the soul into that state and posture which is the fundamental condition of prayer, — humility, deep penitence, utter self-renunciation. With these we may come to God, if we have nothing else. We may have every thing else: if we have not these, our coming to God will be utterly vain and nugatory. The Bible everywhere assures us, in all its principles and precepts and precedents, that this is the one condition he never dispenses with; and this ever the eloquent and prevailing condition; wherever found, there, too, is found God's gracious bestowment. Very natural that it should be so; altogether proper in my coming to God for the faith, the pardon, the righteousness, that I come as one utterly needy, wholly wanting these things; these things to be and to be received as whole gifts at his hand; my very faith, before that standard, to pass into the category of unbelief; and my soul is most heartily willing to have it so, and puts in, with parenthetic adroitness, wherever it can, its plea, *Lord, help thou mine unbelief.*

2. The second condition realized in the sincere offering of the form in the text is, that the soul is brought to place its whole confidence in God. This, further, accounts for the success of the approach. I suppose that all self-confidence, self-reliance, is peculiarly offensive to God. Nothing more often vitiates our doings and thwarts our success; and we do not know that the mischief is lurking and working, so sly, insidious is it. And in order to this, that it may suc-

ceed through insidiousness, it seizes upon something good, something required, some Christian grace, and turns that divinely begotten beauty into an ugly and sore offence. It may be faith: for can the Christian be any thing or do any thing without faith? Can he please God without it? Certainly not. And yet his faith may be the very ground and instrument of his displeasing God. Faith, the great condition of blessings, may be the peremptory shutter-out of blessings from his soul or his family or his friends. Ask you how? Why, he is pleased with his faith. It is so strong and has served him, heretofore, so well; he has so prevailed with God in the exercise of it, that he has insensibly slid into trusting in his faith. Then it is powerless, it is nothing worth. How much better, I was going to say, if he had none at all. Certainly better, if it seemed to him that he had none, because he had so little, and that little so overshadowed and pervaded by the far greater presence and measure of the unbelief; then, as he comes to the throne, all the self-complacency and self-reliance would be abolished, and the whole confidence of the soul would terminate on God, and the whole energy of the soul be gathered and poured forth in the prayer, *Lord, I believe; help thou mine unbelief.*

3. This prepares us to see, thirdly, how another cardinal condition is secured by the state of mind which dictates the form in the text, namely, earnestness. These three things will foster the intensest earnestness in the soul's approach to God: the greatness of the object or interest pending; the fact perceived that the power, the help, is in God; the fact felt by the soul, that there is nothing in itself to be

relied on. If, now, the issue is so amazing; if it is all of God; if my faith is hardly worth the name, so kindred to and clogged by the opposite is it, — can it be otherwise than that my cry to that only Helper should, to the last degree, be importunate; at times, deeply impassioned? The thought I may fail, where failure would be the loss of the infinite; the perception that there is so little reason for or ground of success, here at home, yea, all here within and all in the past discouraging success; yet success may be, for God is able and God is good, is ever ready, and it is wholly with God, — there can be but one way for a soul so circumstanced and so imbued to act; namely, to rise up, with humility, indeed, but with all the resoluteness which humility and faith and the felt want of faith can inspire, and plead and persist, and so take the mighty boon at the hand of God, *Lord, I believe; help thou mine unbelief.*

In view of this subject, I remark, —

1. That the spirit of these words constitutes a good sign in the attitude and experience of a soul in view of its relations to God and immortality. And the hopeful indication lies in the admirable and touching humility they breathe. The great and notable of this world have often and significantly taken to this self-renouncing formula. Mr. Webster, in his heart's inclining to these words, directed them to be engraved on his tombstone, as the symbol of his soul's judgment and confidence. John Randolph, long a reputed atheist, and, afterward, as he hoped, a Christian, found in these words that form and argument of prayer by which, possibly, he prevailed. "It pleased God," he said, "that, after lengths of impiety, my pride

should be mortified; that by death and desertion I should lose my friends, till there should not run, except in the veins of a maniac, one drop of my father's blood in any living creature but myself. I tried all things but the refuge in Christ, and to that, with scourging stripes, was I driven; and I came with the wretched father's cry for his son, often repeating it, *Lord, I believe; help thou mine unbelief.*" "And," he adds, "the Lord's gracious mercy to this wavering faith, staggering under the force of the hard heart of unbelief, I humbly hoped, would be extended to me also."

2. I remark again, how wonderful the touching paradox that sin itself may be turned into the soul's aid and argument in getting delivered from the hateful dominion of sin. Most encouraging the thought, to such as we, that imperfection does not bar our approach to the infinitely Perfect One; that the clogging obstructions of our souls may be turned into lifting helps; that the unbeliefs, often so embarrassing, may be framed into the successive rounds of the ladder by which the soul, in its wrestling prayer, climbs still nearer to the gracious throne. We are only to view these things as God does, as wrong and base and vile, and put them low and put ourselves low on account of them. Thus will they aid us upward; rather, they bring the Deliverer down where we are; and, as sure as he comes, and finds us in our place, he will take us to his own, and make us his own, and we shall see him in his glory.

3. Another remark is, that not only do these words crowd with all blessed encouragements, they also strike away the obstructing excuses; particularly, this

ever present one, that we cannot come aright. It takes this away, by telling you to come as you are. If you cannot believe, or think you cannot, come, and ground your argument before God on that. If you cannot confess your sin, come and confess to God that you cannot confess. Tell him, with dry, rigid bitterness of spirit, that you cannot; that the rock within you will not relent; and ask him to smite the rock, that some penitential drops may begin to ooze from the flinty centre. If you feel, after all, in your earnest but impotent strugglings for a better state, that it must be useless, inasmuch as the very Prince of Evil is in full possession, and high enthroned within you, come still, for the Being you come to is stronger than he. Ask the blessed Lord to hurl him hence and enter and reign in his place.

> "Drive the old dragon from his seat,
> With all his hellish crew."

I would come, and end my sermon with this, the central and blessed idea of my text; and, Oh that God's Spirit would take and imbed it in the centre of thy soul. It tells you to come feeling your depravity, how strong it is. No matter how strong, if you but feel it and confess it, and beg of God against it, pleading, Help this unbelief, break this rock, bend this iron will, bring low this cursed pride: I have been elsewhere, I have been all about, have been to myself, have been to thy disciples, they cannot do it, nor can I. Blessed Master, I come, at last, to thee. Save thou, or I perish. *Lord, I believe; help thou mine unbelief.*

# XXIV.

## THE UNWRITTEN OF LIFE.

*And there are also many other things which Jesus did, the which, if they should be written every one, I suppose that even the world itself could not contain the books that should be written. Amen.* — JOHN xxi. 25

THIS is the closing sentence in the Gospel by John. Some commentators even of the Evangelical type, among the German school, take ground against this unique closing sentence, though they admit all the rest. The ground of the objection is, not that it is wanting in historic authority, — for it has a place in all, even the earliest, manuscripts, — but that the passage is wholly alien from the spirit of John, who is everywhere characterized by a singular moderation of expression; whereas we have here, it is alleged, the most extravagant hyperbole. We admit that it is hyperbole, — designed so to be taken; and if John was ever to venture upon hyperbole, we should suppose it would be when speaking of the works of his Lord, they so transcended record or utterance. And, further, if this apostle were to attempt hyperbole, we judge that the one in the text is very much what he would be likely to produce; it being marked with his peculiar, childlike simplicity. The expression in the text is intended simply to convey the author's conception of the vast quantity, the inexpressible quantity, of books which must be made, if all the Lord did, when on earth, were written, in all the detail of performance and in all the circumstances of interest.

Taking, now, some liberty of accommodation with the text, and some range into the context, I proceed to make some remarks suggested by the Scripture before us.

1. Perhaps one of the first thoughts or emotions, on reading such a declaration as that contained in the text, is of the nature of regret, that such treasures of truth have been lost; for every act of the Lord was truth embodied, — every utterance of his was laden with instruction and wisdom. If all written, it would have been an entire life, with no indiscretion, no impurity, no selfishness or sin to mar or taint it. It being so, that every act was right, every utterance truth, had it only been all written, then we should have had more truth to strengthen and to guide us. At least, the truths we now have we might have had in more convincing forms, with varying illustrations, and more impressive enforcements. There certainly seems to be ground for regret, that such stores of instruction as we should have had, if that prolific and perfect life had been put more fully on record, have been allowed to perish. But the regret may abate, as we think that we have enough now, to form in our minds the idea of a perfect character, and to convince us that Christ is that character; enough to waken our love, reverence, adoration, toward him; enough for all the purposes of his wonderful mission. The decision to record no more, that Divine discretion which allowed no more to

be recorded, furnishes in this very fact of restriction a proof that more was not needed. If more is needed now, more was needed then. If more was needed then, would not that have been the way to supply it, by drawing from that fountain, by calling back utterances which now have been lost, and placing them where they would teach all the generations, even to the end of time?

2. I wish, in the second place, to remark upon the evidence of a divine hand in these records, furnished by the fact, that the writers so wonderfully, so strangely, abstained as they did; that they kept to such terms of restriction. This is not human, this rigid abstinence when set to record a life of One called Wonderful, and who was wonderful through all his life. The evidence of a divine control appears in the meagre quantity or amount that they attempted, — that they touched so *few* of his works, where all were inviting record; that there should be a world of matter crowding, in which the world would be interested, and yet the most of it left out. It appears, further, in the quality, the style of their record, that the statements made were so moderate, putting forth nothing to excite, in narrating the most exciting scenes, using no superlatives in the language, when dealing with supernal deeds, — concise, calm, reciting marvels which altered the course of nature, in the fewest and simplest words. This severely abstinent manner, when ranging in such a field, is not that which belongs to man. It is proof that a Divine Power directed in this thing.

In the many lives of Christ, written at that early time, under the human impulse, there is quantity, — all kinds and measures are put forth into the light.

These apocryphal doings make a perfect contrast to these books we receive and reverence, as brought out by the inspiration óf the Holy Spirit. The divine regimen under which these last were produced, results in such brevity and paucity of detail, such purity, and consequent sublimity often, that we cannot but be impressed, as with the marks of the unerring hand. Thus the very manner of the Gospels becomes one of the strong proofs of their divine origin.

I have sometimes thought that we might gain some alleviation to our regret—if we ever feel any—that we have no more Scripture, when such materials for Scripture have perished, from this fact gain the alleviation; namely, that the tendency is so strong amongst men to misunderstand, misinterpret, Scripture. What a case have we in illustration of this in the context, where the Saviour, in speaking to Peter concerning John, says, *If I will that he tarry till I come, what is that to thee?* This was the exact word of Christ. The meaning, which was received *and went abroad among the brethren* was, *that that disciple should not die.* A false meaning, even where all were friends. And this meaning was got by departing from the very words the Lord used. He did not say that, but something else; yet they took that he did not say. If this occurred among friends, how much more might we look for it among those not friendly. And how much do we actually find of this perversion in those quarters. Very likely, now, an increase of the record would have opened the door far wider for these pernicious misconstructions. Instead of diminishing them, it would have proportionately increased the opportunity, and still more the quantity, of these perversions. It is doubtless true, that we now have a Bible of the right quantity and quality for all the purposes of instruction and redemption.

3. Another remark obviously suggested is this; namely, the amount, the vast quantity, of action, which pertains to a life, even when that life has not been long. The life of Jesus was but thirty-three years. It is true, doubtless, that his life, by an unequalled activity and productiveness, yielded vastly more to record than the ordinary life; incalculably more worthy of being recorded. Still, we say, if there was such a quantity of action in his life as to justify the strong statement of the Evangelist, that the world itself could not contain the books; then how much must there be in every life which lasts a single generation? We may come to this truth of an incalculable quantity of action and life in another way than by inference. We can hardly fail to be convinced of the truth of measureless quantity if we but look within ourselves, and note the busy and prolific working of these faculties we have, ever active as they are, whether the life be one of industry or of idleness. Let any one trace all his deeds, the important and the most trivial; all his words, the useful and the idle; all the thoughts of his mind, in its intent thinking, and in its spontaneous, its almost unconscious, reverie; all the desires, emotions, passions of his heart, — a sea ever showing its slight or its tumultuous swell; and then annex to all this the quantity of mental action which God sees and marks as voluntary and responsible, but of which the person himself, at the time, took no cognizance; let any one trace all the possible detail of his action and history for a day, and

continue the minute and accumulative noting, till it swells to the totality of a year, and, at length, to that of an ordinary life, and he will be convinced, I think, of a quantity, an amount, past the mind's utmost computation or conception. It is, indeed, a serious, not to say most startling, thought, that there is so much proceeding even from the idlest and the most trivial life, — especially startling when we add this thought or truth, that none of this measureless quantity of mental or moral action will ever perish, — not a deed or word or thought, not the slightest affection or evanescent desire or emotion, will be lost, — not one will fail to come up again, and live in our endless experience of joy or of woe.

4. Let us pass, in our next step, to contemplate that portion of life which the divine appointment affects, and even controls; in other words, let us for a moment consider life, as directed or modified by God's providence. Here is something outside of our will or responsibility, making the life of one very different from that of another. We have an instance in the cases of Peter and John, — both faithful disciples, leading apostles, both alike in this respect, but how diverse their lot in the future, as that wisdom which ordains wisely, even when it ordains mysteriously, marked out the course of each; assigning to Peter troublous scenes and a violent death; to John a long life, a serene and beautiful old age, and a peaceful death amid ministering friends. It is difficult, after all, to say which of these is the most favored, — the one sooner cut off, and honored, when he fell, with the martyr's crown; or the one whose sun remained so long ascendant, and at length went so radiantly and tranquilly down. There

is another fact which presents itself, quite probably, to be a fact in our own case; it is this, that the part of the personal history to transpire may be very different, yea, may mark a sharp contrast, to the part which has transpired. Not only did Peter and John greatly differ in the particular just noted; still further, Peter that had been, and Peter that was to be, shows, in respect to the outward arrangement and conditions of his life, an equally marked difference. *When thou wast young, thou girdedst thyself, and walkedst whither thou wouldest; but when thou shalt be old, thou shalt stretch forth thy hands, and another shall gird thee, and carry thee whither thou wouldest not.* The first part, in a temporal respect, prosperous: the hand of adversity nor of persecution was upon him; young, buoyant, free to range as he pleased, in the service of his Master. In the part that remained, these noble impulses of his soul were to be put, now and then, under a painful restriction; himself to follow the Master literally, and finally to the cross. So is it, very commonly, with life, Christian and not Christian; the part that has been, and the part that is to be, very different: as we would have it, for a while, and then the rest as we would not have it. In one case, the satisfactory portion first, and the reverse to follow; again in directly the other order. It is folly to expect the free and the prosperous, the satisfactory portion, to continue throughout life. If we have commenced our course with that, as Peter did, it is wise to be looking and preparing for another sort. If, in the part that has transpired, prosperity has prevailed, that fact constitutes ground for concluding that something is back and to come of altogether another kind. As we are ever arguing contrasts from God's physical arrangements, warmth soon from the present prevalence of cold, moisture from drought, it might be well and safe to expect the same as resulting in his moral arrangements. If our history has been, in the main, as we would have it, prosperous, satisfactory, our own will and desire gratified, then we may wisely look, in what is to come, for a larger mixture of the opposite sort, such as we would not, something of the Lord's assignment, and right against this will, passion, pride, desire; to all this perverse and refractory element of the soul, the Lord saying, as he did to Peter, *Follow thou me* to the cross. And at length, upon the cross, he nails, by his providence, these refractory qualities, and if thou art not crucified, they are. To most of us, who may have got along rather smoothly up to this point, what remains, very likely, quite certainly, if we are Christians, will partake somewhat largely of the painful, and almost bloody, crucifying work. Thou liver heretofore according to thy mind, thou walker when and where thou wouldest, hear the Master speak to thee; for thus, very likely, he will speak: *Follow me.* And it will be good to do so; though bitter at the time, in the end most blessed to do so. The self-willed Peter, the Peter at large, was the denying Peter. And how his heart bled for it immediately after. The girded and bound and imprisoned Peter was the tested, the loyal Peter, his heart the seat of an imperial joy, such as never filled it before. Thus God can make the later and the shadier half far the brighter and the better half. And he will, in case of all who follow him. It is good, then, to be in his hands, to have him apportion our lot, so wonderfully skilled is he in this; namely, in bringing the most unlikely beginning and untoward progress to the most serene and prosperous conclusion. Will we not trust him, and, when it is dark, perplexing, crossing, still trust him, and make it our joy that he reigns?

*And what shall this man do?* This was Peter's question to Christ, prying into the prospective of John. How shall it go with him? There is a great deal of this inquisition forward, to know, if we can, what is to be in our own case and that of others; to read the history, before the material that is to make it has been lived. How shall it go with us in the year we have just entered? It is easy to make statements on this point which will turn out true, having their verifications somewhere in this gathered assembly. But God only can make the personal application. Still it is true, that prophetic declarings like these will find their fulfilment among you. This year now entered, sudden prosperity shall gild thy prospect. Thou shalt retrieve who hast been helplessly sinking. Thou shalt sink deeper in the waves that are now perplexing thee. Mature disciple, thou shalt lay down thy burdens. Thoughtless one, this year thou shalt die. There are details in the plan of God concerning some of us, this year, that would blanch our cheeks were we made now to know them. They will come in their time and order. Our wisdom is to be ready to meet them, to meet whatever shall come.

The year that is gone, its history, the individual, personal history, the acts, thoughts, affections of thy single isolated soul, go by thyself apart, and call it up; the quantity you cannot, the quality you can: in some of the more pregnant and decisive parts you can. And what are they? their moral hue, what? The lines they stamped into your soul, what? And as you meet them in that coming scene, your emotions then, think you, what?

No other year, probably, should you enact the history of a score more, not one to come so important, so influential upon your final state, as the one just ended. In potency of influence, the years grow less as we grow old, except as we do that one work which changes all the rest, reverses all the wrong in the past, and brightens all that is to come; namely, the work of believing on the crucified Son of God. I lift this up, on this new year, as the great work and aim of life. If you have not done it, may God help you to do it. May you summon all within, and lift yourself up with an unalterable purpose; ask help of God to do it, to believe on the Lord Jesus, and make him your friend; to make yourself over to be wholly his; and the blessedness to your soul, as it shall begin here, and swell there, and flow on for ever, no tongue can tell. And it will, doubtless, seem to you, in some remote period, if the whole volume and compass of it should be put into expression, that the world itself would not contain the books it will require to express your joy.

## XXV.

### THE END AT HAND.

*But the end of all things is at hand: be ye therefore sober, and watch unto prayer.* — 1 PET. iv. 7.

THE same apostle says, in another connection, *But the day of the Lord will come as a thief in the night.* There are announcements very similar to the above scattered throughout the New Testament. Paul, writing to the Philippians, exhorts, *Let your moderation be known unto all men. The Lord is at hand.* Writing to Christians at Rome, he says, *The night is far spent, the day is at hand.* James, in his Epistle, says, *Be ye also patient; stablish your hearts: for the coming of the Lord draweth nigh.* In the next verse, he says, *Behold the Judge standeth before the door.* In the Revelation it is written, *He which testifieth these things saith, Surely I come quickly: Amen. Even so, come, Lord Jesus.*

The question here arises, Are these declarations true in the sense which the writers entertained when they penned them? Or are we to suppose that they were permitted to cherish the error — an innocent one, some may think — that the coming of Christ to judgment was literally at hand? Let it be observed, that Paul occasionally uses language of the above import. *The Lord is at hand.* These things *are written for our admonition, upon whom the ends of the world are come.* He seems to speak of the resurrection as an event to occur in his own time. *For the Lord himself shall descend from heaven with a shout, with the voice of the archangel, and with the trump of God: and the dead in Christ shall rise first; then we which are alive and remain shall be caught up together with them in the clouds, to meet the Lord in the air.* This, and other language of the apostle, appears to have been interpreted and understood by many to declare the speedy coming of the Lord; so that, in another epistle, the apostle charges them, that they *be not soon shaken in mind, or be troubled, neither by spirit, nor by word, nor by letter as from us, as that the day of Christ* (meaning the great final day) *is at hand.* Then he goes on to say that it is not immediately to occur, there being some great events to precede it. From this it appears, that Paul certainly, and probably the other apostles, were not cherishing the belief that the day of judgment was literally near. These declarations,— *The coming of the Lord draweth nigh, The Judge standeth before the door, Surely, I come quickly, The end of all things is at hand,*— these and similar declarations were made nearly two thousand years ago, and things have remained as they were; there has been no resurrection, no day of judgment. At the same time, those declarations were intelligently made: they were and are true.

In what sense, then, were they and are they true? It is manifest they had a meaning; and, if they had, they still have a meaning, which is consistent with what, two thousand years ago, was the fact, and is still the common doctrine, that the great day of judgment is not absolutely and literally near at hand.

The language, obviously, has a reference to, and an accomplishment in, successive and somewhat differing events. The Lord is represented as coming in the overthrow of the Jewish state and polity. This was the winding up of the first great dispensation; the first grand period of the Church; indeed, the first grand period of time. This came to its end by one of the most awful judgments God ever visited on any people. By some it is supposed, that Peter, in his remarkable declaration, *The end of all things is at hand,* had reference, primarily, to that appalling catastrophe and consummation. It is certain that Christ warned his disciples of this, his first coming, for purposes of retribution. He gave them definite signs of his coming, and described that coming in language similar to that which is used to invest with majesty and terror his final advent. This consummation and overthrow was, then, literally at hand. It was an event of absorbing, yea, agonizing, interest to every Jewish heart; and one which called for the utmost vigilance and prayer. Admitting this interpretation, the passage is not lost in its palpable bearing upon us. The winding up of the first grand period of the world was manifestly and strongly typical of the far more sublime and awful winding up of the second. The first has passed: the end of the second is to come. It is coming: it is nearing. This is the literal meaning of the word translated *at hand.* The end of all things is nearing. The completion of the first is proof of the coming and certainty of the second. The first coming of Christ, for retribution, in the manner he did, in exact accordance with his own uttered and recorded prediction, is proof that he will come a second time, at the end of the world, in the sublime and glorious manner described in the sacred record. Let any person of seriousness and candor read the twenty-fourth chapter of Matthew, and compare it with the chapter in Josephus in which that historian, an enemy to the Christian faith, describes the exact and literal accomplishment of our Saviour's words, in which he foretold the events of his first coming; then let him read the twenty-fifth chapter, in which the same Lord Jesus foretells and describes his second coming for the purpose of final retribution of quick and dead,—and he cannot, it would seem, resist the conviction, that his second and final coming will take place just as it is predicted; and the history and results of it will be written in the perfected redemption of the saved, and uttered and echoed in the deeper wailings of the lost.

The language, then, has an important meaning, a stirring significancy, as referring to the Lord's coming to judgment. As a great event, transcending and overshadowing all others, ever coming, rapidly nearing, striding, ever rushing on, it may be said to be at hand. Certainly, it appears so to the mind so absorbed in the amazing contemplation as to forget, at the time, all other things. It is really so, in strict truth, when the line between this and the judgment-day is set off against the line which measures the eternity beyond. It is but a step, a point even, to the time when the trump shall sound, the Judge appear, the tenants of the grave come forth and pass the dread ordeal.

But to this great, this final ending, there are other subordinate endings. Death is the end of the world to him who dies; the same to him as if all sublunary things were literally abolished. The glorious sun, the broad, blue sky, the green earth, and the flowing streams, henceforth are naught to him: he will know them no more for ever. With him, it is all ended; the most pregnant and momentous stage of his existence, that on which the whole subsequent eternity depends, is ended. He has gone to his final account, gone to his eternal home. Amazing consummation to the spirit that departs. And how fast are spirits departing. Nearly thirty millions of these consummations occur every year; about eighty thousand occur every day; more than three thousand every hour. Almost every swing of the pendulum crowds a soul into eternity. In this way a whole race is soon gone. The world may remain as it is, a hundred years from this. The sun, moon, and stars will shine with unabated brightness and beauty; but other eyes will see them. The eyes they now enlighten, the bodies they now warm and cheer, will abide in the darkness and corruption of the grave. To all now on the stage it will be ended; a whole race ended; we, as a part of it, ended. May we not say then, and feel it as we say, The end is at hand? How quickly will it be upon you, and upon me, as an individual. This rushing flight of time, these thronging diseases ready to prey upon us, these shafts of the destroyer flying all about us, this wasting strength, this ebbing pulse, this tottering frailty, all say, in the reflecting ear, Mortal, to you the end of all things is near; the termination of all earthly hopes and schemes and pleasures is near; the closing of all these changes, and the entering upon the stabilities of an eternal condition, is near, and not only near, but every day it is coming nearer; death is nearing; judgment nearing; eternity nearing; every step in life is a step towards the sepulchre; the next may be a step into it. This inflexible uncertainty adhering to our condition, gives, if possible, still greater force to the announcement of the text, near, nearing, but how near none can tell. To-day you may be well; to-night you may be contending with nature's great agony; to-morrow you may be laid away in your coffin. When I look at these facts, when I consider this life, how sure and momentous its end; all worldly things, to the departing, ending with it; when I see how quickly a generation passes, as it were, crowded off by a new one rising up to take its place, this again to be crowded off and disappear as soon; one going, another coming, and all bringing on the great consummation; this final end, nearing, ever nearing, with the lightning-like speed of time, — I do feel that there is a meaning and a truth and an amazing solemnity in the inspired declaration, *The end of all things is at hand.*

My next remark upon this passage is, there being a meaning in it to us, it presents a motive for us: it is a great and permanent motive. This consideration of the end at hand has moved myriads who were on the stage many centuries ago. Emphatically was it one of the great moving considerations of the early Christians. These two: first the cross, then the coming. They thought a great deal of Christ's coming, and the end. Their sustained fervor and engagedness were owing, in part, to their vivid apprehensions of the great winding-up scene. Their spirits were kindled and exalted by their visions of that coming glory and majesty. Could we look into the experience of those of every period, who have been eminently active and holy, and see the hidden springs of their piety, we should find, that, like

Baxter, they had been persons greatly affected by an approaching death and judgment.

The next point is, how is this motive to become influential, effective, in any measure proportioned to its greatness and solemnity? How has it been in the case of others? How is it to be in our case? Not, let me say distinctly, by believing in actual, literal nearness, or vicinage. There are some who seem to think, that the great event is nothing, comparatively, as motive, if at a distance. If the judgment be a century ahead, it is of little consequence how we demean ourselves. We are to wake up and bestir ourselves, because, and only because, the scene is actually right upon us. I admit we should bestir ourselves, did we know death or judgment to be literally at our door; but not only for this supposed nearness. It is the very spirit and essence of brutish unbelief, to be affected only by a present, palpable event of this sort. There is no faith about it: we know there is a great deal of praying when death has come to summon the spirit away; but what is praying in sickness and death good for, if there were none in life and health? What is praying in a storm good for; what avails it, if there were none in fair weather? So, in the final day, there will unquestionably be a great deal of praying when the graves are opening and the dead are rising and the world is burning; but what will it avail? An event or motive of this sort made palpable, and brought right upon one with infinite and visible pressure, is enough to make a demon pray; and he would be a demon when he had done. But all the power of an event or scene which is to affect him, in the case of the considerate man, does not lie in the contact of that scene. It is, indeed, a solemn thing to die: it is also a solemn thing to live, and look forward to the hour. It is a solemn thing to be laying by material for the judgment, as well as to be actually judged; to be treasuring up *wrath against the day of wrath*, as well as to encounter its actual and dreadful infliction. On many accounts, it would be better for me that death strike me to-day than that he delay the stroke a quarter of a century, and I pass and close that period in unrepented sin; better for me that the archangel's trump summon me this hour before *the great white throne* than that the time be delayed for me to make longer my line and blacker my account of guilt. Oh that men felt more the solemnity of living: there is motive in living as well as in dying.

But to recur to that great event, — the end; if not by believing in literal nearness, how is it to be made effectual as motive? I answer, as has already been intimated, By the eye of faith looking directly upon it. In this way, it is brought near: it seems near, but a step indeed, to death and the judgment. Faith fixes upon the certainty of the event: whatever else may fail, this will come. Death, judgment, eternity, are assuredly before me. Faith considers the uncertainty of the time. None can divine the time. Men have tried to pry it up from the depths of an unrevealed secrecy; have made their confident calculations, some in this way, others in that; evolving, as they have thought, the hitherto baffling intricacies of prophecy. And so the world has been told again and again and again when the trump shall sound, and the judgment be set; but the event has always proved, and doubtless always will, that *of that day and hour knoweth no man*. Faith looks upon it as a sudden, surprising event; which, when it does come, will come not by arithmetical computation, but *as a thief in the night.*

Faith fixes upon the grandeur and solemnity of the event, and its accompaniments. They will soon be here; and they will indeed be amazing. An amazing scene when the Son of man shall appear in his glory, and ten thousand times ten thousand angels shall be round about him; and the damned coming up in chains from the pit; and all the dead coming forth from the opening graves; and all the living in a moment changed; the heavens rolling together like a scroll; earth and sea and the elements melting and burning; all nations together ascending to stand before the Son of man; a part on the right hand, the remainder on the left; the former to hear, *Come, ye blessed of my Father, inherit the kingdom;* the latter to hear, *Depart from me, ye cursed, into everlasting fire;* and the blessed go through the gates into the golden city; and the doomed go down into the devouring flame, to be for ever with the devil and his angels. Truly, it will be a day of greatness and wonders, equal to all other days gathered into one. As faith fastens upon it, meditates, dwells, gazes thereon, the scene keeps nearing, and swelling out into greater magnitude; and, while thus absorbed and admiring, the believing soul greatly longs for that advent, and that glory, and so hastens unto the coming of the day of God; by the strength of hope and desire, as it were, leaping forth to meet it. All these, the faith, the fixedness, the desire, the grandeur of the scene, its rapid nearing, its certainty as to fact, its uncertainty as to time, destined to burst forth upon an astonished world, — these things, when realized, make out, we think, a strong case, an unequalled pressure of motive.

And here, let me say, is where every man ought to live, with the end before him; death, judgment, eternity, the impending realities of his vision, often painting their mighty image upon the very retina of his soul. So living, how will he live? How will he be affected?

One thing is, his estimate of the present world will be exceedingly reduced and sobered. This estimate, as a general thing, is exorbitant, overgrown. Most think far too highly of the world. It glares upon men, bewilders them, and bewitches them. The difficulty is, it is not viewed enough as Paul viewed it, when he said, *The fashion of this world passeth away.* Let but this simple fact — it passes, the end at hand — be incorporated among the living, productive sentiments of the heart, and every thing about it, every feeling toward it, and every action for it, will be changed. There will be a wonderful coming down and sobering of the whole view and feeling and pursuit. The man has simply come to understand the tenure. This is not my home: nothing here can be long retained. I am not to place my supreme regard upon this sin-deformed, this death-struck scene. I am not going to act the fool before the universe, in scrambling for the baubles of a moment, to the neglect and perdition of my undying spirit. I am not going to barter away the wealth of my immortality for the poor indulgence, the sorry debasement of an hour. Thus he loosens his selfish, his maddened grasp upon the world. The view we have taken goes to moderate all our earthly passions and griefs. *Brethren, The time is short. It remaineth, that both they that have wives, be as though they had none; and they that weep, as though they wept not; and they that rejoice, as though they rejoiced not; and they that buy, as though they possessed not; and they that use this world, as not abusing it.* Every earthly good will have receded, every earthly convenience have been abandoned, and every affliction forgotten, in the oblivion of the grave.

The habit of dwelling beneath these impending scenes cannot fail to quicken the spiritual affections, and give new strength and intensity to the Christian's zeal. What a prize there is for him to win; what an inheritance; what a glory. In his near, full view of it, it seems wonderful; it staggers, it all but overpowers, him. And yet he pants unutterably for that purity and glory. The soul, too, with its vast capacities, redemption, with its interminable results, appear to him in a new light, and call upon him with a new urgency. How many are the exposed; they are all about us; they are on the edge of the precipice; they are pouring into the dark abyss; thousands and millions, to be saved soon, if saved ever. Christ, who died for them, and whose love you have felt, appeals to you, appeals to me. Go, carry my gospel; tell them of, and urge them to, the place of refuge, — the covert from the gathering tempest. The Christian, whose eyes are open to these things, — to that heaven, that hell, that Saviour, that Judge, that judgment, — all near, fast hastening on, if there be any life in him, will be moved to do something for his Lord. He will not, he cannot sleep, any more than he will be able literally to sleep when all the dead are stirring in their graves. He will wake and work; and he will pray God to bless his labor in the Lord.

Christian hearer, try to bring these matters home to

your own heart, your own case. In a little, you pass away, and are here no more. Are you ready? Is your work done, — done in your own soul; done in the field around you, — so that the Lord will say to you, *Well done, good and faithful servant?* Most blessed approval at such an hour, before such a presence. Most dreadful and crushing will be the reverse: some will hear, *Thou wicked and slothful servant.* So live and labor, watch and pray, in the season of effort and prayer, that the welcome, and not the woe, shall be yours; then shall you be for ever with the Lord.

Unconverted hearer, you are not prepared; and yet you may be on the brink of ruin. Have you thought of your situation and of the scene you are to meet? Consider them now: wait not for a literal contact; wait not for the agitation and decay of a death-bed; wait not for the trump of judgment to stir your conscience and move your sensibilities. Ponder, till you feel the truth of that declaration, *The end of all things is at hand.* Though an old declaration, though it has been reiterated for centuries, uttered in ears that have long since mouldered, still it comes fresh and startling to you this day. It will come again. The end will be upon you sooner than you think. You may see it even now, speeding on like the heated courser. Weeks, months, years, come and go; deaths, coffins, graves, crowd on the vision; the inexorable scythe swinging darkly across your path, — how can you be so unconcerned? How can you sleep on, in such circumstances of immense and awful interest and astounding peril? Persist in this, and you are lost. Ere you are aware, will come the unwaking sleep of the shroud and sepulchre; and the soul, neglected, undone, will be driven down to the unsleeping tortures, the agonized, earthquake heavings of the second death. Fall not upon this doom so dreadful; but turn at once and avoid it, and seek that other destiny, listening to mercy's call, and your soul shall live in heaven for ever.

# XXVI.

## CHRIST'S COMINGS.

*But as the days of Noe were, so shall also the coming of the Son of man be. For as in the days that were before the flood, they were eating and drinking, marrying and giving in marriage, until the day that Noe entered into the ark, and knew not until the flood came, and took them all away: so shall also the coming of the Son of man be.* — MATT. xxiv. 37–39.

FOR *as in the days that were before the flood.* There were the days, the years, before the flood, constituting a period of nearly seventeen hundred years, more than one-third of the whole term of time covered by the record of the sacred Scriptures; and yet the whole history of it is compressed into the first six chapters of the Bible. Here all the history there is of this long period; and one of these chapters is filled with the repetition of the sombre fact touching each, that *he died.* Though he lived so long as might seem to establish a right prescriptive of life perpetual, yet, in each case, there comes the same dark dash at the end: *he died.*

He lived nine hundred and sixty-nine years, and he died. All that he did, his honors and his proud gatherings, the whole, is put under the shroud of the single word, *he died.* It took less than two lives to reach through those seventeen hundred years before the flood. Those enormous stretches of life, and those huge, broad facts of contemporaneous abiding, look, indeed, and sound, strange to us. When Methuselah was born, Adam was six hundred and eighty-seven years of age. When Adam died, Methuselah was two hundred and eighty-two years old. The man, then, who lived up to the very year of the flood lived also in the society of the first man two hundred and eighty-two years.

This fact of enormous reach of years, doubtless, had much to do with that other fact which brought on the flood, namely, the great wickedness of the then living world. There was long opportunity to nurture this stalwart growth in violence and crime. And the truth then obtained which later inspiration declared, and all experience has verified, *that because sentence against an evil work is not executed speedily, therefore the heart of the sons of men is fully set in them to do evil.* Under this law of long living, and in this prospect of a remote retribution, all hearts rapidly waxed worse; so that human nature, in the flight of a few centuries, in a period less than of two continuous lives, reached a point of wickedness which made the Creator, as he looked upon it, heartily sick of his work; heartily sorry, that, by his creative fiat, he had ever given birth to the material of such baseness. *It repented the Lord that he had made man on the earth, and it grieved him at his heart.* A grievous sight, indeed, when he looked over the scene, and *saw that the wickedness of man was great in the earth, and that every imagination of the thoughts of his heart was only evil continually;* outwardly, enormous crime, violence, corruption, in all their forms, making it a world fit only to be terminated by a violence of judgment that should answer to the violence of the depravity.

One single pure and bright name breaks that otherwise turbid sea of total blackness. And, on the principle that the righteous alone is remembered, God marks by this name that most apostate period, calling it *the days of Noe.* Noah, doubtless, filled a larger space in the divine gaze and estimation than all the millions beside. That he was a pre-eminently good man we are sure; called of God, *a just man and perfect;* again, set before us as a pattern of faith. That he stood wholly alone in this character and testimony does not appear. His father and grandfather were both living when he began to build the ark. These, it is presumed, were both pious. If so, he had in these, at least, sympathy and encouragement. Still, in one sense, Noah did stand alone; for he was the great operator and leader in the strange and gigantic project. Heroic and sublime his standing, solitary, yet stable, with an opposing world around him. *A preacher of righteousness,* with his lips he proclaimed the great destruction; and his life, his strenuous work, attested the impregnable quality of his faith. A pure man like him, admitted to the secrets of the Almighty, how likely to be right in his tremendous proclamation. Then, those score years of work, every stroke of the hammer, every bolt that was driven into the anomalous bulk, which was to save those God appointed for salvation, all went, we should suppose, to rivet the conviction, — if there were in the sensuous multitudes any thoughtful minds, to rivet in them the conviction, — that the destructive storm was at hand. But no: this earnest testifier, by his words of warning, backed by his deeds of faith, produced no such effect upon that wicked generation; they not repenting, reforming, getting ready. They were doing far otherwise.

How sad the connection of parts in my text. There is set before us the employment of that doomed race, *eating and drinking, marrying and giving in marriage,* no thought of any thing else, knowing, dreaming nothing to the contrary, till the whelming destruction broke over them. Immersed were they in all worldly gratifications, *and knew not until the flood came, and took them all away.* Evidently, they were perfectly at ease, profoundly unconcerned, in the jovial mood, liberal interpreters and livers, not the slightest tinge of fanaticism, or of a sombre, ill-boding piety, in their creed or their constitution; confident, eager in the range of a smiling, and a still inviting future, a sure and joyous future, reckoned by centuries, five, six, seven hundred more years of life: so it was up to the very moment the commissioned elements laid them all together in one liquid grave. That which followed we can think, but who can describe? Who can paint the scene, when the waters began to pour down from above, and break and heave up from beneath? Then belief began, and the wild cry waked, The flood! The flood! and there succeeded frantic fears and passionate laments, imprecations and prayers. Even now the world dies, as it did before, in a sort of succession. Some yield at once: others battle it awhile, and so briefly defer their destiny. The trees and the hilltops are the resorts for refuge. The men who scorned the ark when warned by the man of faith, now, under the terrors of sight, rush for these. How vain. The flood goes over, and they are swept into the insatiate waste. The more brawny arm, that struggles for a footing on a higher peak, has the privilege to breathe a little longer. Upward the waters ruthlessly swelled: *fifteen cubits upward did they prevail; and the mountains were covered.* The work was complete; and this then living world was no more, except the eight souls, saved by faith and works. All the rest believed not, *knew not until the flood came, and took them all away. So shall also the coming of the Son of man be.*

We have, in the preceding, the scene and style of one of the Lord's great comings; his coming, according to his pre-declared word, to destroy the world by a flood. There were to be other notable comings. One was the coming of the Son of man to put an end to the old dispensation and economy, and to destroy the city which was the seat of it, and the temple which was the symbol of it. The flood was typical of this coming; and both these are typical of another, namely, the final coming. As was the Lord's coming to destroy the old world by a flood, so shall be his coming to put an end to the world that now is. The old world met its overthrow by water. The world that now is awaits a destruction by fire. The Apostle Peter states this in all clearness. That *the world that then was, being overflowed with water, perished. But the heavens and the earth, which are now, by the same word are kept in store, reserved unto fire against the day of judgment and perdition of ungodly men.* No one can doubt that it will be literally by fire.

We, of this time, stand between history and prophecy: behind is the fearful past; on, the more fearful future. The things God has done do symbolize and assure to us the things he will do. Our position, then, is singularly favorable for the securing of our safety, if we will. An antecedent world has perished, that we might not perish. So it is, that the principle of vicariousness runs through all God's administration of the world. In every accident, by boat or rail, those who perish give their lives for the greater security of all travellers coming after them on those ill-fated lines. The scores that went down, years since, in that plunge at Norwalk were a sacrifice to the safety of all since at that spot. The same thing God intends in these greater historic affairs. Events of a world-wide knowledge, that throw their lurid glare all across the heavens, arrest and warn all succeeding generations. Thus this now before us, in which the world, according to century-spoken word, went suddenly down, was designed to benefit all who should come after. This comes out in that prospective turn in our text, *So shall also the coming of the Son of man be.* If the destruction is before us in close resemblance, and we may read the detail in veritable and palpable transaction, all divinely recorded for our warning, then, have we not great advantages for escape? And is not God, once so severe in destruction, tenderly good in the revelation? Look back and behold. Look forward and consider. *So shall also the coming of the Son of man be.* What do we learn in this past that is promotive of our escape, our redemption, in that day? What must we learn, admit, and practise if we would escape?

1. We learn, and this let us lay to heart, that the fact of delay in the coming of a judgment, or a retribution, makes not at all against it, as coming at some

time. On this very point there is a great deal of wrong reasoning and concluding. We find it abounding in that earliest antiquity. God spake, he uttered the threatening; and then God waited over the slow track of more than a century for purposes of mercy. This long period, which he gave them for repenting, they spent in proving that the shocking disaster would never come. And this was their one argument, It does not come; a hundred years gone, and no appearance of it. On this premise they all slept together in perfect security; and it did come, and took them all away.

Men, everywhere, are strangely given to reasoning in a like perverse process from God's delaying, showing that he will not because he does not. Peter found them in his day, and he stereotyped their phrase, or their say, thus: *Where is the promise of his coming? for, since the fathers fell asleep, all things continue as they were from the beginning of the creation.* Not quite so far back, ye old cavillers, as the beginning of the creation. There was the flood to break the smooth march of the world's history; and the flood foretold the fire. The delay about the flood explains the delay about the fire; shows that there may be the delay, and yet the burning come. Delay of the punitive stroke is the very reason for the more fearing it; for it is stronger, heavier, more terrible for the delay. Have we not noticed in the storm, the longer the lull the more destructive the succeeding blast; in the play of heaven's hidden artillery, the longer the space of calm and silence the more earth-rocking the explosion that followed? because, in the delay, there was a cumulating and gathering-up of destructive forces. This law in nature seems also a law in life. The hasty man, for example, anger him;

quick as you touch him he goes off, a mere flash; no lead or bolt there. Take another sort of man. Anger him. He takes it quietly, and hides his wrath and purpose down in the secrecy of his nature, and then waits for his opportunity. Such a man is to be considered. It is well to make your peace with him. The comparison, as illustrating the divine principle, or procedure, holds only at this point, that strength and fearfulness accrue to God's judgments from the long delays in his returns of retribution. God is to be especially feared because he is so patient, so slow.

2. I shall lead you to consider, in the second place, how strong are the grounds of belief that this great coming with fire is indeed not far before us. Let us consider these grounds, that we may come to believe profoundly and practically in that coming; that we may cease to disbelieve in regard to it; that we may part with that universal company of the olden time, who, to a man, disbelieved it; and part, too, with that large company of the present time, who try to disbelieve it. The modern disbeliever is far the guiltier of the two; for then there was no precedent. No such thing had been done as destruction by a flood; and there was no rain to do it with. The rain that drowned the earth, it is believed, was the earth's first rain. How unlikely, to a generation that never saw rain, that they would perish by it. Yet they did: we have the precedent. God then said it, and he did it. We have the same word for the greater coming with fire. And we have the fire; a world with all its caverns and bowels filled full of it; and it rages and presses against, and shakes the crust on which we now stand, and it snorts out at all the openings in columns that reach to the clouds, and

quantities that whelm vast tracts with the molten ruin. With the precedent before us of a world's drowning by rain, when no rain had been, can we hesitate to believe that other coming amid deluges and burials of fire, when that same word has said it, and when the material is all in store, yea, when it is probably true, that, if that omnific word did not hold it in check, the next hour it might break out upon us? With such a precedent, — God saying it, and holding the imprisoned fires all ready to do it, my friends, — do not disbelieve it. No matter how many others do disbelieve it. The whole world may disbelieve it, this uttered thing of God will be. In the other case, the entire world did disbelieve it, and yet it fell upon them; when the time came, they all curled down and took it. It is something in the right direction to admit the fact: the disbelief of men cannot make the word of God of none effect. It does sometimes seem as though people thought that God's affairs would go by majorities. Vote him down, and he will not do it. Those ancient presumers tried this to their sorrow. They had millions to one; and yet the Lord proceeded, and did it.

It is a fact that mounts up to the awfully sublime, the forth-standing fact that God's providences, the laws and principles of his administration, do move steadily and inflexibly on; and they will, no matter what men think or say. We may exscind facts, remove the landmarks, deny great principles; but, really, nothing is altered. These great laws and principles of the Almighty still abide; they are marching on; they are executed, and they execute. Sad for any of us, if we are in the way, when the on-going wheels strike to crush. Oh, how they crush, when they strike.

*So shall also the coming of the Son of man be.* It is writ in all history, in the changeless word divine, in the frame and bowels of the earth itself, and on all our living souls, ordained and God-spoken, ere long to be, the final coming of the Son of man. Believe it, and make not God a liar. Believe it, that you may be ready to meet it. There is no arithmetic that will help us in this matter of making out the exact time. It is the one event, now and onward, the one great event which summons to itself the eye and heart of the men of all time. It is sure. It is near. By some law of God's progression I believe it is near. The one vivid word of his warning phrase is, *quickly*. *Behold, I come quickly*. As when strong men step from the tread of business into the presence of God,—*in such an hour as ye think not.*

The storm, it is there. The exposed, it is we. See the ark at hand; behold the living refuge, Jesus, the mighty Deliverer. I announce, to-day, your opportunity. Flee now to him while you may. Take, oh, take him by faith; and the act will be your defence and your joy for ever.

## XXVII.

### DEATH ABOLISHED.

*Who hath abolished death.*—2 Tim. i. 10.

IT is Christ who hath done this. *Abolished death,*—a remarkable expression; *abolished death,*—a remarkble and most beneficent work. What the meaning of this phrase, what the work described? We are, of course, to receive the phrase, and the work affirmed by it, with some limitations. The benefit does not extend to all: it has the limitation which faith gives it. This everywhere declared, and most emphatically in our Saviour's conference with Martha: *Jesus said unto her, I am the resurrection and the life: he that believeth in me, though he were dead, yet shall he live; and whosoever liveth and believeth in me shall never die.* It is, then, in the case of those who believe in Christ, that death is abolished; and even here it is not a literal abolishment. We know of but two followers of God who have been absolved from death. The fact of death, the unalterable necessity, then, abides. All must die, the soul be separated from the body, and the body lie down in the grave and see corruption. The bodily pains of death are not abolished. These remain in their intensity, often, in the case of those to whom the words of our text have their full application.

The sinking, the suffering, the dread convulsion,—these are not done away.

How, then, can it be said that death is abolished. The word rendered *abolished* means to bring to an end, to take away, render void, unproductive, powerless. When we utter the word death, we utter what is evil, the perfection and consummation of all evil: it is a terrible word, a terrible thing. We can say nothing beyond, It is death. Now the essential evil, which gives this event the pre-eminence and the terribleness of death, is taken away. The deadliness of death is removed. Death is abolished, because every deadly element and energy of it is counter-worked, completely nullified; the mischief, the evil, either taken away or turned to advantage.

Let us, in this stage, look at some of the evils, the forbidding, the terrible things in death. It is represented as armed with an envenomed sting; as the enemy of our race; *the last enemy that shall be destroyed;* a king with his prostrate empire, the king of terrors. The pains which are commonly the forerunners and attendants of death,—these scouts of the enemy; these incursions upon our tabernacle; these blows upon the building, knocking away its props, and reducing its strength,—all these are appalling, both in the prospect and the endurance. They give to the scene the repulsive features of death: they make us recoil from the experience and the embrace. Pains which are to attain their climax in such an issue, which are to end only as they end by their own violence, are to most people very formidable. This final pang, the wrench that snaps the cord, is often dreaded when all other disquietude is passed away. Some fear dying, not the being dead, the passion, not the state.

Another source of apprehension in the thought of death is found in its sunderings. It takes us from friends; those long familiar, dear to the heart on account of kindred ties, or social excellencies, or kindly offices. It takes us from sights pleasant to the eye; the green earth, and the vaulted heavens; from all the beauty and magnificence of nature; from anticipations yet to be realized; from plans unfinished, and enterprises on the eve of accomplishment; from estates laboriously accumulated, and comforts industriously brought together, and all ready to be enjoyed. Death as the inexorable alienator of all these, the ruthless sunderer, tearing us away, shutting up the eye, blasting the hope, putting an end to all earthly possession and enjoyment, is a wasting intruder. We find a dread and pang here. There is one item, in this work of separation, to which nature comes only with reluctance and revulsion? It is the parting of the soul and the body, linked as they are by a mysterious tie, made one in sympathy, in suffering, in rejoicing. Having so long dwelt together in concord, in identity even, how can the forcing asunder be but with recoiling and misgiving? For the spirit to leave its dwelling and its organs of communication, become unclothed, and try existence by itself in an unknown scene, is a mighty adventure, a fearful leap. There is another thing under the head of deprivation I will allude to. There is an evil and a pang in death, as it often appears to the good man, that it takes him prematurely, in his full strength, perhaps, from the field of his Christian toils, where there is so much to be done, and so few to do it; where society is corrupting, and millions are perishing, and where every genial seed that is cast bears its hundred-fold. It seems hard for him to die, and leave so much misery behind whose removal he had projected; die with his heart's holy desires so far unachieved; hard for him, in these circumstances, to quit his labors for the awaiting rest, to lay off his armor and put on his crown.

Another formidable feature in death, another source of evil and disquietude, is found in its introductions; not only in what it takes us from, but also in what it takes us to.

It introduces the body to the grave, the spirit to the unseen world. The grave is looked upon very commonly as a gloomy abode. The dishonors there done to this boasted fabric are thought of with no satisfaction. Most regard it as a dreadful necessity which dooms them to the processes and the banquetings of that place; death a most direful thing for its dealings with, and its disposition of, the body.

But the essential evil, the crowning fear of death, lies not here. It is in the soul's introduction into another state. Death delivers over the soul into eternity, to reckon with its Maker, and reap the reward of its deeds. There has been, we will suppose, — ah, how common, — a life of transgression, of forgetfulness of God, and abuse of his mercies, a not living for the great end which God has ordained. Men may deny that it is so, and affirm their own innocence; that they have done no one any wrong, but have lived justly and worthily. But death is an honest hour, a detecting and revealing season, bringing out the thoughts and intents of the heart. Commonly, the verdict conscience rings at that hour through the chambers of the soul is heard. Its true verdict is that sin is upon the soul. This is death's sting. This, more than all other things, makes dying such a work of dread and of agony; not so much the pain of dying as the pain, the sorrow, that lies beyond; the fear, the foretastes, of God's inflicted wrath. Death, as the beginning of this, is a bitter cup; as the door to this, an iron gate. There is something solemn, awful even, in going forth upon an untried scene; in entering upon a new mode of existence, in a new form of being. But to look out upon that region when just ready to launch forth, and know it is an unfriendly region, the Being ruling there in righteousness made our enemy by our impenitent and ungodly living; to know that unerring justice will there deal with us for our sins; that we have come to the very border, and another breath or two, and we are in the midst of the tremendous realities, — this is death. Here is the sting. There have been many instances of this God has made signal, shocking to witness, and we could only describe, by saying, that is death.

This it is which Christ has abolished: not all that is painful, but all that is evil, all that is terrible, all that is stinging in death, he has abolished.

That we may see how this is done, how it is Christ abolishes death; that we may view the admirable and perfect theory of the matter, and at the same time view the admirable fitness, and power, and resources of Christ for this work of our deliverance, — let me recall the essential and fearful evil of death in the three particulars I have mentioned; namely, its pains, its deprivations, and its introductions; and show how each of these is met and counter-worked by the provision and grace of our Redeemer. 1. Changing the order, placing first the last-named particular,—death, as seizing and introducing us into the future, the state of retribution, this called the *sting of death*, the essence and source of all the other trouble,—this is taken away completely, every vestige of it removed. 2. The privations of death are answered by being infinitely more than made up. 3. The pains of death, bitter, protracted, wasting as they may be, are all turned to our advantage. What, then, is left, worthy the name of death?

1. The sting, the venom, the essential deadliness of death, is taken away. And it is done in this perfect and blessed mode. *The sting of death is sin: the strength of sin is the law.* The law transgressed comes upon the soul with its demands, iterates and insists upon the penalty, eternal death; a just demand, a righteous penalty. The sinning soul, in that revealing hour, knows it to be so; and, so far as any thing in itself is concerned, lies under the mighty condemnation. Here the envenomed, triumphing malignity of sin. This Christ has taken upon himself. This cursing, damning strength of the law, expended, yea, exhausted itself, upon Christ, when he was made by his own voluntary offering a curse for us. When death struck his sting, envenomed as it was by the added sins of the world,—when, with his most malignant gust, he struck it thus deep into the body of Christ,—the agony, the death, of that meek victim was dreadful beyond all parallel in the experience of dying. But death lost his sting in the effort, like that venomous creature, who, it is said, stings once,

and deposits and surrenders both his venom and his life together.

Death now has no more power to trouble or hurt, by means of the law, those who have sought refuge in Christ. Paul brings out the whole glorious idea, when he says, *There is therefore now no condemnation to them which are in Christ Jesus.* He comes forth on this point, with an all-challenging audacity, if you please to call it thus. *Who is he that condemneth? It is Christ that died, yea, rather, that is risen again.* Here is a fact and an argument confounding to the fell destroyer. He cannot stand before it; it cripples his strength, and removes all his disturbing and hurting power. Thus the terrible in death, the stinging, the destroying element, is taken away by Christ, enduring it in his people's stead.

2. Then, secondly, the pains attending decay and death are all turned to the soul's benefit, in this, that they are a discipline, they purify through grace; they spiritualize and elevate; they graduate and smooth the descent to the grave, leading gently on to the last conflict, to the disrupting agony, and preparing for it, as they lead the way. Though hard to bear, a heavy and wearying burden, they make heavier the crown of life and the eternal weight of glory.

3. The third item, the deprivations of death are infinitely more than made up. The departing one has friends, we will suppose, with whom he took sweet counsel. He leaves them, parts from them, for a season; but he goes *to an innumerable company of angels, to the general assembly and church of the first-born, which are written in heaven, and to God the Judge of all, and to the spirits of just men made perfect, and to Jesus*

*the Mediator of the New Covenant.* He leaves worldly possessions, but he never regarded them as absolutely his. God made him a steward over so much, and when he dies, he only resigns his office. Well for him, if he has done his duty in the place. What if he does leave accumulated wealth and imposing magnificence; if a Christian, he goes to a *building of God, a house not made with hands*, to an unfading inheritance, to the heirship of all things. He parts from his body, that intimate companion, and instrument of all his functions, without whom he has never existed a moment, and without whom, how he shall subsist, is all a mystery to him. He trusts God, and surrenders the building; but it is only for a season, to be received back again, a glorious and a deathless structure. The burial is but a sowing. Does any wonder, and murmur at God's way in this matter? The rebuke meets his rashness. *Thou fool, that which thou sowest is not quickened except it die.* The corruption to which it is doomed is a refining and preparing process, all carried on in God's hidden but wonder-working laboratory. *It is sown in corruption, it is raised in incorruption. It is sown in dishonor, it is raised in glory. It is sown in weakness, it is raised in power. It is sown a natural body, it is raised a spiritual body.* You see what he lays down, you see what he receives back. No: you do not see that: you cannot imagine it, that *spiritual body*, brought up in power, made like unto Christ's *glorious body*. That you will not comprehend, till it shall be rebuilt, and revealed and restored unto you. Thus the temporary bodily privation shall be incomparably more than made up to him. Death snatches a mean spoil: death's Conqueror restores back a splendid dwelling-place, a building and robe of immortality. Then, again, the life that is surrendered here, that seems to flicker and go out, there is no extinction, no suspension even, no intermediate sleep. It is only a change of place ; the instant it leaves here it enters there. The last throb on earth is followed, in a moment, by a quick and exultant emotion in heaven ; life in its fulness, in its ever-perennial vigor ; in its wondering freshness, in its overflowing, triumphing joys. The death is passed : now it is eternal life.

I ask here, at the end of this argument, every step and turn of which I have taken out of the Bible, I ask, What is there left of death, after he has passed through the spoiling hands of our victorious Emmanuel ? What do you find remaining, that you can properly call death ? We conclude, at once, with a firm logic and a firmer faith, that nothing remains. The work is done almost to the letter. Death is *abolished.* We ascribe the whole work to our blessed Lord. We will do it living ; and if, when dying, we may chose our last faltering utterance, it shall be, *Thanks be to God, which giveth us the victory through our Lord Jesus Christ.*

But let me guard this point. When we say that death is abolished, we would not have it understood that it is a small or light matter to die. With all the alleviations and sustaining hopes, it is a solemn thing to die ; a solemn thing even to die in the Lord, to exchange worlds, to stand before God, to pass the solemn test, to enter upon another state, an opening immortality. It is a great thing to have passed beyond, to have gone over the stream, and be dwelling safely on the other side; to have had the experience, and recorded the pangs, and have written in our own case the whole history of death. Blessed are all those. We trembled for them in the conflict. We looked on in stillness and in sadness. We did pity: we now cry, *Blessed are the dead who die in the Lord.*

The Christian should so improve all his opportunities, all his privileges, all the disciplining events of God's providence, that death in his case, when it comes, shall be abolished; that, when brought to the dread encounter, there shall be nothing for him to do but to yield and to conquer; and so himself become an added fact in the long line of argument that death is indeed done away. Happy if we are found thus ready; happier infinitely than the world can make us, happy as God and heaven with their own imparted fulness can make us.

# XXVIII.

## SPIRITUAL BODY.

*So also is the resurrection of the dead. It is sown in corruption; it is raised in incorruption. It is sown in dishonor; it is raised in glory. It is sown in weakness; it is raised in power. It is sown a natural body; it is raised a spiritual body. There is a natural body, and there is a spiritual body.* — 1 COR. xv. 42–44.

IN the present discourse, I shall treat, not of the fact or doctrine of the resurrection, but of the product of the resurrection.

The fact or doctrine of the resurrection of the body I assume; and yet not altogether assume, but prove it by one text of Scripture; a text which no exegetical torture can make to speak any thing else, namely, this, *Marvel not at this: for the hour is coming, in the which all that are in the graves shall hear his voice,* that is, the voice of the Son of man, *and shall come forth; they that have done good, unto the resurrection of life; and they that have done evil, unto the resurrection of damnation.*

At the present time, we have to do with the resurrection body. And here, at the outset, let me premise two things.

One is, that, in our description of the raised, reconstructed body, we have in view, almost exclusively, the bodies of the just; those which come forth to a resurrection of life. The Bible does this. It does not go into any detail, or particularity, respecting the future bodies of the wicked. From this circumstance the inference has been drawn that the wicked will not be raised. But the fact of their rising out of the grave is as clearly and strongly asserted as the rising of the righteous. The fact is the main thing; and it is the unescapable thing. There is no getting away from the fact that there is to be a coming forth of the body from the grave.

This leads to the other matter I wish to premise, namely, that nothing said on the theoretical part of the subject should be seized and used to prejudice the great fact in the case. The body is to be raised at the last day: it is to be made a spiritual body. These are facts; the rising, and the product of that rising, solemn, incontrovertible verities. But we may think, imagine, speculate, about the qualities of that spiritual body. It is proper that we should glean, as we can, and gather into one ray all the scattered light of Scripture; proper that we gather what intimation we can from reason, and the analogy of things. In this way we frame a discourse upon the spiritual body. But it is liable, on the part of those disposed to pick flaws in our argument, to the charge that it is chiefly speculation, theory, fancy. Furthermore, it is liable to this sophism, that, it being speculation, theory, therefore no reliable truth about it. The sophism, rather the ruinous deception, is in burying the great heaven-descended and heaven-illumined fact beneath the reasonings and the speculations upon the fact. The fact is God's; and it will live and shine when the sun has done shining. We ask you to hold on upon that. If you do not, we tell you that will hold on upon you, and will find you out, every atom of you, when all your bones shall have been powdered. The great fact of a resurrection, the great reality of a spiritual body, we pray you in God's name to receive and respect. Our conjectures and theorizings are another matter, to be tried at the bar of reason and Scripture; and if recreant, let them fall. But here we stand on a platform built by Him who built the world, found in this declaration, *There is a natural body, and there is a spiritual body.* The natural body is what we now have. The spiritual body is what we shall have. What the natural body is, we know perfectly well, namely, this animal body; a body whose functions are all fitted to this animal life; a body nurtured and sustained by natural means. It is the body that suffers, that dies, that we commit to the earth. *The spiritual body:* here we open into a field of mystery. But still we know something, because the Bible says something. Indeed, it utters all the great essential facts, the sublime results in the case.

*There is a spiritual body.* Here we make one point on the authority of Scripture, namely, it is a body. The soul at the resurrection receives a body; in an important sense receives back the body. *This mortal must put on immortality:* language full of striking and wonderful meaning, teaching that human nature, reconstructed from the grave, is to inhabit eternity. As one forcibly remarks, "Not an ethereal rudiment, just saved from the wreck of the former fabric, and just serving to connect, as by a film of identity, the earthly with the heavenly; it is this mortal. The very nature, now subject to dissolution, is to escape from the power of death, and to clothe itself in imperishable vigor." But the phrase, *a spiritual body*, seems to be a contradiction in terms: in other words, a body all spirit. It cannot be a body all spirit, since body necessarily involves the presence of matter. And the extent to which matter may be refined and etherealized we cannot, in our present grossness, fully understand. That the product of the resurrection is a body, a material structure, of wonderful properties, is the basis of all the apostle's reasoning on the subject, — what, indeed, he all along takes for granted. *God giveth it a body as it hath pleased him.* Furthermore, the very doctrine so clearly taught, the resurrection, necessarily implies that they are material structures, which are to come forth and have their place in the heavenly economy. If not, why must the spirit thus come down, and knock at the very grave where lie the mouldered remains of the body it wore? Why disturb that sleeping dust, unless it is to be rebuilt; itself material, therefore some material structure to come from it?

Furthermore, that it is so, the spiritual a material body, is evident from this, that it is to be like unto Christ's glorious body. What this was is declared in his words during that last interview before his ascension: *Behold my hands and my feet, that it is I myself: handle me and see; for a spirit hath not flesh and bones as ye see me have.* And with the same body, and at the close of the same interview, he went up into heaven. The eleven apostles all saw the resurrection body of Christ; it being necessary that they should see him after his rising from the dead. Paul, too, the last of the apostles, was permitted to see the resurrection body of

Christ. He asks, with this reference, *Have I not seen Jesus Christ our Lord?* Have not I, as well as the rest of the apostles, seen the risen Lord? And when? On his way to Damascus, he saw the resurrection body, the glorified body; the body that came forth; the body that ascended; which he could not have seen, had it not been a material, while it was a glorified body. The idea of a *spiritual body*, then, does not preclude the presence and partnership of a material element, but embraces it. The question comes back, Why is it called a *spiritual body?* I answer, for the same reason that the present is called a natural body: this is a natural body, because it is fitted to be an abode and an instrument of this animal life, being earthly and sensuous, like this life. The other is called a *spiritual body*, because it is such, in its material and form, as perfectly fits it to serve the spirit in its higher, nobler, imperishable existence; spiritual, because a body that shall be no burden, require no care, no replenishment; spiritual, as being the spirit's quickener, developing, elevating, helping, the spirit in all its vast operations.

We come now into the region of amazing contrasts. The great facts about the heavenly body we get by contrast. Thus the apostle states the matter in the text, *It is sown in corruption; it is raised in incorruption. It is sown in dishonor; it is raised in glory: it is sown in weakness; it is raised in power.* The first attribute is imperishability. Though matter, though a body, it shall flourish coeval with the inhabiting spirit. We see deposited in the ground a gross, unseemly, dissolving structure. It comes forth incorruptible; no weapon can smite it; no pain can enter it; no form of death can reach it more. We have here matter endowed, as it were, and pervaded with all the salient and springing energies of life; defying the action of time, and all other powers but the fiat of the Almighty. God could bring it down, and bring it to an end. But God's word of promise is, that it shall stand as it rose, incorruptible; onward, onward, a *mortal* that hath *put on immortality.*

Another quality of the reconstructed body is honor; not mean, depressed, but possessing all noble and attractive qualities. As Paul has it, *It is raised* in glory. As committed to its final bed, it is ghastly, deformed, repulsive. It comes up a creation of beauty and splendor, *like unto* Christ's *glorious body.* Here, in this phrase, we have something specific and palpable, something to steady our traversings on this gorgeous sea of mystery. It may be like unto Christ transfigured on the Mount, when his face shot radiance, and his garments glistened, and the whole person put on the image and the overpowering brightness of the heavenly; or like Christ as he appeared in the revelation, when *his countenance was as the sun shineth in his strength,* and his entire form glowed so intensely that the amazed disciple *fell at his feet as dead.* What a glory must that have been to prostrate, and stiffen in the semblance of death, the beholder. It was the glory of Jesus' body. And when his followers shall be like him, then what a glory shall encompass them.

Another attribute of the recovered body is power. Not as it enters the grave; then we see it to be absolutely helpless, every faculty perished, senseless as the clod thrown on to cover it. Power it shall have when it comes forth. Great power there may be of achievement, of producing physical effects. Angels are represented as having this power; power to remove obstacles, to inflict judgments, to execute the most difficult decrees, the most terrible behests. Fetters of iron are as tow in their grasp, and armed myriads as children's playthings before them. One hundred and eighty-five thousand of the enemies of Israel fell before one in a single night. Well may they be called mighty angels, mighty and excelling in strength; but not surpassing the Christian in his glorified body. For inspiration writes on such, *equal unto the angels;* and why not in this power to achieve?

Furthermore, it will be a power to bear as well as to do. What! Burdens in that world do you mean? Yes, this burden, an *exceeding and eternal weight of glory.* As we are now constituted, it would consume us in a moment. When Paul was caught up into the third heaven, whether he was in the body or out of the body he could not tell. We have accounts of some Christians, in peculiar apocalyptic moments, when God has been too lavish in the manifestations of his glory, and too intense a brightness has met their vision, in whom all the wheels of life stopped, and they sunk down at once, inanimate. If they could not bear even that, what would be the case if brought right into the centre and depth of the blazing glories of an unveiled eternity? One text of Scripture would very soon receive its commentary, *that flesh and blood cannot inherit the kingdom of God.* Something more refined, more instinct with vitality, is wanted and is furnished in that body that shall be raised in power; a power to meet the visions and the glories of that place; a power to bathe in those floods of light, and be refreshed and made still stronger by what would otherwise blast and consume it. In short, it will be a power adequate to endure heaven.

But we reach the climax of our text and our subject, in that attribute, spiritual, *raised a spiritual body.* This, indeed, embraces all the rest. It has the qualities of incorruption, immortality, glory, power, because a spiritual body. We began with this in our discussion. We end with it. *It is raised a spiritual body.* Let me take this attribute, *spiritual,* and go forth into the field of its capabilities. *A spiritual body,* — therefore no weariness, no flagging in service, in enjoyment, day nor night; but there is *no night there,* because no needed repose. *A spiritual body,* — therefore endowed with amazing activity and power of motion and communication. This is probable. It is what we know in the case of the angels, great power of motion, darting with the rapidity of light, space presenting no barrier; passing from world to world almost with the quickness of thought, so ethereal are they. We fall back upon the inspired and inspiring comparison, the glorified at the resurrection are to be equal unto the angels. And what a power this will be. What capabilities herein to serve God. What ministries of benevolence, and how swiftly they will be done, when the stride and leap shall be from world to world, as we go now from house to house. Then the circle of fellowship, how it will stretch itself illimitably round; the acquaintance and sympathies and intermingled transports, how they will be diffused through all space where dwells a single pure and loyal subject. What opportunities not only to serve, but to search out, God, to behold and study him in the works of his hands, the powers in question constituting a species of ubiquity, made capable of reaching in a moment the point where the Almighty may be revealing himself in any new work or wonder, there to see and adore; the universe thrown open; an eternity to explore its immensity, ever studying and drinking in knowledge with each eager sense. And though acquisition comes almost with the ease and fulness of intuition, it is kept; all the garnered treasures are retained, while others are ever added, and still new accumulations piled on upon the old. Then this knowledge, all baptized by the spirit of holiness, is used to feed the flame of love to God, the spirit ever loving, and the body ever aiding in the spirit's utmost ardor and outpouring perpetuity of love. In this way, the body as it will be, ministers to the spirit's largest growth of blessedness, takes in God, is filled with all his fulness. Every chord of feeling, every fibre and nerve, shall vibrate with ecstasy, and pour forth an exuberant gladness. Who can tell what a body can do for the inhabiting spirit? We know something of what it has done in its mysterious, mournful connéction in this world. The soul has drooped and sunk with a load it could not bear; and such a case only shows the vital power of the connection. Transfer your thoughts forward to that bright scene and that wondrous union; a perfect spirit dwelling in a spiritual and glorified body. Then there will be a capacity for joy, and an experience, too, such as a spirit alone, a soul disembodied, can never approach to. Doubtless the spiritual body will vastly augment the spirit's blessedness through the cycles of its eternal progression.

Let me remind all who hear me, that this is the work and gift of God; a gift bestowed on a distinctly specified condition. I give it in the words of Christ, *This is the will of Him that sent me, that every one that seeeth the Son and believeth on him may have everlasting life; and I will raise him up at the last day.* This the character, the believer in Jesus, the Christian in heart and life, he shall *attain unto the resurrection of the dead;* he be clothed with this garment of brightness, this resplendent, spiritual body. There is, then, a preparation needed, a meetness of character for it; and you have a responsibility in the premises. Men are not saved in the gospel system by the working of a fatality, nor by the turning of a wheel; not saved by a mechanical process, dug up and saved; not saved by chemical process, striving to bring purity out of putrefaction; but saved by faith, a faith working by love, and the faith and love working out the obedience; saved by two resurrections; the first, a resurrection to newness of life; then, consequent upon this, that final resurrection to a glorified and an endless life.

Another point is, that this matter of being saved is a great matter; saved from sin, from death, from hell; brought out from that penury and infamy and woe, and brought into the possession of astonishing powers, privileges, and prospects; brought up a perfected spirit; endowed with a spiritual body; stamped with God's pledge and seal of immortality; empowered to range the universe, to gather knowledge and wealth from all the works and worlds of the Infinite One. I point you to that product of the resurrection, and ask, Have you thought seriously you could be that? And if you can be that, what else do you wish to be or to have? Is there any thing else in the comparison worth being or having? The height and wealth of that attainment, the resurrection, the spiritual body, is sufficient to dim and dwarf all these gay and painted things the world is so mad after; all little, low, mean, before this supernal splendor. If you succeed in getting them, what have you got? What, as your inventory is read on that day of death's wasting work, and on that other day when death is spoiled, that glorious day of rebuilt forms and fortunes? These are great things, astounding to thought and staggering to faith but for this we get hold of, and hold on upon, — the Promiser and the Performer is God. There put down your anchor and make fast, and look up, and expect that all these amazing things will be done, and these transcendent capabilities be realized in your case, if you are a Christian.

Let me say, further, that not only have you a vast deal to expect, you have nothing to fear. With this hope authentic in your breast, death shall come and bring no terror, his brandished dart shall not move the slightest fibre of your frame. And what is strange, the shuddering and recoiling you feel in the distant remove and dim prospect of this hour shall all depart when you come to the close and fatal grapple; and while you bend and fall beneath that inevitable stroke, your very fall will be a triumph, and the shout go up, *O Death, where is thy sting? O Grave, where is thy victory?*

Inasmuch as Christianity thus honors the body, and opens to this mortal the prospect of immortality, it follows that men have a vast interest and duty here.

And we say in the enforcement of it, Take care of your bodies; and do this by providing for their immortal destination. They must come forth from the grave. Believe with a faith, and hope with an expectation, and live with a discipline, a purity, and an obedience which promise to them a rising to life and glory. Pamper them not. Debase them not. Oh, prepare them not for that other resurrection to *shame and everlasting contempt.* We point you to the good, the glory, the immortality, and ask you to make that your end, your aspiration. If there be any thing manly and responsive in your soul, then reach upward and seize it. Take it. Don't miss it. Make not your final bed with the damned.

## XXIX.

### ETERNAL PUNISHMENT.

*To me belongeth vengeance, and recompense.* — DEUT. xxxii. 35.

*These shall go away into everlasting punishment, but the righteous into life eternal.* — MATT. xxv. 46.

PERHAPS there is no subject, that can be presented from the pulpit, which is received with so little favor by many as the one which relates to the condition, the punishment, of the wicked after the judgment. It seems as though this class of people thought the whole matter turned on this, — namely, whether we who preach make out a case in favor of the punishment of the wicked hereafter, — that the fact would be very much according to the state of the argument in this world or according to the prevailing sentiment; and God would adjust his severity, or his clemency, very much to the judgments and expectations of his creatures. Hence, every person taking a position adverse to any punishment is himself a voice, a vote, an influence, against the infliction of such punishment. Hence, again, the preacher whose argument goes in favor of the punishment of wicked men is supposed to be thereby using an influence which shall increase the probability of such punishment. If not, why are any displeased? The true state of the case is this: the preacher's words and the people's believing have nothing to do with God's recompense as a fact, a reality. It is a reality, or it is not. If it is a reality, nothing is so important as that we know it, and act in view of it. If it is a reality, no man does a more friendly part to you than he who by any means convinces you of it; for if you believe it to be a fact, you will be far more likely to avoid it. Come with me, then, and let us dispassionately inquire after the truth on this subject. What is the reality, the actuality, which lies before us; what will our state be after the judgment, if impenitent and wicked?

1. I lay down this, first, that law is an expressed or implied injunction to do or not to do certain acts, with the alternative of penalty, suffering in some form, if we disobey. It is essential to all law that there be penalty, and necessary to the sustaining of any law that its penalty be inflicted where there is transgression; that is, that the "law be executed."

2. In the second place, I lay down this, which I think no one will dispute, that God is a God of law. Law runs through all the works of his hands. Physical law pervades the whole material universe. As a creature of flesh and blood, if I do thus or so, transgressing a law, the punishment is out upon me. If I put my hand in the fire, pain runs through me for that act. If I open a great artery, the blood streams forth and death ensues. If I abuse these organs by intemperance, they bring down on my head the execution and mortal curse of the suicide. So much for the laws which have relation to the body.

There are also psychological laws, — laws relating to the soul; and these also are inherent, executing themselves. For instance, I commit a sin, violate a moral obligation, and I suffer for it, as a mere natural sequence. There is this natural suffering for sin: all sin brings sooner or later, of itself, suffering upon the soul that commits it. This is not God's penalty as moral governor, but the penalty of transgressing the great psychological law, from which we cannot escape. Thus far we find that he is a God of law in his world of matter and mind; law, penalty, are in both.

I come, next, to look at ourselves, our personalities, as he has made us; and ask, Do we find here any adjustment to a law which is exterior to ourselves? I answer, Yes. We are made with two great departments in our being, hopes, fears; two mighty motives in ourselves, exactly answering to the two great motives without ourselves, reward and punishment. And as these latter are nothing, unless there be within us hopes and fears, so these inner motives or affections are aimless, unless there be the outer, the rewards, the punishments. But all persons are agreed on the side of reward; all believe in this, the bestowing of good. With what consistency, I pray you, if you reject the other, the threat of evil? Thus far we find an outer world, framed by the supreme Creator with incorporate laws, enforced by penalties no transgressor can escape; and man created with a nature exactly answering to the rewards and punishments of law.

Let us now pass on another step, and look at this creature, man, in the social condition and relations. We will enter the smallest realm, the family. Here we find a law-giver, the parent; rules for the children, — rewards if obedient, punishments if they transgress.

It is a necessity that it be so, founded in the system of the almighty Creator, in the very natures he has given us. Pass from the family to the state. Here, also, law with its orderly precepts; punishment, where law is transgressed.

The world has found, again and again, that there is no possible getting-on without the regulations and the retributions of law. This is an unquestioned fact, patent to all of humankind. To advance another step, — we of these natures, made with these hopes and fears, and to whom this regimen of law, precept, punishment, is necessary in these social and civil relations, enter in as parts, subjects, into another and far broader kingdom, of which God is the head, the ruler, the ultimate and absolute authority. This is what all will admit. And all admit, also, that here God has issued laws; rather the great moral law, *Thou shalt love the Lord thy God with all thy strength, and thy neighbor as thyself.* We know this law is laid upon us for our obedience; and we presume, that, like the other laws of God, it had its penalty, its own distinctive penalty. If so, we shall find it expressly declared. We go now to God's Word, the Divine Statute Book, in order to learn what he says about it. Let me recapitulate what we witness as we come along to consult this ultimate authority. We witness, first, in the working of the physical and psychological laws, that both are armed with their penalties. We come to the human statute book, and read there, that whoever violates this law or that, shall suffer this or that punishment. Penalty, punishment of some sort, runs throughout; now imprisonment, now death. The law-makers, and the law interpreters, and all other men agree that it is so; that this language about punishment means punishment. And most will admit, also, the necessity, that the world, no realm or community of it, can go on, and keep together, without penalty; because men are made to be governed, controlled, swayed by law, by reward, by punishment. We pass on another step; leaving man's, we come into God's realm, where he governs on the throne supreme; and what find we here, as we read down the history given in his Word? We find that every law there has its penalty. The law of Paradise had; and it was executed on the very day they ate and transgressed. And the same holds in the law given in the wilderness, penalty if they transgressed; which they did, and their bones were left to bleach on the plains they traversed. It was so in the ceremonial law: penalty, punishment, according to the offence; and there was no escape but through the blood of sprinkling. We pass now from such principles, facts, and scenes to the great law, eternal, supreme over all, which God gives out as the ruler of the universe, the moral law, imposed upon moral beings, in all worlds. And we find the same thing, penalty, the threat of evil to the soul that transgresses. It is written here, *The soul that sinneth, it shall die.* This the great comprehensive principle and statement; afterwards, especially in the New Testament, brought out in varying forms of expression. Let me adduce a few of these. The impenitent, the wicked, the unholy, those who incur this punishment, we read, shall be *cast into a furnace of fire;* shall be destroyed, *both soul and body, in hell;* shall lose their souls; *shall not see life, but the wrath of God abideth on them; shall be punished with everlasting destruction from the presence of the*

*Lord, and from the glory of his power. The smoke of their torment*, it is written, *ascendeth up for ever and ever. Then said Jesus again unto them, I go my way, and ye shall seek me, and shall die in your sins: whither I go, ye cannot come. And they shall come forth; . . . they that have done evil, unto the resurrection of damnation. These shall go away into everlasting punishment.* These are a few specimens of the language used to express the punishment of the wicked in the future state; and the strongest, the most unequivocal of these, are from the lips of Christ himself. Mark the strength, the unambiguous nature of the phraseology, They *shall not see life, but the wrath of God abideth on them.* They shall come forth *unto the resurrection of condemnation.* They *shall go away into everlasting punishment.* And how shall we interpret? We find punishment, the necessity, the threat of it, the fact of it, everywhere else. We come along, and read these words, God's declaration, that the wicked shall be punished from the judgment-seat on without end. And what does this language mean? Is it all virtually a declaration of reward? The fire, the worm, the torment, the gnashing of teeth, — all these the symbols of glory, the expressions of transport and joy, or the aids thereto? Some so interpret. I must dissent from such an interpretation, and take the ground that punishment here, as everywhere else, means punishment; and that everlasting, eternal, when applied thereto, mean everlasting, eternal. If the life, the glory, is eternal, which every one admits, then the punishment, put right by the side, in the same sentence, means eternal punishment. The argument here is simply this, that it is what the language means; that we are so to take it, unless there is an overwhelming reason, compelling us to reduce or alter its meaning. I see none; the reason is on the other side, compelling us to interpret, according to the received significance, the same word assigning an eternal blessedness to the righteous, and an eternal punishment to the wicked.

We so interpret, because, if the language which the Spirit of God uses on the subject does not express the idea of punishment, eternal, literally without end, then no language can express it. If God has not declared it, it never has been and it never can be declared. For language, in God's employment of it, has been put to its utmost tension, its last capacity of expression, on this very subject. No believer of the doctrine, no preacher of it, on this theory of language, has ever yet succeeded in expressing the idea of the endless punishment of the wicked. If God has failed, certainly man has and must. And we add this, that the disbelievers, the rejecters of the doctrine, who have gone away displeased from before the evangelical pulpit, have spent their wrath for nothing. And if there is one here to-day, I say to him, Friend, what is the matter? What the ground of your displeasure and dissent? What have I said? — Said! you have been preaching the horrible doctrine of eternal punishment. — Pray, tell me where and when. You cannot put your finger on the justly offensive sentence. According to your theory and understanding of language, I have preached no such thing as the endless punishment of the wicked. According to your rule of interpreting, this very sermon is redolent with the happiness of all men after death; and every person of that way of thinking ought to be satisfied with it. The fact that he is not satisfied is proof that he is no believer, after all, in his own rule of interpretation; but admits, knows, as everybody else does, that punishment means punishment; and that the Bible, the New Testament, fairly interpreted, does teach the endless punishment of the wicked, the unbelieving, in the future state. I am of opinion that this is the honest, secret belief of nearly all discerning rejecters of eternal punishment, that the New Testament does teach it; and it is the honestly avowed belief of some who stand high in that connection and speak with some authority. One, a metropolitan advocate, has lately put forth this utterance: "And yet I freely say, that I do not find the doctrine of the ultimate salvation of all souls clearly stated in any text or in any discourse that has ever been reported from the lips of Christ." Theodore Parker also says, "To me it is quite clear that Jesus taught the doctrine of eternal damnation, if the evangelists are to be treated as inspired." Mr. Parker says that the doctrine is clearly in the New Testament: he avoids it by rejecting the inspiration and authority of the New Testament. And his case is not a singular one. So far as my own experience has gone, in my personal acquaintance with individuals of this way of thinking, the result is, that those who reject the fact of future endless punishment also reject the Bible as a book coming to them with the authority of a divine inspiration. The reason being, they find the doctrine in the book, and, to avoid the doctrine, they set aside the authority of the book. I take, then, this position, — and it is one, I trust, that will have weight with most before me, — that the inspired Word asserts it; by any fair interpretation, God's Word teaches the perdition of ungodly men. I receive the truth, and am moved to fear, and to strive to avoid the doom, and attain to that life.

Not only all Scripture, but all analogy teaches it. We may reject Scripture; there is a vast deal beside, that will preach to us the truth we want not to hear. The executions of nature, the executions of society, the executions of conscience, will preach it to us. The very existence of evil and misery in the universe suggests it to us. What unmeasured quantities of these, and yet God is only good. Men talk about the divine goodness as being against the endless suffering of the wicked. If the argument is valid against that measure of suffering, it is valid against any suffering, any punishment. "The main difficulty," says a great thinker, and his thought we must all assent to at once, "is not the amount of evil that exists, but the existence of any at all. Any, even the smallest, portion of evil, suffering, is quite unaccountable, supposing that the same amount of good could be attained without that evil; and why it is not attainable is more than we are able to explain. And if there be some reason, which we cannot understand, why a small amount of evil is unavoidable, there may be, for aught we know, the same reason for a greater amount. I will undertake to explain to any one the final condemnation of the wicked, if he will explain to me the existence of the wicked at all."

It is obvious to add, that it is prudent, it is wise, in any one to believe that a fearful retribution awaits the evil-doer in eternity; wise to believe this, because of the vast amount and weight of evidence to the point; evidence enough to prove it, if it is provable; all nature, all law, all revelation, uttering the doctrine, so that it is an amazing stretch and energy of unbelief not to believe it, implying a moral state and position that will not receive it on any testimony, however clearly, unqualifiedly, even to the exhaustion of the capabilities of language, God himself may declare and affirm it. It is wise to believe it, because, believed, it will act as a motive upon you, moving you to do something that you may be delivered from it; not believed, you will be likely to do nothing, to take it easy, and trust to this opinion to save you. If it should turn out to be otherwise, if God was serious in what he said, and will punish the wicked in eternity, then your case will be a hard one. Mark now the consequence in any case. If the doctrine of punishment is not true, and you are one who regards it as true, and repent, reform, and live accordingly, you will certainly be as well off as your neighbor who took the other course. The only loss, in your case, is the inconvenience you may have subjected yourself to in the disciplines and sacrifices of faith and holy living, when you might have had all the gratifications and profits of an impure and fraudulent life, and still have come out safely in eternity. For though your doctrine is not the true one, though the lower and liberal scheme turns out the true one, you fall from the first and that catches you. But if you try the latter, and it proves to be not of God, then you are lost.

The storm, the storm, it is coming, it is near; flee, oh, flee, to the strongholds, ye prisoners of hope.

# XXX.

## HEAVEN.

*And I saw a new heaven and a new earth: for the first heaven and the first earth were passed away; and there was no more sea. And I John saw the Holy City, New Jerusalem, coming down from God out of heaven, prepared as a bride adorned for her husband. And I heard a great voice out of heaven, saying, Behold, the tabernacle of God is with men, and he will dwell with them, and they shall be his people, and God himself shall be with them, and be their God.* — REV. xxi. 1–3.

IN these words, the apostle is supposed to refer to heaven. This is inferred because it is something desirable described, and something which lies beyond the resurrection and the judgment. His eye was permitted, was empowered, to penetrate beyond the day of doom, and to rest upon the condition of the rightous and the wicked in their final state. Not only the place in which this vision occurs, but the phrase in which it is described, leads us to interpret it as a representation of the heavenly state. The future blessedness of the righteous is, perhaps, more commonly described as a state. Hence the question is raised, Is it any thing more than a state?

The main argument for regarding heaven as only a state is, that only state can make heaven. Place alone certainly cannot make heaven. This is admitted, that state — that is, moral character, the affections — is essential to constitute heaven, and in this sense heaven is within you. In this sense, only state can make heaven. Then comes the conclusion, heaven is only a state; but the conclusion is far from being legitimate. When it is said that only state can make heaven, the meaning is, that a right moral state in any one is indispensable to heavenly enjoyment; there can be no such enjoyment where this is not. It does not follow, that the circumstance of place will not heighten the enjoyment, make heaven more heavenly. This certainly may be; this, therefore, is true, that, while place cannot make heaven, in spite of a discordant character it can brighten, and make it more blessed, where the character is in harmony. In other words, we believe there is a locality called heaven.

We all conceive of heaven thus, it being impossible, from the very necessities of our mental constitution, to separate the idea of the created and finite from the notion of locality. Emphatically, when we bring in the fact, that the righteous at the resurrection are not merely spirit, but exist with bodies, these necessarily imply or require place: they must be somewhere; and we naturally suppose that God has provided a where. This thought of being left loose and at large, wandering through immensity, is abhorrent to our natures. While our very natures ask for some locality, abiding-place, city, as our home, our Saviour's words most decisively point to such an abode. In that final welcome we have it, loftily expressed, as that *kingdom prepared for you.* In his prayer for those who should believe on his name, he asks,

*Father, I will that they also, whom thou hast given me be with me where I am; that they may behold my glory, which thou hast given me. Be with me where I am;* where Christ's glory is peculiarly manifested. It is where he went with his glorified humanity. It is where he went *to prepare a place* for his disciples. Here we have it in language which perfectly meets the case, and comes right home to our heart: *In my Father's house are many mansions: I go to prepare a place for you. And if I go and prepare a place for you, I will come again, and receive you unto myself; that where I am, there ye may be also.* There in that place, the high and holy place, where are found the city, the throne of the infinite God, is heaven; and heaven is a place. Thus we can think of its happiness — we love so to do — as in part the result of place. We find a description thereof furnished by an inspired pen, in which are employed the loftiest images of splendor and beauty and magnificence. In the structure of it, the most costly and brilliant things are represented as profusely inwrought; its dimensions are vast; its foundations *garnished with all manner of precious stones;* its walls of jasper; its dwellings of pure gold; its gates of pearl; in the midst of it *the throne of God, and of the Lamb.* Out of the throne flows the *pure river*, the crystal water of life, *and on either side of the river the tree of life.* Allowing all you please for figure, we do have here the structure and the magnificence of place. But place, we have admitted, is not the essential thing. We will pass, then, to designate a few other things, which more vitally help in the conception of the heavenly blessedness, beginning with the negative view.

And the grand negation is, that there is no sin there. Nothing *that defileth, neither whatsoever worketh abomination or maketh a lie.* If you enter there, you enter in a state of perfect and confirmed holiness, all that can taint or disturb you left behind. This consciousness now of an eternal parting with sin, that no deforming stain nor darting pang can ever reach you more; this standing up in heaven erect, and emancipate, finally, from the base and the galling chain; this consciousness and deliverance alone is enough to fill the soul's whole capacity with the most vivid and joyous emotions. Sin away, all the legion evils of its train are put away, all the dishonors of it, the injury and offence to God away; all tears wiped from the eyes; *no more death,* no sorrow, naught to break up those turbid fountains, or feed those flowing streams. The smiting and the hewing and the shaping were all done in this world; the living stones cut and made ready by the sharp discipline of afflictions here, so that they are placed in the eternal building without noise of hammer, there to abide and shine for ever in imperishable beauty.

Again, heaven is frequently presented to us under the image of rest. *There remaineth, therefore, a rest to the people of God. A rest:* a great word this in the compass of its blessedness, greater than we now can know. Not torpid, indulgent ease, but the impossibility of weariness, the absence of assailing temptation, of the beating storms of adversity, of the sweeping blasts of passion; none of these, but the calm, the peace, the rest, of the soul. Rest, refreshment, renewing vigor amidst the ceaseless activities of service, this will be in that world. The idea of activity, service there, is as strongly set forth in the Bible as the idea of rest. *They rest not day and night*, but serve and worship God continually. And yet they rest continually. These two qualities, rest and service, make, as one alone could not, heaven.

Doubtless, the privilege of service, the opportunity of doing good, of kindly office, of communicating happiness, will not be wanting in heaven. Society, companionship, then, is another boon and privilege, we discover, as we look *through the gates into the city*. But while the society is without selfishness, there will unquestionably be distinctions, gradations, and ranks in the heavenly economy. And yet no ambition, no envy; all dwelling in harmony, all rejoicing in any honor or privilege attained by others. These distinctions or honors, like perfumes worn on the person, are more grateful to others who stand near than to the wearer himself. All will be shedding abroad the savor of benignant affections wherever they go. There will be also the intimacies of society, the recognition of friends. What joy to recognize friends in such a scene, and clad in such habiliments; to come together, converse together, live together, with hearts all interfused in the glow of holy love. How transporting to recognize, and associate with, some of the great champions of righteousness, the illustrious names of the past, the reformers and achievers of other days. "I want to go to heaven," said one of the greatest and best of New-England preachers, as he stood in extreme old age on the very threshold, eager to see the glory of God as there revealed, to see the honored co-laborers who had gone before him. Then he adds, "I want to see the old prophets, such as Moses, Isaiah, Elijah, Daniel, and the apostles; but I want to see Paul more than any man I can think of." This longing to see the honored and the good, how it will be gratified, if we come to live in the same high abode with them, where, we doubt not, all obstructions to intercourse will be removed.

Another class of obstructions will doubtless be stricken away, — those to the acquisition of knowledge. I look upon this as among the bright features in the heavenly state, — the opportunities afforded for study, the facilities for gaining knowledge; consequently the large possession and the ever-swelling stock of knowledge. We do not suppose that this acquisition will come without effort. We may reasonably hope it will not be so; for such an arrangement must be taking away one blessed source of satisfaction, one salient spring of joy. The powers there possessed will doubtless be admirable for this service; the mind exalted, the heart made pure, the body glorified, and all adapted to the work; the appetite eager and sharp, and the greatest subjects pressing on the attention. Every inquisitive mind that goes from this world, where he saw *through a glass darkly*, to heaven, has a great many subjects laid by, laid over, for the higher powers and the better opportunities of that state; and we may suppose they will there be the first on his docket of inquiry. These hard-twisted Gordian knots he here could do nothing at all with, these he will untie, if untie he can, even there. Whatever has tried him, overtasked him, and brought him to a stand in this world, he goes there, we may suppose, with a sort of passion to master and to know; and when those higher powers and clearer lights let him into the solution, it cannot be otherwise than that his soul will feel an exultant thrill through all its emotional capacities. How many facts about Christ, for example, we have a desire to know. We can ask the questions, but earth is no place for the answer. How many deep things pertaining to the great scheme of redemption; how many wonderful things pertaining to the works of God and the worlds of immensity, the laws of his physical as well as his moral universe, now beyond and above us, will abide as a study and a scrutiny for that other scene, and that higher state. And can we then come to them and master them, and fill our souls with them, without a heavenly satisfaction; especially when we consider that they all help reveal God, the grandeur of his being, the harmony of his attributes, the ineffable glories of his essence? Can we study them, and be enlarged by them in our conceptions, without also being enlarged and exalted in our blessedness?

We come now to heaven as a place of the immediate manifestation of the glory of the Godhead. It is no circular knowledge we speak of, no matter of remote inference, but direct vision. There are, in the Bible, some remarkable expressions of this kind: *We shall see him as he is;* shall see God *face to face.* The face is where all the attributes and affections concentre, and beam forth as from an unclouded sun. The *back parts* of this, the reflex and half-eclipsed stroke of it, we are told, turned Moses into a fountain of radiance, shining so intensely that his countrymen *could not steadfastly behold.* What a glory it shall be, when, instead of the retreating *back parts*, the near and open face shall be seen. Can you bear it? Yes, then and there. Can you imagine the effect? It will be to make you *like him.* You cannot compass all the meaning of those two words, *like him,* — bringing you into a resemblance and a vital union, pervading you and flooding you with his glory. It is this which elevates and refines the character, and which will make you, if there, a very partaker, putting you in possession, of the divine holiness; and, what is more wonderful still, putting you in possession, making you a *partaker of the divine nature.* And this must open upon you the floodgates of the divine blessedness. The glory of God becomes your glory; the rest of God, your rest; the joy of God, your joy. The mandate was, the stride now is, to enter into the joy of your Lord; to take the possession; to let it surround and fill you. And how full it will fill you; and how strangely it will ravish you; and the joy shall grow *unspeakable, and full of glory;* and love shall wake up all its intensest ardor, and praise call into service all her sweetest strains. There will be in heaven worship, doubtless, in its gentlest song, and its loudest and universal acclaim; all the involved and enrapturing harmonies of music exhausting the powers of its eloquent expression in that work of praise, when the redeemed shall cry, *Worthy is the Lamb that was slain to receive power and riches and wisdom and strength and honor and glory and blessing.* Then the sublime response, the thundering chorus from innumerable voices shall be heard, *Blessing and honor and glory and power be unto Him that sitteth upon the throne, and unto the Lamb for ever.*

I might here consummate and crown the description by two or three comprehensive heads of thought.

One is the thought of what they once were, poor, vile, wretched, doomed; then the thought of what they now are; and then, again, the thought, so far as thought can reach, what they are to be. They were once sinners, plunged deep, perhaps, in the mire and slough of sin, helpless, condemned, miserable. Now they are free; the denizens and inheritors of the universe; partakers of the nature, the holiness, the blessedness, of God. What a contrast. And who has done it for them? Who brought them there? Their Deliverer, who? He is right before them, in his glory, — that Christ their souls do admire; his love, the intensest ecstasy of their heart; his presence, the brightest spot of their heaven. Their view of him, their song to him, never wearies, but ever freshens, and more and more deeply thrills on every repetition. Their character, position, possessions, employments, all pure, enriching, enrapturing, heavenly. Then the prospect, eternal confirmation in the amazing inheritance; the prospect reaching on vaster and brighter and still more blessed, the blessedness of the possession and the blessedness of the prospect put together into one. Can you, in conception, get up to that? And have you seriously thought, and succeeded in faintly realizing, what it will be, by and by, to find yourself in heaven? We read, *There was silence in heaven about the space of half an hour.* The first half-hour there, to you, to me, if we reach there, will be, so far as we are concerned, methinks, the silence of unutterable amazement. Amazement and gratitude that we are indeed there.

Has some friend of thine, the servant of God, gone

there? And do you mourn for him; mourn that he is in heaven; mourn that he went there too soon? And would you disturb him if you could, dislodge him if you could, and bring him down from that society, that you may again enjoy his presence? Would you do it, or let him stay where he is; and bless God for the evidence of being ready thy friend gave, and thy God ratified, when he took him and made him one of his own jewels?

Have you a hope of heaven, expecting to be there? And how is it with you? Are you all captivated with this world, carried away with its fascinations, buried up in its cares, covered and defiled with its sweat and its dust? It is not right, not fitting. Beware, or you come short. See to it, that you do not. See that yours is a heavenly spirit, a heavenly life; then the end shall be heavenly, glorious.

My hearers, do you believe in that world, that place, the heaven of the Bible? That is infinitely brighter and richer than the one I have described. Mine all dim and low and mean in the comparison; the reality, as God has made it, more glorious and precious than language can utter, or the mind can know. You believe in God, believe also in that. Have you done any thing worthy to obtain a title to it, a home therein? Is there one here, before hesitating and lingering, now ready to rise up and try for it, in God's name and strength? Run, wrestle, for that crown. Strive, agonize, to enter into that glory. That Eye that sees us all, sees it one such?

# XXXI.

## THE SUFFERINGS AND THE GLORY.

*For I reckon that the sufferings of this present time are not worthy to be compared with the glory which shall be revealed in us.* — ROMANS viii. 18.

THE same apostle speaks in a similar strain in his second Epistle to the Corinthians. *For our light affliction, which is but for a moment, worketh for us a far more exceeding and eternal weight of glory.*

The present is a state of afflictions and trials. They fall somewhere; they come at some time. The apostle, in the context, represents the entire world, as in a burdened and suffering condition; not only Christians, but all men; not only the rational creation, but the irrational, and even the inanimate. *For we know*, he says, *that the whole creation groaneth and travaileth in pain together until now. And not only they, but ourselves also, which have the first fruits of the Spirit, even we ourselves groan within ourselves, waiting for the adoption, to wit, the redemption of our body.* In the text the apostle speaks of sufferings here; of a glory to be revealed; and of the comparison between the two.

I. The first thought presented is *the sufferings of this present time.* There may be here a reference to the peculiar tribulations of Christians in that cruel and persecuting age. But the language is no more confined to that period than the sufferings of Christians: as I have said, they are the lot of all time. There are, first, the sufferings peculiar to the Christian character and experience. As the disciple of Christ has joys with which the stranger intermeddleth not, he has sorrows which the mere worldly mind has no experience of. His sufferings from the presence and working of sin within are often keen, sometimes overwhelming. He is not yet delivered from sin, but he hates it, watches and prays against it; and, if endowed with the Spirit of the Master, he will resist it *even unto blood.* There is suffering in these conflicts, these wrestlings, with the enemy; and if sin gets the advantage, as it sometimes does, and he is thrown down and defiled, there is greater suffering still. David calls it the anguish of broken bones; occasionally, even the agony of a broken spirit; all this, because he is a Christian of so decided attainments, that sin has become to him the greatest possible evil and offence. The Christian sometimes suffers from the assaults of Satan. We know that Christ's sufferings from this quarter were very great; no greater came upon him, save those connected with the scene of the crucifixion. As it was with the Lord, so it will be with the disciple. The great enemy will assail him, and turn, for a season, all the springs of his happiness into waters of wormwood.

There are sufferings to the Christian, from an opposing, not to say persecuting, world. The world does not love the pure gospel of Christ, but dislikes it for its claims, its restrictions, its penalties. And those who have professed it have, in times past, encountered all the ills human malice could dispense. They have had *trials of cruel mockings and scourgings, yea, moreover, of bonds and imprisonment.* They have been *stoned;* they have been *sawn asunder; tempted, slain with the sword;* all the instruments and engines of death have been often employed, and their utmost capabilities, in the work of torture, have been exhausted upon the followers of the Lord Jesus. Multitudes, in these periods, have tested the whole fearful meaning of the declaration, *that we must through much tribulation, enter into the kingdom of God.* But there is a more refined persecution which strikes not the body,—the taunt, the sneer, the shaft of ridicule, the uttered blasphemy wounding the soul. Christ's saying has been verified in every period of the Church, that *a man's foes shall be they of his own household.* And perhaps no suffering for the cause of the Master can exceed that of those who cannot be Christians, with toleration, at home; who have not only no sympathy there in their best hopes and joys, but even forfeit affection, and are subjected to an outbreaking opposition and an unnatural hate from those most dear to them, simply because they love the Saviour and choose to keep his words.

The Christian, in some instances, suffers intensely from the fluctuations of experience. The light is withdrawn from him, and hope is almost extinct, and there comes over him the dreary sense of divine abandonment. He feels, in his measure, as Christ did when he exclaimed, *My God, my God, why hast thou forsaken me?* Or much as David did, when he uttered those dismal interrogatives: *Will the Lord cast off for ever? and will he be favorable no more? Is his mercy clean gone for ever? doth his promise fail for evermore? hath God forgotten to be gracious? hath he in anger shut up his tender mercies?* And he may add with the psalmist, *This is my infirmity.* It is his infirmity,—a mysterious disease reaching to the seats, and rudely sweeping all the chords of feeling; or, operating as an iron shutter to all the windows of the soul, to keep from the imprisoned tenant the descending beams of day, so that every thing is shrouded in gloom. The prayer attempted seems all heartless and scattering, a mockery to the great Being addressed; the hope long cherished, a baseless delusion; God appears only as awful in justice and holiness; Christ, only as the armed and avenging king; the Comforter, as the grieved and banished spirit; death, the personification and embodiment of all conceivable terrors. Such the working of the infirmity, and the anguish in such a case. Who but the sufferer knows it? But the sufferings thus far described are those peculiar to the Christian faith and profession.

There is another class I will advert to,—those of a providential nature. With these the Christian is visited in common with the rest of mankind. Equally with others he is exposed to the vicissitudes of the world; to the defeating of earthly plans and hopes; to the evils and deep distresses of a remediless poverty. Even *the Son of man had not where to lay his head.* There are also the sufferings arising from sickness and decay. These, at some time, in some form, all must encounter. If any have lived years without feeling the wilting hand of disease upon them, let them be thankful, and not presume that it will always be so. The Christian may have great consolation in the season of his trial, but he cannot escape it. Not that God afflicts willingly, but he has kind purposes to be answered by the laying on of the stroke. Sometimes it seems as though the Christian were more certain than others to suffer in this mode. Not unfrequently do we see the ungodly and profane passing quietly out of life, having *no bands in their death;* whilst others, eminent for holiness, linger and wear out by the simple force and process of tormenting pain. God's reasons for so doing we will not undertake to penetrate. It may be to show the power of godliness, the sustaining energy of the Christian's hope. It may be a discipline, the kindling of a fire to purge away the remaining dross of sin. It may, in part, be a chastisement; light strokes administered in a momentary but corrective displeasure for some offences or neglects which cannot be passed wholly by. Whatever the cause, the sufferings are sometimes great. The Christian's death-bed, while it may be a place of inward peace or positive triumph, the last struggles of a crowning victory, may also be a place in which centre the sharpest piercings, and over which roll the heaviest billows of pain. There are the sufferings attendant on bereavement, the removal by death of beloved friends. The cords of attachment grow strong, and very closely bind heart to heart. The parental, the filial, the fraternal, the conjugal tie seems often to pass around and encompass every other joy; and, when sundered, it is as though every thing were taken. The circumstances, perhaps, all administer to the heart's deep anguish. He sunk down amid strangers; he sleeps in a foreign grave, or on the coral bed; a favorite child, perhaps, who died and gave no evidence that he was prepared. The Christian knows that it is all right, even wisely and kindly done; but, he feels the cleaving stroke, and in the fresh intensity of his sorrow, in the first tumult of his grief, does not realize the assuaging power of the divine considerations. He dwells only upon what he has lost. His memory recurs, and fixes with a mournful tenacity upon those objects which are the most directly fitted to harrow still more the already torn and bleeding sensibilities. The room, the seat, the loved one occupied; all the little arrangements as he left them; the books as he marked and laid them away; the garments where he hung them; the trees those hands did plant; the ground those feet did tread, — each is made to contribute its pang in the ministry of grief, till the heart can hold no more; till, in its paroxysms, it swells and heaves almost to bursting. Such the anguish of bereavement, sometimes, before religion has had time to soothe by its healing appliance.

I will not dwell longer upon the sufferings of this present time, but turn, in the second place, to that other and contrasted scene.

II. *The glory which shall be revealed in us.* And what can we say here? The sufferings are matters of experience; the glory, now known in part, of faith. The nature of it admits of no literal disclosure; nor can we, as yet, bear an open manifestation. Mortal eye cannot behold, nor ear hear, nor heart conceive *the things which God hath prepared for them that love him.* The spirit of inspiration, tasking language to its utmost, can only shadow forth the coming blessedness of the Christian. It is a *glory that shall be revealed in us*, a glory in the presence of God, *the glorious liberty of the children of God*, an *exceeding and eternal weight of glory*. Here we have Paul's magnificent and laboring utterance; hyperbole upon hyperbole, literally a greatness excessively exceeding, *a far more exceeding and eternal weight of glory*. We are also told of the life, the *eternal life*, the *crown of life;* of *an inheritance incorruptible and undefiled, and that fadeth not away;* of *an enduring substance; a kingdom which cannot be moved; a building not made with hands, eternal in the heavens*. Christians are to *walk in white;* they are to reign with Christ; they are to have bodies *fashioned like unto his glorious body*. These various modes of description are, obviously, intended to set forth to our minds a state of great exaltation and happiness. That state is the Christian's sure possession; toward it he is borne on the swift wings of time; a state in which there will be no sin, none of these sufferings and conflicts and bitter mournings; where all tears will be wiped away, all trials merged in triumphs; a state of renewed intercourse with redeemed friends, and high companionship with saints and angels; a state of enlarging and striding knowledge, where *we shall be like Him; for we shall see Him as he is;* when we *shall know as* also we *are known;* a state in which love will be perfected and all-pervading and all-blessing with its hallowed intensity. But why attempt to describe that state, that *glory which shall be revealed*, when all our attempts are futile, and we can only retreat upon Paul's doubled hyperbole, and gain a little relief to our minds in the use of his masterly superlatives? — crying out, and wondering as we repeat, *a far more exceeding and eternal weight of glory*.

III. Having considered some of the sufferings, and

glanced at the glory, hereafter, we might pause, in the third place, long enough to institute a comparison between the two. But there is no comparison of a momentary sorrow with an infinite and eternal joy. The Apostle thought so amid the heavy trials of his lot, charged as he was with an unwonted responsibility, carrying about with him that dread infirmity, surrounded with enemies, traduced, beaten, *killed all the day long*. The sufferings were present and almost without a parallel in Christian endurance; the glory future, and apprehended only by faith. He weighed the matter, he calculated carefully, he balanced the account; and this was his settled judgment: *I reckon*, I account, *that the sufferings of this present time are not worthy to be compared with the glory which shall be revealed in us*. And can any one hesitate in coming to the same conclusion? We might refer the question to one of far feebler faith and in deeper trouble, one on whom the hand of affliction was pressing most heavily, and the glory seemed dim and far away. The affliction for a moment, the felicity eternal. The affliction light, the glory unmeasured in weight and worth. Can the depressed and most sorrowing heart hesitate in the judgment, *not worthy to be compared?* Suppose we pass to the other side of the scale, and put the question to one of those spirits before the throne, who have come *out of great tribulation, and have washed their robes, and made them white in the blood of the Lamb*. Be the umpire one who encountered every form and variety of earthly trial; the direst malignancy of persecution; the most desolating strokes of bereavement; the tortures of a racked and groaning body and the still keener anguish of a wounded spirit.

That spirit, thus tossed and troubled, is now resting in the embrace of infinite and protecting love. That heart, which at times drooped beneath the weight of its sorrows, now swells with the fulness of unutterable joys. It has felt its last pang; now it is perfect peace. Thus that purified intelligence has tried both sides; has had experience of the sorest sufferings of time, and the opening and growing blessedness of eternity. Ask him his judgment, and what think you he would say? As he looked down upon this little point and speck of trouble, and as he thought of the immeasurable felicities of his present and secured immortality, what would he say? He would say, with the utmost reach of language and strength of emphasis, — and all the redeemed would join in and peal forth their intense agreement, till those eternal pillars should tremble with the utterance, — *not worthy to be compared.*

IV. But, though there is no comparison, there is a connection, between the present suffering and the coming glory. Let me now remark upon the beneficent nature and working of this connection. We see in it the blessed hand of God, here, as everywhere, bringing good out of evil, plucking from the very jaws of sorrow a shining tribute of joy; all things, all trials, all bitter pangs, made to work for good. These afflictions, when the mind comes out from them ascendant, work into the character an element of strength and assurance, a conscious supremacy over the assailments of trial and evil; producing a character that has met the storm, and now firmer stands for the blasts it has successfully sustained; a character refined and made purer by the fire, and more shining from the rough and hard attritions. *These light afflictions*, by working these things in us, work out for us that *far more exceeding and eternal weight of glory;* mightier for these light afflictions. So, also, the future glory gives strength to bear the present trial. That coming glory, let it shine back and put to shame and silence every rising murmur. If ever tempted to say, or even feel, that God is unkind in putting upon you so great a trial as has come upon you, pause long enough to think of the glory, and especially of the sacrifices, he has made to open your path unto it. God unkind, that he did not spare you that visitation, when he *spared not his own Son, but delivered him up for us all?* God unkind in the discipline he employs to cleanse your soul, and fit it for that high state? Look up, and think again of the glory, and you will discover in all nothing but a Father's solicitude, and an overflowing goodness. If ever ready to faint and give over, saying, All these things are against me; every event an adversity; every new scene a trial, — remember still to look up, and think of the glory, and gather from above strength and courage, and so hold on your way, ever struggling to reach the goal and gain the prize. Then all these things, here so much dreaded, will prove helpers to your deliverance, added gems to your crown, new richness and sweetness in the cup of your blessedness. There is another thing I will suggest, that while the future glory gives strength to bear the present trial, the present trial in turn will heighten the fruition of the future glory. I have said no comparison can be instituted; but there is a contrast which the delivered soul will feel, so sudden, so perfect, as to fill it with wonder. Mark that weary disciple, who had a long and sorrowing experience; whose sensibilities were mostly ministers of pain; whose clayey tabernacle was often turned into a prison by thick and brooding infirmities; whose faith was small and his fears frequent; conflicts, doubts, sufferings, for years his bosom companions, till he seemed to cling to them, as though they were his inheritance. The hour of redemption at length arrives; the submerging waters are past; and, in an instant, the celestial glory stands all revealed. As the darkness settles heavily here, the light opens transportingly there; and, as the body is sending out the last moaning sounds of death, the spirit begins to hear, and even join in, those heavenly melodies. To such an one,—to one coming out of that tribulation, rising above those billows, parting for ever with those pains and glooms and labors, but remembering them all,—how refreshing must be that rest; how sweet that peace; how glorious that triumph; how immeasurably heightened all that joyous possession and experience, by the scenes which have been gone through. We are lost here; we know but little. Blessed shall we be, if we reach that state, and learn by experience the riches and the mysteries of its glory. We see here the firm ground for the grace of patience. How lovely is this grace; how desirable that we possess it; that it grow stronger; that there be put into it firm nerves and sinews, so that we be able to bear the afflictions we cannot shun; not only the momentary, but those wearying burdens which can only be laid down with the burden of our mortality. Happy those who thus endure to the end, and show, through all, *the patience of the saints.*

In conclusion, we cannot fail to see, that every thing in God's providence, and in the Book he has given us, goes to diminish the present, and to heighten and greaten what is to come. If now these are *light afflictions;* these joys of sense are light joys; these possessions of time are shadowy and vain possessions, — oh, how small and mean to be set as the supreme object of pursuit to those made in the image and for the service of God; and how these things will look, in the retrospect of a lost eternity. If lost, you will see them then as the price of your soul. You will know that you bartered heaven for that now perished baseness. You will behold it in the distance, a floating trifle, a dim, receding speck, and yet it was the price of your soul. Bear in mind, that soon you will leave the little things, the gildings, the baubles, the vanities, and go forth to the substantial, the weighty, the eternal. Awake, watch, strive, or this lying world will work out for you, and lay upon you, a dreadful burden, — the burden of your Maker's curse, because you would not heed his counsel, and embrace his Son. You will lie under it for ever, a far more exceeding and eternal weight of infamy and misery.

THE END.



---

Cambridge: Printed by John Wilson and Son.

www.ingramcontent.com/pod-product-compliance
Lightning Source LLC
LaVergne TN
LVHW020106110826
845151LV00001B/76

* 9 7 8 1 4 2 5 5 4 4 1 3 3 *